Engaging Adversaries

Engaging Adversaries

Peacemaking and Diplomacy in the Human Interest

Mel Gurtov

ROWMAN & LITTLEFIELD
Lanham • Boulder • New York • London

Published by Rowman & Littlefield
A wholly owned subsidiary of
The Rowman & Littlefield Publishing Group, Inc.
4501 Forbes Boulevard, Suite 200, Lanham, Maryland 20706
https://rowman.com

Unit A, Whitacre Mews, 26-34 Stannary Street, London SE11 4AB,
United Kingdom

British Library Cataloguing in Publication Information Available

Library of Congress Cataloging-in-Publication Data Available

ISBN 978-1-5381-1112-3 (cloth : alk. paper)
ISBN 978-1-5381-1113-0 (pbk. : alk. paper)
ISBN 978-1-5381-1114-7 (electronic)

♾ ™ The paper used in this publication meets the minimum requirements of American
National Standard for Information Sciences Permanence of Paper for Printed Library
Materials, ANSI/NISO Z39.48-1992.

Printed in the United States of America

To my wonderful sisters,
Judi Harris and Ellen Simons

Contents

Preface

When I started work on this book, the idea of engaging adversaries was actually being implemented under President Barack Obama. Now, one administration later, President Donald J. Trump has relegated engagement to history—with the exception of Russia. Why, then, persist in working on a strategy of engagement? Because I believe the time will come when engagement will again be viewed by policy makers in the United States and elsewhere as a wise choice, preferable to the use of force or threat. In that event, this book will provide some points of reference to what has worked, what might work, and what hasn't worked.

If Obama was only partially successful, it was owing as much to domestic politics in the United States and in the adversary's country as to strategic factors and changing international circumstances. Yet when we examine world politics at this moment, one can only applaud his achievement of historic breakthroughs in a few places. Every one of the international relationships examined in this book is worse now than when Obama left office, and the threat of a major war hangs over humankind once again. Traditional realpolitik has much to answer for.

President Obama's overtures to various adversaries were often cast as idealistic, and I suppose the same can be said of my book. Idealism does animate my study; I believe humane values, such as empathy, mutual respect, nonviolence, and social justice, must occupy an important place in any discussion of international relations. But the principles and practices of engagement—working on the basis of win-win solutions, mutual interests, and common security—are also entirely realistic if practiced with consistency and seriousness of purpose. They serve both national interests and the human interest in a just and peaceful world order.

In writing this book I had the benefit of advice from some wonderful friends and colleagues. Mark Selden not only critically reviewed key portions of the manuscript but also was pivotal in facilitating its publication. Peter Van Ness, Miroslav Nincic, Walter Clemens, Birol Yesilada, Stu Thorson, and two anonymous reviewers offered valuable comments on particular chapters. Milton Leitenberg once again provided press and journal articles that I would otherwise have missed. I would also like to thank Hyung T. Hong and the East Asia Foundation in Seoul, Korea, for financial support of a conference on engagement that I organized at Indiana University on April 19–20, 2013. Many thanks, too, to folks at Bloomington, Indiana, who hosted and helped bring the conference to life: Gil

Latz, Melissa Biddinger, and the Australia National University-Indiana University Pan Asia Institute.

Finally, my deep appreciation—to my wife, Jodi; my children, Ellene, Marci, and Alia; and my grandchildren, Brynn and Gavin—for their love and support. This book is really for them—and especially for the children and all children, everywhere. Their futures will not be secured by war, ignorance, or neglect. They deserve our best efforts to ensure that they will live in peace, safety, and good health. In that endeavor, may they always seek to understand and learn from others.

Deadwood, Oregon, August 19, 2017

ONE

The Global Citizen and Engagement

ANALYSIS IN THE HUMAN INTEREST

With this book I hope to contribute to the study of international peace-making. It is rooted in prioritization of the human interest in international affairs. To apply that priority to peacemaking—specifically, to a proposed strategy of engagement between adversarial governments—requires stepping back from one's nationality and speaking as best one can from the standpoint of a global citizen. Even though most of the cases reviewed here concern US foreign policy—and even those that do not involve the United States playing a pivotal role—I take pains to avoid framing the cases in terms of US interests and objectives, or for that matter any other nation's, political party's, or corporation's interest. I write with sensitivity to ordinary citizens, their communities, and the progressive agenda for human rights set forth in the Universal Declaration of Human Rights 1948.[1] Seeking to engage one's adversaries is a way to protect and promote the human interest.

Events since the supposed end of the Cold War buttress the need for a global perspective. Far from providing a respite from international (state-to-state) and global security problems, the period following the Cold War has been characterized by multiple and intersecting crises: unstoppable global warming, collapsing ice flows and coral reefs, an enormous increase in refugees and widespread resistance to accepting them as fellow citizens, development of new nuclear weapons rather than an agreement to abolish them, wars and interventions in the Middle East, the great and growing divide between rich and poor—and the prospect of new cold wars involving the United States, Russia, and China. The response to these crises has largely been politics as usual: spasmodic, self-interested, costly, and grossly inadequate. A sense of urgency, even emergency,

1

about the state of the world is therefore a prime motivator of my analysis. In a word, we still need to devote a great deal more attention to peace-making and peacebuilding.

From a global citizenship point of view, these peace projects require a reassessment of values. "There is enough for every person's need," said Gandhi, "but not enough for every person's greed." Notions of sufficiency, sustainability, respect for nature, community, fairness, responsibility, and service flow from that statement and stand in contrast to the satisfaction of the endless "needs" and "wants" that characterize modern-day materialism and the constant quest for more—more energy, more land, more profit—by nations and corporations. Pope Francis's encyclical on the environment carries forth Gandhi's idea of "enoughness." In the human interest we must protect the planet from disastrous climate change and other abuses of our inheritance; otherwise, we cannot find peace.[2] Environmental protection is thus as much a part of the engagement agenda as any other aspect of human security.

Looking at the world through the eyes of a global citizen was the foundation for my book *Global Politics in the Human Interest.*[3] At the time of that book's initial publication, the notion of global citizenship was well outside the mainstream. But no longer; polling by the BBC shows that majorities in eighteen countries, including China, Russia, and the United States, identify as global citizens.[4] What this entails is giving priority to the needs and aspirations of the global majority, the world's politically and economically powerless. They are characterized by very low income, literacy rates, and access to health care, as well as by vulnerability to the whims of governments, armies, and big business. Serving the human interest means that the richest and most powerful countries, social groups, and institutions must undertake, as a priority task, the responsibility to make the world safer and more equitable for the global majority.

I contend that the human interest perspective amounts to a new realism, better suited to analyzing the main challenges of our times than standard realism's focus on maximizing power and promoting the national interest. This perspective fits within a conflict resolution framework, as I show below, and has a prescriptive element—engaging adversaries—that I elaborate on in chapter 2. Engagement is an alternative to seemingly endless wars and intractable disputes; as a strategy, it aims at building trust and reducing tensions between adversaries, with due regard—even empathy—for the other party's political, socioeconomic, cultural, and historical circumstances. Relations between the United States and Iran or Cuba (chapter 3) demonstrate that a thoughtful engagement strategy seriously pursued can work. China-US relations (chapter 4) have not been as successful—I call this "halfway engagement" because we see both numerous points of positive interaction and ongoing tensions—but opportunities abound to deepen engagement. Then we have two cases of disengagement (chapter 5): US-Russia relations, which were once on the verge of a "reset" but now are in a deep freeze, and US relations with North Korea, which remain highly contentious and increasingly perilous. Finally, I offer studies (in chapter 6) of relationships trapped by history: China-Japan and Israel-Palestine.

I argue that thinking in terms of mutual gain, incentives, and multi-level diplomacy may promote positive steps toward international problem solving: deepening engagement in thus far successful cases, reversing cases of disengagement, and finding mutually beneficial outlets for relations trapped by historical grievances.

SITUATING ENGAGEMENT IN CONFLICT RESOLUTION

Management If Not Resolution

The task of resolving, or at least mitigating, international conflict must take into account not merely the type of conflict but also its players, phases, histories, and other specific features. In practice and in theory, many potential tools are available for addressing disputes of all kinds. But having a large and diverse toolbox is not the same as being able to use it. Every conflict is unique in origins, evolution, and perceived opportunities for settlement. Moreover, in many conflicts critical tools such as money, impartial interveners, and officials dedicated to peacemaking are not available. The relationship of the parties may be too intensely hostile to make a peacekeeping effort possible. It does, after all, take two to tango. Often the apparent causes of a conflict hide the actual ones, and the immediate causes hide the deep roots. This is one reason conflict resolution is less about identifying causes than about focusing on the *conditions* of conflict. Typically, the causes have been present for a long time. We want to know what combination of circumstances, between the disputing parties and around them, is bringing conflict to the surface. Resolving or managing conflict, in short, is not about eliminating its roots but about damping down its worst consequences.

Timing is everything; identifying early warning signs of impending conflict is obviously preferable to waiting until tensions boil over. But government and international bureaucracies typically do not focus on, much less heed, early warning signs; they wait until conflict is under way, at which point outside intervention may be futile and is certainly more expensive. Moreover, in the real world of multiple conflicts, there are *too many* warning signs. Identifying those that portend violence and might be amenable to management is problematic. Likewise, identifying "ripeness" for settling a dispute is theoretically optimal, but being able to spot that moment and take advantage of it has proven to be no easy matter. Often we must await a "hurting stalemate," the point at which both parties are too exhausted to go on, to take hold before the parties are ready to sit down with each other.

Perhaps most problematic of all is that the path to bringing conflicting parties together is strewn with all kinds of political obstacles. These may be domestic, such as lack of public support or legislation (e.g., concerning human rights) that would constrain or undermine actions national leaders might want to take. Internationally, the obstacles might include security commitments to one of the parties to a dispute, reliance on a coalition of outside parties instead of a willingness to proceed unilaterally, or threats such as red lines and economic sanctions.

Engaging adversaries enters the picture here. My particular interest is *preventing conflict from turning violent or, if it is already violent, turning the conflict to dialogue.* I want to ascertain when and how a dispute can be diverted to a nonviolent path, even if the dispute cannot immediately be settled. We know from considerable research that in fact the full and final settlement of long-standing, sometimes intractable international conflict of the sort explored in this book is rare. Agreements break down over differences of interpretation, minor incidents are treated as major ones, new leaders challenge settlement terms, war may again look more promising than peace, peacekeepers and honest brokers are unavailable, and so forth. *Conflict resolution* therefore is a hope far more often than a reality, which is why *conflict management* may be the more appropriate characterization, particularly in the kinds of long-standing adversarial relationships studied in this book. Even so, finding ways for the parties to a dispute to reach common ground, and on terms that may be *sustainable,* is a worthy goal. Engagement is one strategy for reaching that goal.

Toward Peace and Common Security

When successfully managed, engagement reduces tensions and shows a pathway to eventual peace. It is, after all, the art of the possible: tensions and frictions may never be eliminated, but neither will they become so serious that violent conflict is seen as the only way out for one or both parties. Meaningful incentives create value for ongoing, deepening engagement. Engagement is most effective before open conflict breaks out. But one can imagine engagement occurring anywhere along the conflict timeline: preconflict, during the dispute, on the threshold of violence, postconflict, and in the process of normalizing relations.

The *conflict type* and *relationship of the parties* certainly influence what engagement might accomplish and how it might be carried out. One involving nuclear weapons, such as between the United States and North Korea or between India and Pakistan, clearly poses many obstacles to reaching out, particularly in view of the power disparity between the parties and their history of enmity. Absence of direct, regular, high-level communications is a further complication. The *level of the actors* may be relevant if, for example, local leaders or nongovernmental organizations (NGOs) are in a position to participate in meeting with counterparts and create grassroots relationships. Their work can contribute importantly to the vital process of trust building, but success usually depends on the willingness of their governments to provide meaningful incentives.

Incentives, whether at the official or unofficial level, give substance to a party's effort to reach out, conveying that a peaceful resolution is better than perpetual conflict. But the choice of peace must also mean acceptance of a long-term process of building trust, backed by the notion that security between adversaries will be *mutual*. An Indian scholar recalls Prime Minister Jawaharlal Nehru's wise words when defining the inclusiveness of the new India. It would not be a "Hindu Pakistan," he said.

> Whatever the provocation from Pakistan and whatever the indignities and horrors inflicted on non-Muslims there, we have got to deal with this minority in a civilized manner. We must give them security and the rights of citizens in a democratic state. If we fail to do so, we shall have a festering sore which will eventually poison the whole body politic and probably destroy it.[5]

Nehru's observation is just as applicable to interstate as to internal security relationships: giving the other side security or facing constant insecurity. That circumstance has still not happened in India-Pakistan relations. Creating mutual security is fundamental to the engagement project between the two Koreas, Israel and Palestine, and all the other cases explored in this book.

Trust ultimately depends on the willingness of state leaders and their people to bury or at least put aside past animosities. George Washington so advised in his Farewell Address in 1796. Though the address is best remembered for his warning to avoid "entangling alliances," he also urged avoiding partiality or animosity toward any particular country. He said that

> nothing is more essential than that permanent, inveterate antipathies against particular nations and passionate attachments for others should be excluded, and that in place of them just and amicable feelings toward all should be cultivated. The nation which indulges toward another an habitual hatred or an habitual fondness is in some degree a slave. It is a slave to its animosity or to its affection, either of which is sufficient to lead it astray from its duty and its interest.[6]

Washington's advice is clearly relevant to all the engagement cases I address, for example raising questions about negotiating with "evil," finding a path to peace through the thicket of each side's politics, and acknowledging an adversary's grievances and security concerns. Excessive reliance on one country or persistent hostility toward it was, to Washington, equally risky, compromising foreign policy flexibility on the one hand and promoting domestic insularity on the other. Better to "observe good faith and justice toward all nations. Cultivate peace and harmony with all." Idealistic advice for our times, to be sure; but on the other hand, no one has come up with a better plan for sustainable peace in international relations.

NOTES

1. Lest we forget, the Universal Declaration of Human Rights speaks for all people and cultures in seeking "a world in which human beings shall enjoy freedom of speech and belief and freedom from fear and want . . . as the highest aspiration of the common people."

2. Pope Francis, "Encyclical Letter *Laudato Sí* on Care for Our Common Home," May 24, 2015, http://w2.vatican.va/content/francesco/en/encyclicals/documents/papa-francesco_20150524_enciclica-laudato-si.html.

3. *Global Politics in the Human Interest*, 5th ed. (Boulder, CO: Lynne Rienner Publishers, 2013).

4. Naomi Grimley, "Identity 2016: 'Global Citizenship' Rising, Poll Suggests," April 28, 2016, www.bbc.com/news/world-36139904.

5. Ramachandra Guha, "India's Internal Partition," *New York Times* (hereafter *NYT*), August 15, 2007, 25.

6. Quoted in Henry Steele Commager, ed., *Documents of American History*, 6th ed. (New York: Appleton-Century-Crofts, 1958), 173.

TWO

Engaging Adversaries

ENGAGEMENT: A THIRD WAY

During his initial presidential campaign in 2007, Senator Barack Obama suggested that if elected he was prepared to meet immediately with the leaders of five countries with which the United States had hostile relations, including the Democratic People's Republic of Korea (DPRK, North Korea) and Iran. "It is a disgrace that we have not spoken to them," Obama said. Senator Hillary Clinton, his principal challenger, derided the idea, characterizing it as "irresponsible and frankly naïve." In fact, the two were not that far apart on the subject, since both believed then (and later) that nothing is wrong with meeting adversaries so long as the ground is well prepared ahead of time.[1] Nevertheless, this tempest in a teapot underscored just how sensitive an issue engaging adversaries is, at least as much for domestic political as for foreign policy reasons.

Talk of engaging one's opponents can be treacherous business, all the more so for present and future American leaders. The accepted language of US foreign policy calls for faithfulness to national security interests; toughness with adversaries; military power "second to none"; and determination to spread democracy, liberty, and free markets throughout the world. Engagement has little to do with any of those ideas; its chief aim is to serve the cause of peace, nationally and internationally. Thus, leaders in the United States and elsewhere must take care, for if they choose a public engagement strategy, they probably will need to balance it with reassurances of their commitment to their nation's security and its traditional political values.

Those who speak the language of power will always have the upper hand over proponents of engaging enemies. Condoleezza Rice, for instance, once wrote that "great powers don't just mind their own busi-

7

ness." Indeed, they don't. Great powers—meaning only the United States, so far as she was concerned—respect the sovereignty of states only when it is in their interest to do so. When it is not, they react in ways as diverse as diplomatic isolation, economic and military sanctions, deployment of troops, and attempts at regime change. Operating on realist principles, great powers presume that enemies are permanent and friends are transitory. The normal way of "doing business" in the harsh world of power politics therefore calls for diplomacy backed by military power and preparedness to act unilaterally "in the national interest" when coalitions prove difficult to form or unwieldy to direct. Bridge building, it seems, is the exception that proves the rule of realism.

But realism has its limits, imposed either by the international situation or by a country's domestic politics. Coercive diplomacy, as Robert Jervis has argued, fails more often than it succeeds, often at great cost in lives, money, and credibility—for example, for the United States twice in Iraq, as well as in Serbia, Syria, and Afghanistan.[2] Indeed, one of the psychological pitfalls of coercive diplomacy is that increasingly dire threats—red lines—undermine any prospect of improved relations and in fact lead the target of coercion to become more resistant to threats than before. North Vietnam's willingness to endure years of intensive US bombing rather than end what it saw as a war of national liberation is illustrative, as is North Korea's defiance of United Nations (UN) sanctions on its ballistic missile and nuclear weapon tests. Such cases do not in and of themselves dismiss the option of coercion; ever harsher threats might create a tipping point in favor of an adversary's giving in. But then the threatening party must be prepared to use force without knowing how much force it must use, a hazard underscored by the endless "global war on terror."

Realism also falls short when it relies on worst-case hypothesizing. Presuming the worst of an adversary and arguing on the basis of that adversary's most malevolent intentions sets up impossible barriers for an engagement strategy. Some China studies illustrate the point: the underlying assumption is that China's power will rise in a constantly straight line, ending with it becoming the world's leading economic and military power and hence also a threat to its neighbors. Missing from such analyses (see chapter 4) is attention to China's serious domestic problems, which are a source of weakness and a constraint on action. Those problems may well mean that China's rise will not be indefinitely sustainable; that China's neighbors will resist pressures to accommodate it; and most important, that deeply engaging China might deflect it from any aggressive ambitions.

An alternative to projecting power is to use the levers of globalization. In today's global economy, virtually all states want to partake of foreign investment, trade, loans, aid, and technology transfers. To countries willing to play by globalization's rules—that is, the rules of the World Trade

Organization (WTO), the International Monetary Fund (IMF), the World Bank, and the governments that exercise controlling influence in them—there is the promise of financial rewards, and these can be used as incentives to engage. Bringing Russia and China into the major international financial and economic institutions certainly facilitated a reaching-out process by the West. But economic interdependence more often comes with a price. Recipients of financial assistance must abide by the rules of the "Washington consensus": they must privatize state-owned assets, liberalize investment terms, and remove trade barriers. If they don't, loans, aid, and investments will not be forthcoming from the global financial institutions. Nor is that the worst of it; governments that flout the rules are liable to be subject to credit squeezes, disruption of aid, travel restrictions, high tariffs, a hold on bank accounts abroad, and other sanctions.

Engagement is a third way to deal with unfriendly states that are considered threatening. The purpose of engagement is not to sanctify or otherwise reward a particular government. Rather, it is to improve security—national, regional, and global—by finding a cooperative path to peaceable relations. That requires according an adversary respect, giving it *the space* to change course, and even enhancing the adversary's own sense of security. In this book I identify a number of difficult international relationships in which a strategy of engagement might spell the difference between war and peace, between unending tensions and cooperative—or at least live-and-let-live—relationships.

WHAT IS ENGAGEMENT?

Engagement as Process and Strategy

> It's all part of their [the conservatives'] narrative that "we will keep you safe, cuz we're the real men who aren't afraid to send your kids off to die in wars of choice. And the Democrats are a bunch of nancy-boys who think of war as some sort of last resort. They believe in engagement, and other pansy concessions that could lead to dialogue, or even worse, peace."[3]

Engagement is a process more than a policy, a strategy more than a tactic. It proceeds from the determination to catalyze new directions *for* policy that will set the stage for a more positive relationship with an adversary. To seriously "engage," therefore, is to create an environment conducive to changes of perspective and behavior on *all* sides by focusing on actions (joint as well as unilateral and multilateral) that will move the parties away from destructive conflict. To be effective, however (i.e., meaningful to the other side), engagement should be undertaken strategically—as a calculated use of incentives with the expectation of *mutual* rewards, namely in security and peace.[4] As one of President Obama's foreign advisers reportedly said, "Engagement should be judged as a means to an end, not as a policy goal itself."[5]

"Engagement" is often misused when characterizing a government's direction. What the media, public officials, and many scholars call "engagement" is in fact simply *contact* or *nonviolent dealings* with an adversary. American diplomats reference "deep, or positive, engagement" with China, for example, when discussing the many ways the United States and China interact.[6] International relations scholars talk about engagement as America's enduring grand strategy.[7] Writing on President Obama's early diplomacy, one reporter defined engagement as "shorthand for 'talking to your enemies,' or at least to countries with which you have profound differences."[8] In that vein, US officials were reported to be considering "a fresh effort at engagement" with North Korea, when in fact they weren't.[9] Such misuse of the term exaggerates the content and misses the purpose of engagement, implying the presence of a substance and an aim that do not exist.

Engagement should also be distinguished from instances in which adversarial countries realign their interests and establish friendly relations. Such turnabouts in international relations do occur from time to time. But are they the result of an engagement strategy? They might be, provided they lead to a deeper effort at mutual accommodation, such as by seeking to right past wrongs, creating a dialogue on security concerns, and exchanging concessions. Otherwise, the realignment is likely to be merely a response to changing circumstances and therefore temporary and subject to reversal. A country's decision to embrace a new *process* for dealing with an adversary is key.[10] For example, starting late in 2015, Turkey and Russia had a serious falling out over Syria, made worse by Turkey's downing of a Russian plane. But a year later they reconciled as each side modified its objectives in Syria: Turkey by focusing military activity on the Syrian Kurds rather than on the overthrow of Bashar al-Assad, and Russia by avoiding that part of the border area while continuing to protect Assad's government. This dual shift made it possible for both sides to deal quietly with the assassination of Russia's ambassador to Ankara in December 2016, in what otherwise would have been a major crisis.[11] But I argue that Turkish-Russian *engagement* did not occur; it was merely a marriage of convenience for the purpose of avoiding conflict between them in Syria. Absent deeper interaction, chances are the two countries will have another falling out sooner or later.

Strategic Engagement

All these distinctions underscore the difference between true engagement—a *strategy* of conflict prevention—and interactions that fall short of it. By defining engagement as strategic, I mean to suggest a calibrated plan that is carried out methodically and deliberately for as long as it yields positive results. One country's effort to engage invites reciprocity, thus setting in motion a succession of positive changes in policy and outlook.[12] Reciprocity does not necessarily mean exchanges or concessions of equivalent value. Nor need reciprocity come immediately. The greater the gap in real power between contending sides, the greater the obligation of the more powerful side to create an inducement to engage and to be patient in expecting positive returns. At some point not too far down the road, a reciprocal gesture is to be expected; but at its early stages the main purpose of a unilateral act is to build trust and *invite* a positive response. The literature on reciprocity suggests a variety of categories.[13]

Engagement is not an easy strategy. Both parties seeking to engage need persistence, forbearance, ingenuity, and a tough skin for dealing with critics at home and abroad.[14] In short, engagement *is* for "real men" (and real women) who want to avoid war if at all possible. Practitioners must be sensitive to how much of foreign policy is driven by domestic politics everywhere and not only in their own backyards, as discussed in more detail later. Like negotiation and mediation, engagement relies on credibility, flexibility, and other qualities that enable access to the other side and the opportunity to talk or bargain. This is why engagement signifies a *process* as well as an outcome: sticking to the plan, so to speak.

But there is a difference between engagement and negotiating. Engagement is a long-term strategy that may involve negotiations but embraces a good deal more, including unilateral steps, multilateral formats, and exchanges below the official level. Face-to-face official talks between adversaries may result in give and take leading to agreement; but they may also get nowhere, particularly if the actual purpose of talking is to *win* instead of to find common ground. At the same time, agreements reached by an NGO with an adversarial government may contribute importantly to engagement. Moreover, if official talks are undertaken from the standpoint of engagement, they can bring rewards over time even if they do not result in settlements. Examples are the Six Party Talks on North Korea's nuclear weapons, the Association of Southeast Asian Nations (ASEAN) "habit of dialogue,"[15] and the Israeli-Palestinian talks at Oslo in 1993. None of these produced enduring agreements, but they did show that persistent talking in an atmosphere of mutual respect is capable of creating small breakthroughs, probably more so than if pressure tactics had been used. As the speaker of the Iranian parliament said, in the same breath with which he endorsed the idea of a nuclear Iran: "We may be sure that the Americans are our enemy. Working with enemies is part of world politics. I believe that a strategy of curbing and reducing disruptions and normalizing relations is itself beneficial."[16]

Sanctions

Since the 1990s sanctions have gained favor as a way for Western governments, individually and within the UN, to promote liberal political reforms and change the behavior of an adversary that flouts international norms. We might think of sanctions as negative engagement—seeking to pressure an opponent back to "reality"—meaning, in official parlance, rejoining "the international community." Apart from frequently hurting the wrong (read: innocent) people, sanctions more often accomplish precisely the opposite of their intended political purpose. If the message to an adversary is that talks are possible once the adversary changes its behavior, as the United States and others have communicated to Iran and North Korea, economic and other sanctions send another message entirely: *dis*engagement.[17] Even where two parties have numerous points of contact at every level, official and unofficial, as in US-China relations, sanctions imposed on government entities can seriously hinder deeper engagement.[18] And where sanctions are entirely relied on to change a regime's behavior, without the "carrot" of negotiations or other incentives—examples are US relations with Saddam Hussein's Iraq, Bashar al-Assad's Syria, and Vladimir Putin's Russia—failure is fairly predictable. Using sanctions to move a regime toward respect for human rights, for example, is more likely to result in greater repression.[19] Sanctions may sometimes be appropriate for *moral* reasons, as in the disinvestment movement against South Africa under apartheid, or in response to a regime that commits aggression. But as a strategic move, sanctions historically have rarely accomplished their political goals.

In terms of popular support and elite cohesion, sanctions are more likely to strengthen than weaken the targeted regime, as has happened with US and UN sanctions against North Korea. Escalating punishment, such as restrictions on economic aid and trade, will not hurt those in power, but it will incite nationalism and increase dependence on the regime. A regime under sanctions will use that situation to justify resistance to foreign pressure, and the more of one, the more of the other. As one expert has noted about US sanctions against Iran:

> Since 2003, Washington has relied on sanctions to bring Iran to the international bargaining table. . . . Rather than pushing for a negotiated solution to the crisis, Washington has often seemed to be holding out for Iran to simply capitulate. But that only undermines the original purpose of the sanctions—to resolve the crisis without war—because sanctions can be a two-edged sword. The more pressure they exert, the more suspicious Iran's leaders get about America's real intentions. The more suspicious they are, the more they want a nuclear program. And the closer they get to their nuclear goals, the more they feel able to resist new pressure.[20]

In fact, that is exactly the Iranian response to sanctions to this day. As Iran's foreign minister said in 2017, threats don't work in gaining Iran's cooperation. Iran prefers "the language of respect, the language of mutual interest."[21]

There may be times when sanctions can become an inducement to engagement, provided they are used with that end in mind. Consider the case of Iran's insistence on the right to enrich uranium. In December 2007 an impasse in talks occurred when the Iranians once again stonewalled the major powers by stating there was no nuclear problem and that the government would only deal with the International Atomic Energy Agency (IAEA).[22] Iran was well within its rights to take that position; but it gave the United States and its European Union (EU) partners the opportunity to impose new sanctions to bring it back to the negotiating table. They sent Iran the message that sanctions were firm but removable if a nuclear deal could be worked out. Such a tactical, rewards-based use of sanctions is different from imposing sanctions to bring down an opponent's regime or cause its economy to collapse.

Myanmar may be another exception. The military junta has taken steps to reform its political system, notably by permitting parliamentary elections in 2015 that enabled Aung San Suu Kyi to return to the political scene after fifteen years under house arrest. The United States and the EU responded by easing some sanctions and restoring ties: diplomatic relations, aid facilities, and official visits.[23] They are waiting to see how far Myanmar's reforms will go, and they have an eye on China, which has been Myanmar's chief economic partner. Here we have an excellent example of carrots before sticks: sanctions will be reimposed if Myanmar backslides on reforms, but if the military refrains from committing major abuses of human rights, it will be rewarded. Unfortunately, the Myanmar military failed the test in 2017, when it carried out a campaign of terror against the minority Rohingya Muslims that has led to pillaging of villages, atrocities, and the flight of over 600,000 people to neighboring Bangladesh. Targeted sanctions on the military, such as an arms embargo, now seem likely.

Sanctions are among the negative steps that, far from supporting engagement with an adversary, will more likely be the death of it. Other examples are providing weapons and economic assistance to disputing parties as incentives to engage, such as US military aid to Israel and Egypt, or to India and Pakistan, and seeking to influence a government's choice of engagement by intervening in its politics, such as by bribing officials. As Charles A. Kupchan has written, "the historical record confirms that accommodation, not confrontation, is usually the essential ingredient of successful rapprochement."[24]

Modes of Engagement

As mentioned, a chief purpose of engaging enemies is to promote one's own security, in the course of which others' security may also be strengthened. Difficult, unpredictable relations need to be put on a businesslike, stable, reciprocal basis, with the common understanding of the parties that adherence to mutually acceptable rules will bring shared (though not necessarily the same or equal) benefits. Common experiences will presumptively create positive grounds for wider ties using different formats—unilateral, bilateral, and multilateral—and different levels (or tracks) of international relations: official (Track I), semiofficial (Track II), and nongovernmental (Track III). These options can be pursued using any number of methods: diplomatic (such as through official recognition, the establishment of formal relations, or institution building within regional and global organizations, all of which are unique to Track I), economic (such as trade, aid, and investment), military (confidence-building arrangements), and dialogue (via exchanges of ideas and people).[25] Every conflict situation is unique, and one cannot say in advance which format, level, and method of engagement should be applied and at what point in the engagement effort which of them will work best.

Table 2.1 shows a a simple matrix that may prompt thinking about the kinds of symbolic, diplomatic, and substantive actions governments, businesses, NGOs, and other entities might take to open a path to an enemy or rival. Table 2.2 displays some of the many modes or tools of engagement, most of which apply in any of the three tracks.[26]

Table 2.1.   Levels of Engagement

	Unilateral	*Bilateral*	*Multilateral*
Track I	Diplomatic	Diplomatic	Diplomatic
	Economic	Economic	Economic
	Military	Military	Military
Track II	Economic	Economic	Economic
	Military	Military	Military
	Dialogue	Dialogue	Dialogue
Track III	Economic	Economic	Economic
	Military	Military	Military
	Dialogue	Dialogue	Dialogue

The Challenges of Engaging

Should a democratic government engage with "evil?" The decision to engage an adversary, like talking with hostage takers, is difficult and will always prompt second-guessing. After all, engagement is not always an acceptable option. There are times when it is a morally and strategically

Table 2.2. Tools of Engagement

Initial Material Steps	Initial Nonmaterial Steps	Later Material Steps	Later Nonmaterial Steps
Inducements	Emissaries	Trade-offs	Formal arrangements
Exchanges	Negative incentives	CBMs/CSBMs	Personal relationships
Informal understandings	Honest brokers	Functional cooperation	
	Signaling	Tracking	
	Symbolic gestures	Cooperative structures	
		Follow-on inducements	

See note 26 for definition of terms.

foolish pursuit, when in fact disassociating from an aggressive country, sanctioning it, and in the extreme case using force in a collective security action to save large populations may be the right and necessary thing to do. A government that engages in genocide, ethnic cleansing, or other heinous crimes does not deserve to be "engaged," for what is there to bargain about, and why legitimate criminal behavior? How can common ground possibly be found when a leader's interest is to cement a dictatorship, wipe out opponents, and perhaps seek to conquer neighboring countries? Engagement, after all, does not spring from pacifism. Bishop Desmond Tutu, the Nobel Peace Prize winner who headed resistance to apartheid in South Africa, said about this: "When you are faced with a Hitler, I don't think he listens to moral persuasion. And when he pushes people into gas chambers, you have to do something to stop it. I think there are things you have to fight for and maybe be killed for."[27]

In our times we have had several candidates who are undeserving of engagement, such as Pol Pot in Cambodia, the Serbian leaders Radovan Karadžić (president of Republika Srpska) and Slobodan Milošević (president of the former Yugoslavia) during the Bosnian war, Robert Mugabe in Zimbabwe, Bashar al-Assad in Syria, and Abu Bakr al-Baghdadi of the Islamic State in Iraq and Syria (ISIS).[28] These individuals were or are absolutists; they are all about power: preserving it, expanding it, and abusing it without limit. They are not in the least interested in bargaining away or moderating their power. They tolerate no challenges to their authority and view outsiders' peacemaking overtures with disdain. Contact with them may sometimes be necessary, as happened with Assad in a failed US attempt in 2013 to get him to destroy his chemical weapons and then, in 2015–2016, bring about a cease-fire with Russia's support.[29] But accepting the legitimacy of such leaders and plying them with incentives to cease killing and repression is useless. On the contrary, these are cases in which the use of force or pressure is the only thing that stands between their crimes against humanity and perpetual despotism.[30]

Yet I argue in this study that directly engaging some dictators and authoritarian governments, such as North Korea's and Iran's, may sometimes be the preferable road to take. What's the difference between dealing with leaders of those countries and not with the others just mentioned? Iran is under the repressive rule of an ayatollah and his Revolutionary Guards, and North Korea's notorious gulag invites comparisons with the Khmer Rouge torture chambers and Stalin's labor camps. But those governments are not hell-bent on expansion, value international acceptance, and have proven open to negotiations on security issues. They have a record of compliance with agreements (as well as cheating), and they have not deployed weapons of mass destruction. Their international conduct, though sometimes provocative, often arises out of defensiveness and insecurity, which are strongly related to a long history of US threats and interventions. Iran's well-educated population has elements of civil society and prodemocracy forces that an engagement strategy would encourage. While it has a supreme clerical leader, Iran also has an elected president, parliament, and city councils, with both men and women able to vote. North Korean leaders have shown a willingness in the past to exchange greater regime and state security for denuclearization and economic aid, which over time might bring about improvements in the lives of ordinary people and constrain the country's nuclear weapons ambitions.[31] Take away the US threat, and both countries' security pictures improve immeasurably. In a word, these leaders need the United States as much as they fear and despise it.

Should only "nice guys" be engaged? "Nice guys" are easy to engage; tough adversaries are the kind that need attention. One has to keep in mind the endgame, which in the first instance is to keep conflict from turning violent. That goal invites a basic question from adversaries: Who is the evil doer? *They* (our enemies) are the ones who have sanctioned and pressured us, sought regime change, imposed sanctions, rejected our overtures, and failed to fulfill agreements. *We* are the ones under constant threat. *We* are the ones who were provoked to retaliate. *They* persist in behaving as though the Cold War were still around. These are all charges that major-power leaders, particularly in the United States, have had to face, whether they have been interested in engaging an adversary or not. The fact is that some of these charges are accurate and must be addressed: by talking, not by confronting.

The Limits of Engagement

Engagement is not an act of charity or a weak-kneed attempt to postpone the inevitable; it is a process chosen because of its expected benefits. As a kind of soft power, it may open other societies to new ideas—not crass commercialism, but civil society, good governance, respect for human rights, and resource conservation, to name a few. Practicing engagement may also create greater mutual security, create opportunities to settle outstanding issues (such as territorial and financial disputes), improve economic conditions and terms for doing business, and reduce armaments. But any and all of these benefits must be seen by both sides as *incentives* to begin a rapprochement.

Just as it is easier to go to war than to achieve a lasting peace, it is easier to make threats than to craft believable promises. Historical animosities, and sometimes actual fighting, are invariably present in interstate disputes; they alone create exceptional difficulties when it comes to one set of leaders believing the promises of an adversary. Belief requires developing a trusting relationship and, as Nicholas J. Wheeler has written, a trusting relationship requires that one side expose its *vulnerability*. A government must take a risk for peace in order to demonstrate that it is trustworthy.[32] Unilaterally reducing or redeploying one's forces or weapons, for example, or stopping military aid to an ally while providing economic aid to an adversary, demonstrates good faith by reducing one's security and increasing the other's security. However, one side's notion of good faith may not be interpreted that way by the other side, so incentives for peace must be devised with the opposing leadership's priorities clearly understood, and as Wheeler reminds us, while somehow also sidelining influential domestic players who might sabotage a trust-building initiative.

Engagement adversaries also need to ask: What are the consequences of refusing engagement? There are opportunity costs for rejecting engagement, such as *denial* of the benefits of deeper contacts—not just punishing sanctions but also dissociation, such as reducing or eliminating aid or refusing to support the rival's case in international organizations. The country that rejects diplomatic engagement, trade relations, and opportunities for exchange needs to know that the other party will read its rejection as a hostile act, thus deepening suspicions and possibly setting the stage for costly reprisals. But the more powerful party that seeks engagement may also pay a price. For example, US failure to reach new understandings with North Korea has led Pyongyang to continue testing and refining ballistic missiles and nuclear weapons, raising the distinct possibility that it will eventually have a nuclear-tipped missile capable of reaching US shores. Failure to engage Iran at the Track II and Track III levels has meant lost opportunities for business, educators, and politicians hoping for a democratic revival. Nonengagement will embolden the most hawkish elements in those countries' leaderships, providing them with further evidence that nuclear weapons are the only real security against an untrustworthy America. Finally, failure to engage North Korea and Iran ensures lasting hostility, reflected in these regimes' support of terrorist and other militant groups, export of missile components, undermining of relations with neighboring countries, and incentives for some of those neighbors to arm to the teeth and even "go nuclear."

THE POLITICS OF ENGAGEMENT

Friends and Foes at Home

Perhaps the greatest barrier to the party that initiates an engagement strategy lies on the home front, in the domestic political environment. Enemies abound: in the opposition party or faction, in journalistic circles, in a nationalistic public, in the military, and perhaps even in the leader's inner circle. These opponents will go to great lengths to undermine engagement policies, and their ability to do so is at least as great as the ability to reach out to the other side. The more successful opponents are at painting engagement as a flawed process or worse—as appeasement, for example—the more risk averse they make the leadership.

On the other hand, a one-sided approach to engagement—something akin to peace at any price—does warrant critical scrutiny. It is one thing to reset relations with an adversary and quite another to pretend that there are no serious differences with it. In contrast with Obama, who tried and failed to "reset" relations with Russia (see chapter 5), Donald Trump consistently praised Russia's leader, Vladimir Putin, and treated Russia uncritically despite harsh criticism from Republicans and Democrats. Trump found that the politics of engagement leaves little room for going soft on an adversary. The difference between him and Obama is that Obama held to *terms* of engagement—a mutual bargaining format— whereas Trump simply hoped that goodwill could be restored without demanding any satisfaction of US interests in return.

Or consider relations between the Republic of Korea (ROK, South Korea) and Japan, which have a history—Japan's colonization of Korea from 1910 to 1945—just as troubled as those between China and Japan. At various times, South Korean officials have said they would be "future-oriented" with Japan and drop references to past grievances. President Kim Dae-jung agreed with his Japanese hosts to look only to the future when he visited Tokyo in 1998 and announced, with them, a new friendship declaration. In 2008, following the election of Lee Myung-bak, his ambassador to Tokyo again pledged to seek "future-oriented relations" with Japan. "President Lee advised me not to be trapped in the past and obsess with small issues," an official told Korean reporters. "He also said we should form future-oriented relations with Japan and become its close friend and a fair competitor."[33] Unfortunately these statements aroused the ire of human rights groups in South Korea. Shelving disputes proved politically impossible; these groups preferred to keep the pot boiling. Lee wound up making a provocative, first-time visit by a president to Dokdo, a disputed island. His successor, Park Geun-hye, went a step further by ignoring Japan when it came to summit diplomacy; she visited China instead.

When Secretary of State John Kerry put together a new framework for a final settlement of the Israeli-Palestinian conflict in 2014, the greatest obstacle to Israel's agreement lay in Prime Minister Benjamin Netanyahu's own backyard. As Thomas Friedman wrote at the time, the risks to Netanyahu's leadership were daunting:

> [A]lthough Netanyahu has started to prepare the ground here for the U.S. plan—if he proceeds on its basis, even with reservations, his coalition will likely collapse. He will lose a major part of his own Likud Party and all his other right-wing allies. In short, for Netanyahu to move forward, he will have to build a new political base around centrist parties. To do that, Netanyahu would have to become, to some degree, a new leader—overcoming his own innate ambivalence about any deal with the Palestinians to become Israel's most vocal and enthusiastic salesman for a two-state deal, otherwise it would never pass.[34]

As Friedman put it, Netanyahu would have had to make a political U-turn to accept the US plan, essentially making enemies of his supporters and supporters of his enemies. He refused to do so.

If only for domestic political reasons, engaging an unfriendly state has a time limit. The political opposition and public opinion may not tolerate unreciprocated generosity for very long, least of all when a dispute has cost lives or when a government has developed a well-earned reputation for repressing its citizens. Oppositional politics places expectations on engagement efforts to produce reciprocity, if not immediately then soon. Thus, while engagement may begin with unilateral acts to inspire good feeling and generate trust, at some point the other side needs to demonstrate good faith and respond with positive measures of its own. In the early 1990s, for example, relations between North and South Korea were relatively harmonious: President George H. W. Bush authorized withdrawal of tactical nuclear weapons from the ROK, and the two Koreas signed accords on denuclearization of the Korean peninsula and exchanges of goods and people. The DPRK agreed to join the Nuclear Nonproliferation Treaty regime and open its lone nuclear reactor to inspection. The future of inter-Korean relations looked rosy. But the discovery of an enrichment facility in the North brought on a crisis in US and South Korean relations with the DPRK that nearly resulted in a US attack on the North's nuclear facility. The crisis also left a lasting legacy of North Korean cheating that plagues arguments (including my own in chapter 5) for reviving negotiations.

The specific domestic forces that may come into play in any internal debate on engagement are many and varied. Democracies, with their checks and balances and competing political forces, pose particular hurdles for leadership on engagement. *Bureaucratic politics* may pit different government agencies against one another and may find agency heads taking positions on the basis of narrow self-interest (e.g., increasing missions and budget) rather than the national interest. *Public opinion* can be influential even in the most authoritarian country. *Media*, including *social media*, have as many ways to challenge and undercut official policy as to support it. *Nongovernmental organizations* may lobby for or against engagement depending on their philosophical view and objective. *Businesses*, domestic and foreign invested, usually have a strong interest in engagement if their stake in a country is, or could become, important.

The salience of any of these forces depends, needless to say, on the visibility and immediacy of the issues at hand, on how strongly engagement impacts the interests of specific groups, and on competing issues of the moment. Presidential politics also matters greatly; a popular president, or one who (like Obama when engaging Cuba) is at the end of his term, will surely have more leeway to attempt to engage an adversary than an embattled president in midterm.

Politics on the Other Side

The country that is the target of engagement has its own assortment of antiengagement forces. Critics of engagement will always have the upper hand when political leaders are embarking on a new course that involves discarding old stereotypes. As does the engager country, the "engagee" inevitably has people who will show impatience with the absence of results. They will charge that engagement is a recipe for a sellout of national interests, by which they often mean it will threaten a particular bureaucracy, career, or business. Engaging the enemy may also undermine the ruling ideology and may turn public opinion against a regime. We can be sure that there are plenty of Chinese, North Korean, Iranian, and Cuban analysts and officials who seek to prevent a closer relationship with the United States or the West in general. It doesn't take much to upset engagement efforts or arguments for them: an incident at sea; an unintended diplomatic slight; a military exercise; or a critical comment by an official or news organization on the country's leadership, economy, or belief system.[35]

Allies of the government that seeks to engage may also become formidable foes. When allies believe themselves threatened by a partner's engagement efforts, they start whining about their vulnerability and demanding some sort of compensation for it. No sooner was the nuclear deal with Iran concluded, for example, than the Israelis, Saudis, and other US Middle East partners criticized it as representing abandonment and emboldening Iran to become a stronger meddler in its neighbors' affairs. All sorts of dire predictions were made about horrendous consequences, clearly intended to influence the Obama administration to give these folks something for their pain, such as money, arms (both of which they received in abundance), and especially new defense commitments.

When allies make such demands, they count on support in the engagement-initiating country from people who feast on threats and specialize in worst-case hypothesizing. Once engagement is underway, these critics are in full throttle, talking as though engaging a former enemy amounts to something just short of treason. It takes exceptional leadership to overcome such charges. We saw this drama on display in the Iran case: Israel under Netanyahu constantly railed against Obama's conclusion of a nuclear accord with Iran and predicted that the Middle East would completely unravel because of it. In such circumstances, the burden is on the president to resist such pressures. Obama knew from the outset of negotiations with Iran that reaching an agreement that had the ayatollah's blessing was only half the battle, that the other half was at home and with Iran's enemies in the Middle East. With Donald Trump in office, however, Netanyahu found an ally in moving back from engagement with Iran.

Leadership on Engagement

One should not think, however, that state leaders are entirely at the mercy of opponents of engagement. Leaders have plenty of ammunition to override or preempt opponents, starting with the leaders' popularity at home and whether or not they are subject to reelection. Their other significant weapon is secret diplomacy, carried out by executive decision and without consulting other parts of the government. Examples include Henry Kissinger's secret trip to China from Pakistan in 1971, Obama's backdoor diplomacy with Iran via Oman in 2012, and the lengthy behind-the-scenes US-Cuba talks in Canada and the Vatican that led to normalization of relations at the end of 2014. These unilateral steps isolated or sidelined domestic forces, at least temporarily, including people within Obama's own administration; they also added to the predictable angry backlash of engagement's opponents, who shouted betrayal.

The sad fact is that when it comes to engagement, the more open and consensual the policy-making process, the more vulnerable engagement is to defeat. Operating secretly affords the power to frame the policy narrative. Obama's communications team put out a story, which the president repeated, that the 2015 nuclear agreement with Iran was crafted over a two-year period that coincided with the election of Hassan Rouhani as Iran's president. In fact the process had begun much earlier. But it was politically useful for the president to portray the agreement as the result of the coming to power of a "moderate" Iranian.[36] Selling the agreement then became a matter of tailoring all news related to Iran to specific audiences at home and abroad and in the most optimistic terms.

Changing the narrative—finding the appropriate language to signify a shift in relations—is another tool available to engagement-minded leaders. It means abandoning the blame game. Depicting the other side as being totally responsible for ongoing conflict and insisting that only its changed behavior can lead to a resolution may seem necessary for internal reasons. But if engagement is the aim, a one-sided narrative is highly unlikely to promote it, especially when the other side's narrative calls for resistance to attempts to dominate it. Until the Obama-Castro rapprochement, the prevailing US narrative had been that Cuba's communist dictatorship needed to be eliminated so that democratic change could be unleashed, whereas the Cuban narrative had been that US sanctions were responsible for Cuba's economic ills and required repression of those who threatened the revolution. In Western relations with Iran, Trita Parsi notes, "a language of Western power and control" always stood in the way of progress in negotiations. It was always the Iranians who had to "meet their international obligations and find a peaceful solution to this issue, and the ball is in their court," as one US official said. Iranians see such language as a matter of Western permission. "Iran is essentially at the mercy of the West, the narrative suggests."[37] And in US relations with the DPRK, the choice given North Korea has invariably been between "joining the international community" and remaining isolated—and heavily sanctioned. North Korean officials will undoubtedly say that only US hostility prevents their country from fully joining the international community. Their response to the US narrative is therefore predictable: denunciations and counterthreats.

A leader committed to engaging enemies must prove herself to the other side at the same time that she establishes her nationalistic bona fides to the satisfaction of domestic critics. That poses quite a problem for the engagee as well. How credible is the offer to engage? Is it well-meaning or just a disguise? Communicating the desire for engagement to an authoritarian system is even more complicated. While a government may be seeking to open up dialogue, its scholars, journalists, and politicians may be loudly debating ways to punish the other side. How are those attacks perceived by a regime that makes no distinction between the public and private spheres and therefore may see advocates of sanctions (or worse) as speaking for the government? Obviously, in a democracy such antiengagement advocacy cannot be silenced. But the engagement-minded leader will be hard pressed to persuade an adversary that the critics do not speak for her administration.

Timing, context, and above all genuineness are essential when seeking to justify engaging an authoritarian rival. The engager must demonstrate that it prefers engagement to confrontation, that there are real rewards for compliance, and that further diplomatic efforts will take place in both bilateral and multilateral settings. Richard Nixon was able to normalize relations with China because the strategy of befriending "the enemy of my enemy" (the Soviet Union) made sense not only to the US public, to many members of Congress, and later to the business community, but also to China's leaders. Nixon and Kissinger exploited the so-called strategic triangle. Presidents since Nixon have all engaged China to one degree or another and have had public support for doing so. But that has not been the case with Cuba, North Korea, Iran, or Russia. A full explanation would cite China's obviously greater importance than any of the others: it is larger, more influential, and more economically and geopolitically important. China looms so large on so many international issues that all US administrations have avoided a confrontational policy with it. While engaging China has its detractors in the United States on both the Left and the Right, it also has strong domestic constituencies. All these considerations apply as well from the Chinese perspective; cooperation with the United States so far outweighs any benefit that might derive from confronting it.

By contrast, other authoritarian states are easy marks for domestic critics, who can count on the US public to support tough policies and can undermine engagement efforts by charging appeasement. Russia is the leading example today. Unlike China, such governments lack a strong US domestic constituency to argue their case; in fact there are plenty of groups and influential individuals who will consistently line up against them. Engagement-minded leaders must "prove" that engaging "rogue" or "aggressive" regimes is in the national interest, which is perhaps an impossible task, made all the more difficult by the failure of these regimes to consistently behave in ways that would make engagement look workable.

In sum, the strategy of engagement is built around *preventive peacemaking*: identifying concrete steps that the parties take—first, to avoid violent conflict and recourse by one or both to coercive behavior, and second, to kick-start a positive, mutually beneficial relationship through incentives that may build trust and test each side's intentions. If there is a golden rule here, it is to climb the ladder of incentives before climbing the ladder of escalation.

"WE APOLOGIZE"

Officially apologizing is one option in an engagement strategy. It is a politically charged element, readily open to criticism from both the side offering the apology and the recipient. That fact limits its actual employment. Yet a proper apology can send a strong signal of hope for a new start in an international relationship. I offer an extended discussion here of apologizing, not to suggest its universal applicability but to illustrate why, like any other engagement option, it has dynamic possibilities.

Who Apologizes?

When state leaders do apologize—I list a number of examples below—it is typically a long overdue response to terrible, illegal, heinous acts that resulted in thousands, sometimes millions, of deaths, mostly of civilians. But such apologies remain rare. Major instances of state aggression have never been apologized for, such as the Soviet interventions in Afghanistan and Czechoslovakia, both the US and Chinese interventions in Vietnam, Iraq's invasion of Kuwait, the Iran-Iraq conflict in the 1980s, and the latter countries' efforts (with the Turks) to wipe out the Kurds. Nor have we heard apologies for enormously destructive internal wars and repressions, such as the Chinese government's Cultural Revolution and Tiananmen bloodbaths, the Serbs' atrocities in Bosnia, the Khmer Rouge genocide in Cambodia, and the Argentine military's "disappearing" of its enemies. On a global scale, governments and corporations share responsibility for desertification, seemingly irreversible climate change, and other acts of wanton destruction of the planet's environment. They have yet to apologize.

Apologizing isn't *necessary* for engagement between enemies to occur, and demands for an apology by one side may even undermine chances for engagement. The United States and Cuba have normalized relations without exchanging apologies. China and the United States have not apologized for their war in Korea and other close calls, yet they have engaged on a number of issues. Still, apologies would be very much in order in those and all the other cases studied here. Why so few apologies? Leaders of states don't want to appear weak, they don't want to injure national pride, and they don't want to run afoul of their political supporters or competitors. Of course they will often insist that they are the wronged party; it is the other side that must apologize. Winners of conflicts also do not apologize, nor do great powers, win or lose (like the United States in Vietnam). Those who ordered secret missions to assassinate foreign leaders such as Patrice Lumumba in the Congo or Cuba's Fidel Castro, the beheading of "infidels," the suppression of Tibet, the abduction of Nigerian girls, or the seizure of Crimea probably will never have to account for their decisions, let alone make an apology. On the contrary, some victors who engaged in criminal behavior will mete out "justice," as they did at the Nuremberg and Tokyo war crimes trials.[38] War crimes, genocide, and crimes against humanity are defined in well-established international covenants, and the International Criminal Court now exists to implement them. But although we may find American, Russian, Chinese, and Europeans defining and deciding the law, we will not find their political leaders in the dock to answer for their own international crimes.

Japan's Elusive "Sorry"

To illustrate how agonizing apologizing can be when it is embedded in politics, I examine Japan's official discounting of its aggressions in World War II and the sexual enslavement of Korean "comfort women." Ian Buruma's *The Wages of Guilt* is a marvelous comparative study of the different ways Germans and Japanese, in positions high and low, have reacted to the aggressions of their governments in the World War II period. Where the Germans have for the most part faced the past forthrightly, the Japanese have reacted with embarrassment, obfuscation, and self-righteousness. The prime minister of Japan will not be like Willy Brandt, who went down on his knees in the Warsaw ghetto to apologize. Nor is the leader of Japan's parliament likely to give his countrymen a history lesson in how the country became a "criminal state," as Philipp Jenninger, president of Germany's Bundestag, did in 1988—for which he was widely criticized. Japan is often holding the other end of the stick, as senior officials manage to find ways to obfuscate the apology issue, such as with assertions of moral equivalence: the atomic bombing was another Holocaust, or Japan's imperialist adventures simply followed the example of Western colonizers, thus excusing or at least mitigating the crimes of the emperor and his military chiefs.

To be sure, Japanese officials have at times apologized for past transgressions, and to some observers they have squarely faced up to the past.[39] When Emperor Akihito paid the first-ever visit of a Japanese emperor to China in October 1992, he expressed "deep sadness" at the "great suffering" inflicted on the Chinese people. In the so-called Kono Statement of 1993, a cabinet official admitted that the military had resorted to sexual slavery, and in 1995 socialist prime minister Murayama Tomiichi acknowledged Japan's aggression in World War II. Prime Minister Obuchi Keizo, in a joint statement with South Korea's president Kim Dae-jung in 1998, expressed "deep remorse and heartfelt apology" for the "tremendous damage and suffering" Japan had caused. On the fiftieth anniversary of Japan's defeat, August 15, 2005, Prime Minister Koizumi Junichiro said: "Our country has caused tremendous damage and pain to the peoples of many countries, especially Asian countries, through colonial rule and invasion. Humbly acknowledging such facts of history, I once again reflect most deeply and offer apologies from my heart." And again, on the one hundredth anniversary of Japan's annexation of Korea in 1910, Prime Minister Kan Naoto said: "For the enormous damage and suffering caused during this colonial rule, I would like to express once again our deep remorse and heartfelt apology."[40]

But Japan's ultranationalists and various government officials have consistently objected to the statements and would clearly prefer that they be disavowed or at least forgotten. Under Prime Minister Abe Shinzo, excuses for the past have sometimes given way to outright attempts to bury it. Ominously, Abe's resistance to apologizing has unleashed right-wing assaults on intellectuals and the liberal press, among whom regret over Japanese imperialism's rampages and support of Article 9 of Japan's "peace constitution" remain strong.[41] Politics rules; the Abe administration took advantage of anti-Japanese sentiment in China to gain a sympathetic hearing among the Japanese public against further apologizing. Yoshihide Soeya quotes one senior Japanese government official as acknowledging that it is harder to deal with Japanese conservatives than with people in Beijing or Seoul on the issue. "You always have to be careful about friendly fire from behind," he said.[42]

Abe, a neonationalist, wants the Japanese to take pride in their history, upgrade the military's role in national security, and change Article 9 to allow the military to engage in collective security actions abroad. Abe established himself as a history denier in an earlier term as prime minister, saying, for example, that there was no proof that the Imperial Army forced "comfort women" into prostitution or trafficked in them.[43] He has not fully reversed that position today. So, while Abe has finally shaken the hand of China's leader and vowed to "learn from" the past, he has avoided numerous opportunities to face up to that past and fully support previous Japanese statements of regret.[44]

Abe's best opportunity came in 2015 on the seventieth anniversary of the end of World War II in the Pacific. In a long-awaited address that many hoped would clarify his stance on apologizing, Abe recounted Japan's "wrong course" to war and said: "I express my feelings of profound grief and my eternal, sincere condolences" to all the innocent victims. Abe also expressed personal sorrow over "women . . . whose honor and dignity were severely injured" in the war, as well as "deep repentance" and a promise not to repeat Japan's actions. But as for personally apologizing, Abe walked a fine line. "Japan has repeatedly expressed the feelings of deep remorse and heartfelt apology for its actions during the war," he said. "Such position articulated by the previous cabinets will remain unshakable into the future." The inevitable contrast that observers drew was with Abe's predecessors, who did make personal apologies. Abe, with his domestic audience in mind, would not go that far, thus once again giving critics (e.g., in Beijing) an opening to charge that he was merely playing with words.[45]

It Can Be Done

There are precedents for official apologies, or at least statements that tend in that direction. Some examples over roughly the last twenty-five years are the British government's acknowledgment in 1997 of its role in bringing on "The Great Hunger" in Ireland between 1845 and 1850; President Ronald Reagan's formal apology to Japanese Americans who had been interned after Pearl Harbor by order of President Franklin D. Roosevelt; North Korean leader Kim Jong-Il's apology in 2002 to Prime Minister Koizumi for his country's abduction of twelve people from Japan in the 1970s and 1980s, in return for which Koizumi expressed "deep remorse and heartfelt apology" for Japan's thirty-five years of colonial rule over Korea; the Australian government's apology to its aboriginal people in 2008 for the degrading actions of the government over many years, in particular the removal of many thousands of aboriginal children from their families as part of a policy of forced assimilation; President Bill Clinton's statement that the United States was "wrong" to support the right-wing Guatemalan government's attacks on Mayan villagers and leftist guerrillas in the 1960s; the Irish government's apology in 2013 to more than ten thousand women who, over about seventy-five years, had been detained and forced to work without pay and under harsh conditions in laundries in which the state had an interest; the apology of Pope Francis in 2015, while on a tour of Latin America, for the "many grave sins" of the church "committed against the native people of America"; and the apology in 2016 of Taiwan's new president, Tsai Ing-wen, to the island's aboriginal population for centuries of maltreatment.

Note, however, certain common elements in these apologies and regrets. They were long overdue and were the subject of frequent political wrangling before finally being issued. Political opposition to apologizing usually centered on the argument that only the government that caused the harm could legitimately apologize—a feeble excuse, but one that carried the day for many years. Except for the interned Japanese Americans and the Japanese abductions, none of the apologies was offered with compensation to the victims and their survivors. (In the latter case, it was the Japanese government that paid, but in the form of economic aid.) Finally, in no case was the harm caused declared a crime as a warning to then-present or future officials.

Engaging an adversary by apologizing does not cancel out the terrible wrong that has been inflicted. Nor does it remove the possibility that some wrongs could have been prevented by concerted action, including military action. In other words, a distinction must be made between preventive steps in the case of potential mass murder and the opportunity for the perpetrator to begin making amends to the victims by apologizing. Both the failure to act and the consequences of the act require apology. Two cases come to mind: Rwanda and Srebrenica.[46] The international community failed to act against a looming genocide in both cases; only in the Rwanda case was an apology offered (by President Clinton in 1994) for inaction and the consequent genocide. Neither Rwanda's Hutu *genocidaires* nor Serbia's president, who authorized the killing of some eight thousand Bosnian Muslims, apologized for the crimes committed in their names. And who will apologize for the destruction of Aleppo, Syria, and the slaughter of so many thousands of its citizens?

Apologies Matter

Does apologizing matter? Britain's apology to Ireland may have helped in the settlement of the conflict in Northern Ireland and the demobilization of the Irish Republican Army. (In 2002, the IRA also offered "sincere apologies and condolences" to civilians it killed during the thirty-year war in Northern Ireland.[47]) Might not history have been different if Washington had apologized to Iranians for US training and support of the SAVAK (the Shah's secret police) and other costly interventions in Iran's political life? Wouldn't Turkey's stature have risen if it had finally, on the one hundredth anniversary of the genocide against Armenians in 2016, expressed remorse for its near-universally accepted responsibility? If tomorrow Japan were formally and unequivocally to apologize for aggressions and atrocities, wouldn't its international image and relations with its neighbors measurably improve? More important, Japan's sense of self might be different; apologizing would begin a process of healing, even as it would also exacerbate divisions between generations and political factions. Ian Buruma may be right that while Japan's victims want apologies, a fundamental political transformation is the necessary first step. But counting on such a long-term prospect only defers the day of reckoning, which a few choice sentiments could greatly shorten, to the country's immediate benefit.

If we (whoever "we" are) want others to apologize, and say it often, with feeling and just the right words, shouldn't we set an example? Chinese leaders are quite self-righteous about Japanese apologies, but when it comes to apologizing for repression of Tibetans and other ethnic minorities, Beijing has nothing to say. Leaders of the United States might follow the example set by Bill Clinton and offer a heartfelt apology to the people of Hiroshima and Nagasaki. And why not also apologize for US use of torture in the "war on terror"—it's an international and domestic crime, after all—and bring to trial those political and intelligence officials and contracted psychoanalysts who devised and approved it? After all, the United States has essentially apologized for complicity in other states' use of torture. President Obama did so on a visit to Argentina, when he acknowledged wrongful support of that government's "dirty war" against leftists in the 1970s and later declassified documents on "Operation Condor."

Contrition for having inflicted great pain and suffering on other people is the human thing to express. It reveals empathy, a feeling sorely lacking in international affairs. Contrition can also be the pathway to self-analysis and potentially the precondition of policy change. A government that sincerely apologizes hopefully wants to understand what it did and is willing to say, "never again." Who knows? An apology might even help disseminate a new value of nonviolence and global responsibility.

Fearing to Apologize

Apologizing is difficult, even when the governments involved are amenable to doing so. The foremost reason is their publics, where the thinking is likely to be either "we have nothing to apologize for" or "why should we believe them?" After years of hating the other, empathizing and making amends may seem like weaknesses for both the offending party and the victim. And there are other issues that may invite opposition to apologizing: the question of adequate compensation; the credibility of a promise not to commit a crime again; the unspoken preference, usually on the part of politicians, to have an enemy as a convenient target of blame; and the usefulness for budgetary and military purposes of sustaining the notion of a foreign threat. Even if these essentially domestic obstacles can be overcome, the politics of apologizing may have an additional external one: how to apologize in a way that's certain to be accepted. After all, apologizing does take two to tango.

An intriguing question arises: Can "negotiating" over acceptable wording of an apology resolve the issue? Might it be a way to get past political use of apologizing as a lever, as China has repeatedly done? What risks does a negotiated apology carry for both parties? The short answer is that negotiated apologies are not ironclad assurances that grievances will be buried forever. Take South Korea's long-standing anger toward Japan over the comfort women. In December 2015 the two governments reached an agreement on a "final and irreversible resolution" of the issue. The agreement included Abe's "most sincere apologies and remorse" on behalf of Japan (but not himself) and a one-time "consolation" payment of 1 billion yen into a compensation fund for the surviving victims and their families. Even though the South Korean government distributed the money, the two sides remain at an impasse. Pressure from Korean civil society groups led Seoul to insist on "renegotiating" the agreement, which Tokyo has adamantly refused to do. Koreans have erected two memorial statues to honor the comfort women, both in front of Japanese diplomatic missions, as reminders of their continuing outrage. In January 2017 Japan responded by withdrawing its ambassador to South Korea. Some grievances are simply intractable, and some apologies are simply never enough.[48]

Against this background of engagement—the philosophy that defines it and the strategy that animates it—we turn to the cases, which are current and evolving. I begin with the most hopeful ones: US relations with Iran and Cuba. Though apologies have not been prominent in these cases, what was prominent is the reexamination of their history with each other, with the result that historical animosities gave way to agreements to engage in spite of the considerable political obstacles.

NOTES

1. Patrick Healy, "Clinton and Obama Campaigns Spar Over Debate," *NYT*, July 25, 2007. The other three countries were Cuba, Syria, and Venezuela. Most references to the *New York Times* in the notes are from the online edition, which lacks page numbers; references that have page numbers are to the hard copy edition.

2. Jervis, "Getting to Yes with Iran: The Challenge of Coercive Diplomacy," *Foreign Affairs* 92, no. 1 (January–February, 2013): 105–115. Syria should now be added to the list.

3. "Bill Maher Takes Apart the Right Wing's Fake Machismo," January 25, 2014, www.dailykos.com/story/2014/01/25/1272362/-MUST-SEE-Bill-Maher-takes-apart-the-right-wing-s-fake-machismo.

4. The premier work on incentives or inducements is Miroslav Nincic, *The Logic of Positive Engagement* (Ithaca, NY: Cornell University Press, 2011).

5. Denis R. McDonough, quoted by Mark Landler, "On Several Foreign Policy Fronts, Events Force Obama to Turn to Plan B," *NYT*, September 27, 2009, 13.

6. For example, the comment by an Obama administration official: "I certainly think we tested the limit of how far you can get with China through positive engagement." Mark Landler, "Obama's Journey to Tougher Tack on a Rising China," *NYT*, September 20, 2012.

7. For example, Stephen G. Brooks, G. John Ikenberry, and William C. Wohlforth, "Lean Forward: In Defense of American Engagement," *Foreign Affairs* 92, no. 1 (January–February, 2013), pp. 130–142.

8. James Traub, "Obama's Foreign Engagement Scorecard," *NYT*, December 19, 2009.

9. Mark Landler, "U.S. Considers Possibility of Engaging North Korea," *NYT*, August 27, 2010.

10. Miroslav Nincic offers a different perspective, distinguishing between a quid pro quo form of engagement (such as the realignment of interests in the Turkey-Russia example) and a structural change in one party, such as in post-Mao China, that facilitates engagement. Nincic, *Logic of Positive Engagement*, 58–87.

11. Max Fisher, "Turkey, Russia and an Assassination: The Swirling Crises, Explained," *NYT*, December 19, 2016.

12. On strategies of reciprocity, see Charles Osgood, *An Alternative to War and Surrender* (Urbana: University of Illinois Press, 1962).

13. See, for example, Carolyn Rhodes, *Reciprocity, US Trade Policy, and GATT* (Ithaca, NY: Cornell University Press, 1993); Robert Keohane, "Reciprocity in International Relations," *International Organization* 40, no. 1 (Winter, 1986): 1–27; and Michael Mastanduno, *Economic Containment* (Ithaca, NY: Cornell University Press, 1992).

14. Charles A. Kupchan, "Enemies into Friends: How the United States Can Court Its Adversaries," *Foreign Affairs* 89, no. 2 (March–April, 2010): 120–134.

15. As defenders of the "ASEAN Way" say, one thing the organization has achieved is the virtual elimination of the possibility of war among its members. That is certainly an important achievement, though it might be pointed out that *disputes* among the members have not been eliminated, and important differences on particular issues, such as labor migration, Burma's human rights abuses, and transboundary pollution, have often been buried or sidestepped rather than addressed.

16. Ali Larijani, quoted by Ray Takeyh, *Guardians of the Revolution: Iran and the World in the Age of the Ayatollahs*, reviewed by Roger Cohen, "Into the Eye of a Storm," *NYT*, August 5, 2009.

17. Nincic, *Logic of Positive Engagement*, 16–31. Nincic offers the same negative assessment of so-called smart sanctions targeted at a regime's assets rather than at the country as a whole.

18. David E. Sanger, "In Step on 'Light Footprint,' Nominees Reflect a Shift," *NYT*, January 8, 2013.

19. Dursun Peksen and A. Cooper Drury, "Economic Sanctions and Political Repression: Assessing the Impact of Coercive Diplomacy on Political Freedoms," *Human Rights Review* 10 (2009): 393–411.

20. Vali Nasr, "Why Iran May Be Ready to Deal," *NYT*, March 17, 2013.

21. Richard Engel, interview with Mohammad Javad Zarif, foreign minister of Iran, February 19, 2017, www.nbcnews.com/video/javad-zarif-foreign-minister-of-iran-full-interview-with-richard-engel-880666691718.

22. See Elaine Sciolino, "Iranian Official Pushes Nuclear Talks Back to Square 1," *NYT*, December 2, 2007, 3. By this time, according to Mohamed ElBaradei, Iran had already put three thousand centrifuges into operation and prevented IAEA inspectors from determining their purpose.

23. US Department of State, "U.S. Relations with Burma: Fact Sheet," January 27, 2017, www.state.gov/r/pa/ei/bgn/35910.htm.

24. Kupchan, "Enemies into Friends," 123.

25. The distinction between trust building and confidence building measures merits a brief explanation. Though the two are often intertwined and are mutually reinforcing, they are different. Trust building typically involves face-to-face contact over a period of time so as to create, as the ASEAN process puts it, the "habit of dialogue." CBMs are more concrete actions that involve visible means of communicating nonviolent intent, such as hot lines, troop withdrawals from disputed areas, and prior notification of military movements.

26. *Inducements* include aid, trade, and energy assistance, with additional *follow-on inducements* of the same kind. *Exchanges* may be cultural, educational, scientific, sports, people-to-people, and other tools of public diplomacy. *Informal understandings* can be nonbinding pledges, joint statements of resolve, and other unofficial acts. *Emissaries* are peace missions led by very senior deputies to signal seriousness and respect. *Negative incentives* include assurances against attack, punishment, or use of threats. *Honest brokers* are third parties (international organizations, third countries, or trusted individuals) that have a reasonably good working relationship with the disputants and can transmit credible incentives and messages. *Signaling* means sending up a trial balloon to show interest in engagement. *Symbolic gestures* demonstrate cross-cultural awareness and sensitivity to national pride, for example by apologizing, shaking hands, using correct names of countries and correct titles of leaders, erecting (or taking down) memorials, giving "face," and avoiding negative stereotyping. (Raymond Cohen, *Negotiating Across Cultures: International Communication in an Interdependent World*, rev. ed. [Washington, DC: United States Institute of Peace Press, 1997]). *Trade-offs* are quid pro quos, such as territorial or prisoner swaps. *CBMs (confidence-building measures) and CSBMs (confidence and security building measures)* can be hot lines, troop pullbacks or redeployments; codes of conduct; and steps to promote transparency (e.g., weapons reports and advance announcements of military maneuvers). *Functional cooperation* involves joint projects, such as research, construction, program administration, and space exploration. *Tracking* entails creating "situational awareness" (as in space) and sharing of data. *Cooperative structures* are multilateral institutions and projects designed jointly by the parties, for example, environmental protection projects such as resource sharing, joint management of forests and waterways, and early warning systems to safeguard vulnerable environments. (See United Nations Environment Programme, "From Conflict to Peacebuilding: The Role of Natural Resources and the Environment" [Nairobi: UNEP, 2009]). *Formal arrangements* are official undertakings such as treaties, framework agreements, and bans. *Personal relationships* refer to establishing trusting relations with an adversary's counterparts. (As Abraham Lincoln once said, "I don't like that man. I must get to know him better.")

27. *Los Angeles Times*, May 12, 1985, 26.

28. Documents compiled on Syria by the independent group International Justice and Accountability link "the systematic torture and murder of tens of thousands of Syrians to a written policy approved by" Assad. They constitute "a record of state-sponsored torture that is almost unimaginable in its scope and its cruelty." Ben Taub, "The Assad Files," *New Yorker*, April 18, 2016, 36. On Zimbabwe, see Robert I. Rotberg, "Mugabe Über Alles: The Tyranny of Unity in Zimbabwe," *Foreign Affairs* 89, no. 4 (July–August 2010): 10–18.

29. The perilous effort to negotiate with evil became clear in the spring of 2017 when the Syrian regime used sarin, a nerve gas, against a city, killing eighty people (including numerous women and children) and wounding hundreds. The attack up-ended the Obama administration's claim in 2013 that an agreement with Assad had resulted in the total destruction of Syria's chemical stocks and avoided war. Assad could not be—and should not have been—trusted to keep his promises. See Peter Baker, "For Obama, Syria Chemical Attack Shows Risk of 'Deals with Dictators,'" *NYT*, April 9, 2017.

30. On the choices in Bosnia, for example, see Richard Holbrooke, *To End a War* (New York: Random House, 1998).

31. These "mutual gains" are essential to answering positively the question whether or not to negotiate with those some consider evil. The North Korean and Iranian leaderships must, of course, evaluate the situations they face in the same way. See Walter C. Clemens Jr., *North Korea and the World: Human Rights, Arms Control, and Strategies for Negotiation* (Lexington: University Press of Kentucky, 2016), 144–149; and comments by Professor Clemens to the author.

32. Wheeler, "Trust-Building in International Relations," *Peace Prints*, www.wiscomp.org/pp-v4-n2/nick%20wheeler.pdf.

33. *JoongAng Daily* (Seoul), April 19, 2008.

34. Friedman, "Why Kerry Is Scary," *NYT*, January 28, 2014.

35. An example is the fallout from the wiretapping revelations of Edward Snowden, a contract worker for the US National Security Agency. Snowden's leaks of high-level documents showed the scope of US spying not only on domestic communications but also on some Chinese and Russian officials and institutions. Two immediate conse-quences were that US criticisms of China's hacking of US industrial and military computers lost force, and that neither China nor Russia was willing to seize Snowden and turn him over to US authorities when he fled to Hong Kong and then Moscow.

36. David Samuels, "The Aspiring Novelist Who Became Obama's Foreign-Policy Guru," *NYT*, May 8, 2016.

37. Parsi, "Iran Deal More than a Nuclear Issue," *Middle East Eye*, December 7, 2014, www.middleeasteye.net/columns/iran-deal-more-nuclear-issue-1767492686.

38. I am here referring to apologies for large-scale offenses, not incidents that may bring loss of life. Governments are far more likely to apologize for the latter than for the former, as for instance when the United States apologized to Iran when a US warship mistakenly shot down a commercial aircraft in 1988 or to China for the EC-3 air collision over Hainan in 2001.

39. Yoshihide Soeya, "A View from the Inside on Japan's Perpetual Trust Gap," *Global Asia* 8, no. 3 (Fall 2013): 38–41.

40. Martin Fackler, "Japan Apologizes to South Korea on Colonization," *NYT*, August 11, 2010; "Japan's Apologies for World War II," *NYT*, August 13, 2015.

41. As Chung-in Moon observes, some moderate Japanese academics have knuck-led under, dodging the matter of Japan's direct responsibility for atrocities by compar-ing Japan's behavior to that of Great Britain, France, and other colonial powers that never apologized. Moon, "Apology Still a Distant Dream," *Korea JoongAng Daily*, March 17, 2015, http://koreajoongangdaily.joins.com/news/article/article.aspx?aid= 3001991.

42. Soeya, "A View from the Inside," 41.

43. See Mindy Kotler's excellent article, "The Comfort Women and Japan's War on Truth," *NYT*, November 15, 2014.

44. See the interview with Abe in the *Financial Times*, March 27, 2015, 7.

45. Text in *NYT*, August 15, 2015.

46. Edward P. Joseph, "Are the Lessons of Srebrenica Being Forgotten?" *NYT*, July 10, 2015.

47. Brian Lavery, "I.R.A. Apologizes for Civilian Deaths in Its 30-Year Campaign," *NYT*, July 16, 2002.

48. Keeho Yang, "The South Korea-Japan Agreement on Comfort Women: Mending the Past, Building a Future," *EAF Policy Debates*, July 11, 2017, www.keaf.org/book/ EAF_Policy_Debate_The_South_Korea-Japan_Agreement_on_Comfort_Women:_ Mending_the_Past_Building_a_Future?ckattempt=1.

THREE

Successful Engagement

US Relations with Iran and Cuba

Engagement is typically an uneven process, marked by optimistic ups and pessimistic downs. I judge US-Iran and US-Cuba relations as successful cases because they demonstrate concrete steps aimed at overcoming historical enmity and adversarial policies. But they also contain the possibility of backsliding due, above all, to political opposition within each country. Both these cases are marked by well-known histories of US interference that led to decades of hostility, barriers to contact, and conflict in areas near and far. I provide some background, but in the main I focus on the transition from mutual suspicions to the point where engagement opened the door to nonhostile relations, if not friendship.

THE UNITED STATES AND IRAN

Before Obama: Toward Regime Change

The back story to Iran's agreement with the United States and several other countries on reining in its nuclear weapons capability is strikingly similar to the US-led international effort to restrain North Korea's nuclear weapons program (see chapter 5). Despite the significant difference in facing a country with nuclear weapons as opposed to one capable of producing them, the problems confronting engagement have many similarities. First, mutual mistrust cultivated over many years led US officials to give priority to regime change and led Iran's leaders to seek some kind of modus vivendi. Second, the United States missed an exceptional opportunity to reach a deal with Iran, due mainly to far-right resistance in Washington and in Israel. Third, under Obama as under his predeces-

35

sors, sticks (sanctions) invariably had first place over carrots (negotiations). Yet broader sanctions only produced more resistance within Iran to reducing tensions over its nuclear program. The option of negotiations was consistently undermined by putting the onus on Iran for changed behavior.

Historians will rightly say that the story of estrangement between the United States and Iran since World War II should begin with Washington's support of the dynasty of Mohammad Reza Shah Pahlavi, who ruled Iran from 1941 until the Iranian revolution of 1978. The shah took full power following the CIA-engineered coup in 1953 that removed the nationalist premier Mohammad Mossadegh. The overthrow of Mossadegh and then of the shah by the Shiite clergy led by Ayatollah Ruhollah Khomeini cemented the role of the United States as Iran's main enemy. By the same token, US hostility to the Iranian revolutionaries, intensified by the seizure of its embassy personnel in a hostage crisis that lasted 444 days from 1979 to 1981, ensured that US leaders would again target Iran for regime change.

Notwithstanding the abiding mutual enmity, the United States squandered an opportunity for peace in 2003.[1] By then US forces had quickly overthrown Saddam Hussein in Iraq. Neoconservatives in and around the George W. Bush administration were full of themselves, believing that with Iraq subdued, the moment was ripe for going after Iran. Israel strongly supported the idea. Sensing the danger of encirclement, Iran resurrected a Geneva Channel in 2002. Its top leaders prepared an offer — "in mutual respect" — that they never again repeated, but the neoconservatives moved quickly to sabotage any dialogue. Iran's proposal, communicated through the Swiss in May 2003, called for an end to "US hostile behavior" (such as being on Bush's "axis of evil" list), removal of all sanctions against Iran, "full access" to nuclear energy and other technologies, recognition of "Iran's legitimate security interests" in the Middle East, and repatriation of a group the Iranian leadership considered terrorists.[2] In return, Iran promised not to develop or possess weapons of mass destruction, to allow international inspection, to provide "full cooperation" against al-Qaeda and other terrorist groups, to stop support of Hamas and other Palestinian opposition groups, and to work with the United States to create a nonreligious and politically stable Iraq. Iran also said it would adopt a two-state approach to the Israeli-Palestinian conflict favored by the Arab states and thus would recognize and make peace with Israel.

Knowledgeable people in Washington and Europe[3] recognized the extraordinary, groundbreaking nature of Iran's proposal; it was certainly more than enough to warrant direct talks. But the neocons, led by Vice President Dick Cheney, made the classic dismissal: "We don't speak to evil." There would be no negotiations with Iran. As Trita Parsi writes, "These officials opposed a deal with Iran no matter what the ayatollahs offered because, they said, America could get what it wanted for free by simply removing the regime in Tehran."[4] Had these officials taken Iran's offer seriously rather than been guided by ideology, they would have seen a chance to establish an entirely new relationship with Iran that would have had major positive implications for security and political relations throughout the Middle East. Instead, what they got was Iran's support for militant anti-Israel groups and direct Iranian involvement against the United States in nearby conflicts, including Iraq.

The US rejection of a deal surely confirmed to Iran's leaders that the United States was indeed "the Great Satan"—essentially a mirror image of US depictions of Iran—and that Iran should learn from Iraq and North Korea about the virtues of quickly acquiring a nuclear deterrent. The timeline is significant: Iran's nuclear program, which began in 1985, did not achieve significant results until around 2002–2003, when Iranian scientists succeeded in enriching uranium in multiple centrifuges. Iran later admitted to having received help from Pakistan and North Korea.[5] By 2006, although Iran's government publicly pledged that it would never make a nuclear bomb, it announced enrichment in 164 centrifuges—modest progress but, according to experts at that time, far behind the curve of North Korea's nuclear program.[6] In fact, the US intelligence community concluded in 2007 and 2008 that Iran had stopped trying to produce a nuclear weapon *in 2003*:

> We judge with high confidence that in fall 2003, Tehran halted its nuclear weapons design and weaponization activities, as well as its covert military uranium conversion and enrichment-related activities, at least for several years. . . . Iran made significant progress in 2007 installing centrifuges at Natanz, but we judge with moderate confidence it still faces significant technical problems operating them.[7]

The intelligence community concluded that Iran's work on enrichment technology for nuclear energy (and *possibly* weapons) was continuing, as well as on deployment of ballistic missiles that would be capable of delivering nuclear weapons.

These assessments were not as decisive as the Bush administration wanted to hear, especially after the CIA's failure to prove that Iraq had weapons of mass destruction—the famous "slam dunk" that wasn't. As in Iraq, Bush turned to the Pentagon, where Cheney's neocon colleagues held sway.[8] The administration urged European allies not to relax on sanctions.[9] It was at this point that "regime change" entered the official vocabulary, helped by the fact that Iran had hidden its nuclear ambitions for nearly twenty years.

Now in its second term, the Bush administration chose to apply full-court pressure on Iran, rejecting urging in Europe, Russia, and China to seek direct talks with Tehran and also rejecting an "invitation" from Iran's president to Bush for a discussion of principles of proper international behavior.[10] The US failure to pacify Iraq became another argument for regime change in Iran, and not just in doctrine. Bush authorized covert Pentagon operations in Iran, including drone probes,[11] evidently to acquire intelligence for a possible strike against Iran's nuclear facilities. Pakistan and Israel assisted in the planning and execution of the US operation, whereas Congress was kept in the dark, just as it had been during Bush's futile effort to find nuclear weapons in Iraq.[12] Iranian exiles based in Iraq, the Mujahedeen Khalq, as well as other resistance groups, sought aid from allies in the Pentagon despite being officially labeled a terrorist organization by Washington.[13] Secretary of State Condoleezza Rice led the way in pushing for millions of dollars in aid to these groups, contending that it was a way to promote democracy.[14] Hearings were conducted on Capitol Hill on Iran's human rights conditions to support the neocons' determination to undermine the Iranian regime. At some point Bush authorized deployment of a computer worm, "Stuxnet," developed jointly by Israelis and Americans, to undermine and delay Iran's ability to produce a nuclear weapon. This cyberweapon, coupled with US sanctions, evidently did put Iran's nuclear program back by many months.[15]

Covert operations were coupled with threats directed at Iran's nuclear weapons program.[16] Bush said Iran should not have even the knowledge to make a nuclear weapon, much less a weapon itself,[17] and prophesied that a nuclear Iran might mean "World War III." Bush said "the whole strategy" was to "keep the pressure on" Iran and "continue to isolate you in the hopes that at some point somebody else shows up [in the leadership] and says it's not worth the isolation."[18] The Bush team warned Iran often and harshly that nuclear weapons were a red line, that all US options were "on the table," and that Iran would not be offered any incentives for turning away from the nuclear option.[19] Various publications produced stories of US nuclear strike plans, presumably leaked by the administration, and Cheney hinted that Israel might attack Iran's nuclear sites on its own.[20] The neocons' position, communicated to Iran, was simple: no negotiations unless and until Iran "fully and verifiably suspend[s] its enrichment and reprocessing activities."[21] Iran, said Condoleezza Rice, was entitled to a civilian nuclear energy program, and if it did as the United States demanded, it could expect economic benefits. But Iran would not get security assurances, and if it did not suspend the nuclear program, it could expect "a set of penalties, or a set of sanctions." She refused to answer a reporter's question about whether or not the United States was seeking to "overthrow, undermine the Iranian government." In fact, threats were barely disguised: "We have options," Rice said, "that are very near-term options should they [Iran] not make the right choice."

Carrots Over Sticks

But by the time the Obama administration took office in January 2009, reality had set in. Despite widespread agreement in Washington on basic policy—the threat posed by Iran, the need for tough sanctions on Iran, and rejection of negotiations unless Iran essentially gave up the nuclear option—enthusiasm for a military attack on Iran had declined. American officials apparently came to their senses about the practical difficulties and wider implications of a new war, helped along by Russian and Chinese opposition. As one senior US commander put it, "This constant drumbeat of war is not helpful, and it's not useful." Regime change became containment, with the accent on deeper sanctions even though there was no indication that Iran would change course.[22] The case for engagement was out there, but it had a very small audience.[23]

Obama's approach thus amounted to more carrots and stronger sticks. The attack option was still on the US table, and the Stuxnet cyberwar operation continued. But simultaneously, the search was on for a start to negotiations. Thus, at the same time that Obama's staff was reciting the reasons for hanging tough on Iran—and in early 2009 that position was influenced by Iran's launch of a satellite into orbit—the president was telling an Arabic-language television station that "if countries like Iran are willing to unclench their fist, they will find an extended hand from us."[24] Iran responded, President Ahmadinejad saying that "the Iranian nation is ready for talks, but in a fair atmosphere with mutual respect."[25]

As in the past, however, the same forces that had worked against direct talks between the United States and Iran during the Bush administration came to the fore again, producing a stalemate.[26] Israel kept up a drumbeat of protest against any weakening of US nuclear policy, arguing that Obama should not allow Iran to enrich uranium and should step up sanctions. The anti-Iran "lobby" in Congress, well funded by pro-Israel and right-wing millionaires and groups, ensured that sanctions would tighten and the possibility of an Israeli attack on Iran would get plenty of publicity.[27] Politics in Iran further complicated US policy making. A contested presidential election in June 2009, in which Ahmadinejad was reelected amid charges of fraud and huge protest rallies, led to charges of US interference. In all, throughout Obama's first term and into his second, prospects of negotiations with Iran looked very unlikely. Time and again Obama refused to discard the military option, at one point even saying, "I do not have a policy of containment. I have a policy to prevent Iran from obtaining a nuclear weapon." His audience, not coincidentally, was the American Israel Public Affairs Committee (AIPAC), the major pro-Israel lobby in Washington.[28]

Most troubling about the US position was the very narrow conception of diplomatic possibilities. As we shall see again in the case of North Korea, diplomacy was intended to be about containing Iran's nuclear ambitions; only afterward would negotiations move on to subjects of importance to Iran. Experts on Iran in the United States were generally pessimistic. As one wrote in 2012, "Obama's embrace of engagement with Iran is a distant memory. . . . Instead of buckling under the pressure, Iranian leaders have promised to retaliate against American interests. U.S. officials maintain that negotiations remain the preferred path forward, but it is hard to imagine a constructive dialogue between Iran's revolutionary theocrats and the nation that has set out to collapse its economy." But while cautioning that any deal would carry significant risks, the author concluded that a negotiated outcome was the only option—one that conceded Iran's right to enrichment in return for "verifiable assurances that Iran's nuclear activities are constrained from militarization." That view proved to be a key part of the path to agreement.[29]

The US approach changed in 2013, at a time when Track II dialogue was reinvigorated. In part, these unofficial meetings, which fed into technical aspects of a nuclear deal, owed much to the election of President Hassan Rouhani and Mohammad Javad Zarif's return to the foreign ministry in Iran.[30] The changed US position may also have been due to the views of the Iran Project, a bipartisan panel of senior diplomats and foreign policy experts. The Iran Project pointed to the failure of sanctions and covert operations to alter Iran's behavior and urged greater emphasis on diplomacy.[31] The group argued that although Iran's nuclear program may have been slowed down, US policy may have hardened Iran's "resistance to pressure" and "may be sowing the seeds of long-term alienation between the Iranian people and the United States." The policy recommendation was for a deeper US commitment to finding common ground even while maintaining the option of using force if Iran decided to produce a nuclear weapon, which the group thought highly unlikely. Perhaps most important, the recommendation was that the United States proceed with mutual respect and noninterference in Iran's politics, be prepared to accept Iran's low enrichment of uranium for peaceful purposes, and seek broader agreement on conflict management in the Middle East.

Ayatollah Khamenei helped by reiterating Iran's policy on nuclear weapons and talks with the United States: "We believe that nuclear weapons must be eliminated. We don't want to build atomic weapons." If the United States wanted to talk, he said, "crippling sanctions" had to be lifted—they amounted to seeking "the surrender of the Iranian nation"—and Iran's right to have a nuclear energy program had to be respected. "This is the only way to interact with the Islamic Republic of Iran, and in that case the U.S. administration would receive a proper response."[32] That hopeful note may have prompted President Obama to make a well-publicized phone call to President Rouhani in September 2013, at the conclusion of the opening UN General Assembly session. Obama said afterward that a verifiable nuclear agreement with Iran would bring "relief" from existing sanctions.[33] The two leaders never got to the point of a handshake or direct talks, but the phone call was a sign of a possible breakthrough.

Lessons Learned

In trying to parse the reasons for the successful negotiations between the United States and Iran, let me introduce John Limbert, who was a political officer in the US embassy in Tehran when the nightmare hostage crisis unfolded in 1979. Out of his captivity has come a seminal guide, *Negotiating with Iran,*[34] which reflects his deep background in Persian studies and his commitment to dialogue and mutual understanding. Limbert's book examines several cases of crisis in Iran and then offers fourteen lessons for successfully engaging the Iranians. I have selected seven of them to highlight here and have added one of my own.

Avoid legalisms; seek solutions based on "mutually agreeable standards" that Iran can claim as a victory. Having two MIT scientists who knew one another on each side's negotiating team facilitated a focus on scientific technicalities rather than on politics. As for claiming victory, while Secretary of State John Kerry and other US officials could cite major concessions by Iran, Foreign Minister Mohammad Javad Zarif could boast that Iran would keep its centrifuges and nuclear enrichment program, its major nuclear research site at Fordo, and some of its uranium stockpile.

"Be aware of Iran's historical greatness" and past grievances based on humiliations by foreign powers. President Obama *was* aware and showed his attentiveness to Iran's history and culture. He pointed to the Ayatollah Ali Khamenei's mention of Iran's unhappy history with the United States and made respectful comments about Iran's greatness and right to acknowledgment as a major regional power.[35]

Clarify lines of authority: be sure to talk with the right people, but also present a common US position. This was a challenging lesson to follow, inasmuch as the ayatollah deliberately kept in the background, letting his negotiators do their thing but without committing himself to the outcome. On the US side, Republicans' and others' sniping presented obstacles for negotiators, in particular when forty-seven US senators signed a letter to the ayatollah warning that any agreement was subject to congressional review. Nevertheless, the "right people" were evidently at the table and were able to craft an agreement that on Iran's side the ayatollah did not negate and that on the US side amazed even some conservative critics.

Understand Iranian interests. Obviously, removing the sanctions was essential to a deal, but not at any price. Iran's insistence on keeping fuel rods at home and not shipping them to Russia was essential face-saving, and US negotiators did not allow that position to halt the talks. The same approach applied to the centrifuges: the United States negotiated down their number, but Iran was still left with several thousand.

Do not assume the Iranians are illogical, uncompromising, untrustworthy, duplicitous. Respect your adversary. For the Americans to engage with us, President Rouhani said, they must accept Iran's legitimacy: "To have interactions with Iran, there should be talks based on an equal position, building mutual trust and respect, and reducing enmity. I hereby say this explicitly, that if you expect a suitable response, you should talk to Iran with respect, not the language of sanctions."[36] The US response did not consistently follow that advice, often urging Iran "to act quickly to resolve the international community's deep concerns over Iran's nuclear program," after which the United States would be a "willing partner" in finding a peaceful solution. But eventually mutual respect did become the norm.

Ignore hostile rhetoric and grandstanding; be businesslike and professional— and be willing to stay the course. Here, establishing personal relationships, such as Kerry did with Zarif, was clearly instrumental in breaking through the rhetoric and past grievances.[37]

Remember that there were successful US-Iran talks in the past, for example in 2001–2002 over Afghanistan following the fall of the Taliban.

Be ever-conscious of the politics of a deal: the fact that on each side, it must be *sold* to wary buyers and outright opponents who want to see it fail.

The Politics of Engaging Iran

The definitive story of the negotiations between Iran and the United States remains to be written.[38] But one thing is clear: both sides had to overcome substantial obstacles within their own political systems. As noted in chapter 2, engagement threatens some individuals and bureaucracies and benefits others, but usually in disproportionate ways. After all, who wants to be seen as openly siding with "the enemy"? As Bill Keller of the New York Times wrote, "Iran's rejectionists and our own have much in common." Both, for example, "equate compromise with surrender," and both hoped the nuclear talks would fail. They lay low while the talks proceeded, but they were clearly ready to pounce, either to denounce an agreement on the basis that the other side would never abide by it or, should talks break down, to proclaim that negotiations with the enemy were never worthwhile and should never have been tried.[39]

Obama took major political risks to engage Iran, a country that brings to mind many years of US political interference for Iranians and, for Americans, the hostage crisis of 1978. The president and state department obviously saw merit in trying to stop a suspect Iranian nuclear program that would greatly complicate Middle East politics if it led to an arsenal of bombs such as North Korea had acquired. On the president's side was an Iranian American community that wanted to end sanctions on Iran; see US-Iran relations normalized; and make possible a return to an earlier time when business, educational exchanges, and family visits were conducted without huge barriers. Big Oil was first in line when it came to those corporations that wanted to see commercial barriers with Iran removed. Also supportive of the administration was a coalition of seventy-two peace, church, and friendship groups that wrote an open letter to the US Senate opposing sanctions.[40]

The president's first order of business was to get past opponents of engagement in and around him. They included supporters of Israel (AIPAC in particular), whose government considered Obama naïve about Iran; hardliners in the Congress who pushed for passage of the Nuclear Weapon-Free Iran Act of 2013 that formalized sanctions; Republicans and others on the right who sensed a political opportunity to deride engagement as a strategy of the weak if not another Munich; and some former diplomatic and intelligence officials, who believed Iran would lie again just as it had lied before about its nuclear activities.

Obama dealt with the Republican lawmakers who wrote to the ayatollah warning that Congress had the final say on a deal by going around them and concluding the deal by executive agreement. But he could not prevent the Republicans from inviting Benjamin Netanyahu to address the Congress on the nuclear deal, giving him an opportunity to attack it and embarrass the president. Pressure also came from former US officials and outside experts. Nineteen of them, meeting under the auspices of the conservative Washington Institute for Near East Policy, wrote an open letter in June 2015 that argued for tougher terms in the nuclear agreement, such as more intrusive inspections of and data gathering from Iran's military and civilian facilities. If Iran did not comply? "Precisely because Iran will be left as a nuclear threshold state (and has clearly preserved the option of becoming a nuclear weapon state), the United States must go on record now that it is committed to using all means necessary, including military force, to prevent this."[41]

Crafting a nuclear agreement had its own set of political challenges. With Congress, Obama and Kerry had to deal with pressure to come up with a deal with Iran that would be virtually (and probably impossibly) ironclad. And they had to do so quickly, or watch US senators' patience evaporate. Some senators wanted demands made of Iran that would obviously scuttle a deal, such as frequent and highly intrusive inspections of its nuclear facilities. How to satisfy members of Congress who preferred stronger sanctions, and obtain support from enough of them to revoke or soften sanctions as part of a nuclear deal with Iran, was a major challenge for the Obama administration.[42] When the IAEA found, for example, that Iran was enriching uranium at a fast clip, with many more centrifuges than had previously been thought, Obama was hemmed in by pressures from Israel to draw a red line, from hard-liners in Congress, and from Mitt Romney's presidential campaign to go beyond sanctions and employ force. Israel was threatening to act unilaterally against Iran's nuclear sites, using Netanyahu's personal relationship with Romney (who had recently visited Israel) to force Obama's hand in an election year.

When the Obama administration reached the initial stage of an agreement with Iran in 2013, opponents immediately sought to derail it by threatening to impose new sanctions, all the while claiming that by playing good cop, bad cop, they were actually strengthening the president's hand. The president and secretary of state pleaded for time to see if Iran would honor the agreement. Obama had to reiterate the administration's red line on Iran—that it will never be allowed to have a nuclear weapon—and Kerry had to promise congressional critics that he would push for new and deeper sanctions if the agreement fell through. How much of an impact pro-agreement lobbying had is unclear, but in the end the 2013 sanctions bill was defeated, and the administration's argument, framed so as to cast supporters of sanctions as warmongers, won out.[43]

On the other side of the Iran story, the role of Ayatollah Khamenei was politically mischievous. At home, he seemed to be playing both sides of the engagement issue against one another, probably with an eye on the implications of engagement for Iran's regional competition with Saudi Arabia and Turkey. On the one hand he seemed to back his president, Rouhani, but on the other he warned that Iran had options if it did not get a nuclear deal to its liking. (For example, in a speech in 2014 he approvingly noted that Obama had taken military options against Iran off the table; but he also warned against US interference in Iran's internal politics.[44]) By staying involved but above the fray, he protected himself against failure while positioning himself to benefit from success, a formula for ingratiating himself with either the liberals or the hard-liners, depending on the outcome of talks with the Americans. At the same time Khamenei's standoffish approach abroad was actually giving ammunition to US Senate advocates of sanctions, whose resistance to engagement could only weaken Obama's hand.[45]

On the front line of Iranian engagement was the foreign minister, Javad Zarif, who was appointed following the surprise election of Rouhani in 2013. Zarif had to move carefully to avoid being sidelined by Iran's hard-liners—all the more so as several US government figures who came to know him praised him to the skies.[46] Educated in the United States (he holds a doctoral degree from the University of Denver's School of International Studies), Zarif was an obvious target for people whose careers and economic interests depended on continuation of tensions between the United States and Iran, including elimination of the Track II dialogue that Zarif favored.[47] For those people, the more reforms took hold inside Iran, the less influence they would have over policy, whether domestic or international. Rouhani, too, had to contend with political forces in Iran that were just waiting for the deal to fail. He was reported to be so upset with his critics that at one point he assailed them for "cheering on the rival team," which he characterized as "sabotage of national interests and favor for partisan politics."[48]

Bureaucratic politics also influenced the Iranian position. When Zarif reportedly said that "just a couple of [US] bombs" could eliminate Iran's defenses, the commander of the Islamic Revolutionary Guards told him to mind his own business. Indicating his distaste for the interim nuclear agreement Iran had reached with the United States, the commander said Iran had "given the maximum and received the minimum." Iran has its own red lines, he warned, meaning the right to enrich uranium accorded to all countries under the Nuclear Nonproliferation Treaty. "If the other side takes such an approach [of crossing the red lines], we will return to the past."[49]

The Deal

Politics aside, President Obama wanted to add to his legacy of engaging adversaries with an agreement that would at least significantly delay Iran's ability to produce nuclear weapons. The Ayatollah Khamenei wanted to end all US sanctions immediately in return for forgoing the nuclear option. Both leaders wanted a final agreement that would look like a victory in order to overcome powerful domestic resistance. The terms of the final agreement in April 2015 could never satisfy all the critics, but it was a milestone in international arms control.[50]

The agreement reached by the United States and five other countries (Great Britain, France, Russia, China, and Germany) with Iran—officially, the Joint Comprehensive Plan of Action (JCPA)—should be remembered as one of President Obama's notable foreign policy successes. But the agreement was in many ways a victory for Iran as well, not just in the technical sense but also in political terms. Leaders in Tehran could claim that they had preserved the means of developing nuclear energy—the centrifuges, uranium, and research facilities—and (though left unsaid) of going nuclear if a final agreement could not be reached. American leaders could claim that they had achieved a sharp reduction in the number of centrifuges and intrusive international inspections, ensuring against a sudden nuclear "breakout" by Iran. Perhaps as important, Iranians could claim that they had won the respect and legitimacy they had demanded, and the Americans could argue that the combination of carrots and sticks had worked.

To be sure, the devil is always in the details, and there is no guarantee that the JCPA will hold over the fifteen years during which Iran will be nuclear weapon free. But to reach this point after more than thirty-five years of on-again, off-again talks when other administrations had either failed to cut a deal or refused to try was nothing short of extraordinary.[51] And in the case of Iran, the nuclear agreement came at a crucial moment, not merely in terms of Iran's nuclear weapons potential but more broadly with respect to the chaotic shape of Middle East politics.

A group of twenty-nine scientists and engineers well known for their expertise on nuclear weapons and arms control wrote an open letter to the president that summarizes the Iran agreement's main achievements:

> It limits the level of enrichment of the uranium that Iran can produce, the amount of enriched uranium it can stockpile, and the number and kinds of centrifuges it can develop and operate. The agreement bans reconversion and reprocessing of reactor fuel, it requires Iran to redesign its Arak research reactor to produce far less plutonium than the original design, and specifies that spent fuel must be shipped out of the country without the plutonium being separated and before any significant quantity can be accumulated. A key result of these restrictions is that it would take Iran many months to enrich uranium for a weapon. We contrast this with the situation before the interim agreement was negotiated in Lausanne: at that time Iran had accumulated enough 20 percent enriched uranium that the required additional enrichment time for weapons use was only a few weeks.[52]

The letter points to other innovative terms, including challenge inspections of Iran's nuclear facilities, a ban on nuclear weapons research and not simply manufacture, and verification procedures that last through 2040. The IAEA is given an exceptionally intrusive role in verifying Iran's adherence to the agreement. The scientists and engineers were convinced that the agreement was a model for nuclear nonproliferation efforts, and they, like the Obama administration, believed that if Iran were to cheat, discovery would be much easier than before, and a strong US response would always be available.

To meet Iran's concerns, the Obama administration began lifting economic sanctions, specifically those affecting Iran's energy, banking, and automobile sectors. The agreement also lifted a UN ban on arms sales to Iran and Iranian arms exports after five years and on nuclear-capable ballistic missiles after eight years. Iran may enrich uranium, but with limitations on enrichment level, centrifuges, and locations. Finally, in a side deal, Iran was able to recover about $1.7 billion in frozen assets in return for the release of four Americans held in captivity.

The bottom line of the agreement is that, in Winston Churchill's famous words, "jaw, jaw is better than war, war." For many military leaders, including Obama's service chiefs, a diplomatic resolution was far preferable to war planning. As thirty-six retired generals and admirals wrote in support of the nuclear agreement:

> The international deal blocks the potential pathways to a nuclear bomb, provides for intrusive verification, and strengthens American national security. America and our allies, in the Middle East and around the world, will be safer when this agreement is fully implemented. It is not based on trust; the deal requires verification and tough sanctions for failure to comply.[53]

In fact, as of 2017 Iran had not cheated and was fully in compliance with the agreement, whereas the United States was very slow to ease sanctions.

Concluding Thoughts

Three questions have a particular urgency: Is the United States better off with a nuclear deal that has shortcomings or no deal at all? Should worst-case thinking apply to presuming that Iran will cheat while the agreement is in force and will pursue nuclear weapons once it lapses? Did sanctions and not just engagement bring about the agreement?

In answer to the first question, the history of arms control strongly suggests that perfection is out of reach. Agreements to reduce or eliminate arms, whether nuclear or conventional, are not the same as legal contracts enforceable in court. The devil is in the details, and the wiggle room is invariably substantial. That said, the opportunity for both the United States and Iran to significantly delay, if not end, Iran's nuclear weapons potential in exchange for an end to US (and perhaps later, UN) sanctions, immediately or in stages, is far more attractive than a confrontation that might lead to war. Right-wing hawks provide the best reason for reaching an imperfect deal: they are ready to bomb Iran's nuclear sites, with Israel's help, and risk war. This must not happen. But in order to counter a vote in the Senate to express disapproval, Obama constantly had to refer to the option of ramping up sanctions if the agreement fell through.[54] The vote did not pass, but the arduous process showed once again the difficult political road engagement must always follow.

On the second question, a common criticism is that the agreement with Iran does not prevent it from acquiring nuclear weapons once the ten- to fifteen-year period lapses. Omitted from this criticism is the salience of what happens in US-Iran relations during those years. If relations move toward normalization in that time—economic ties are restored, cooperation on common regional issues such as ISIS is achieved, quiet diplomacy leads to the two countries' embassies reopening—Iran would have no incentive to go nuclear and every incentive for deeper engagement. Of course, if relations do not improve because of cheating, a failure of one side to honor its commitments, or continued friction on one or another Middle East issue, we will be back to square one, with a guarantee of more US-Iran tensions than previously. That's the challenge, and the proper context for evaluation.

Critics of engaging Iran, and even some supporters, also err in putting their entire focus on Iran's capacity for troublemaking. This is so despite all the evidence that Israel and Saudi Arabia, among other US partners, are also guilty of troublemaking—and that Israel has never been pushed to open to inspection, much less reduce, its nuclear arsenal. Nor have the Sunni Arab partners, all autocracies, been pressed by the United States to reform their political systems so as to be able to accommodate their many sources of inequity, which the Arab Spring evidently did not accomplish. Haven't they ever heard of burden sharing? Failing to confront these realities leaves the United States precisely where it is now: having to prove its "resolve" and its "leadership" by deepening its already steep, multifront military involvement in the Middle East.

Regarding the third question, a common belief is that Iran was forced to negotiate because of sanctions: both their actual impact on Iran's economy and the threat of even tougher ones. The Obama administration contended, correctly, that reintroducing sanctions would ensure the demise of the nuclear agreement—and, we might add, the engagement strategy. Ayatollah Khamenei, even while excoriating US foreign policy generally, seemed to support Obama's direction when he said: "The enemies think they imposed the embargo and forced Iran to negotiate. No! We have already said that if we see interest in particular topics, we will negotiate with this devil in order to eliminate trouble coming from it."[55] Foreign Minister Zarif put Iran's perspective differently, arguing that "sanctions produce negative economic results, but they do not produce a change in policy." "The nuclear agreement," he went on, "was based not on mutual confidence but on mutual *lack* of confidence," which is why the agreement contains so many elements designed to ensure compliance.[56]

In short, there is plenty of evidence that sanctions rankled with Iran's leaders and exacted a painful toll on its economy and military establishment. But the key reason an agreement eventually was reached was US "respect" for Iran and recognition of its important role in the Middle East, matters that John Limbert's study emphasizes. The Obama administration demonstrated these qualities in several ways, by abandoning the military option, rejecting the Bush administration's demonizing of Iran, accepting Iran's right to enrich uranium, and sidelining the UN restrictions on Iran's ballistic missile tests. All these shifts made it possible for Iran to "live with" an agreement even though it did not end economic sanctions.

The nuclear agreement is an opportunity that an American administration should use as an opening wedge in a broader policy shift that seeks normalization of relations with Iran and a new era in US relations with the Middle East. Though the Saudis, the Israelis, and some other professed friends of the United States will strenuously object, a cooperative US-Iran relationship is a critical piece in the overall puzzle to establish regional peace. As one Middle East expert has written, US engagement with Iran can have a number of positive consequences for Washington elsewhere in the Middle East: showing "respect for a Muslim state's sovereignty," allaying fears of Iran in Sunni-majority Arab states, stabilizing conflict in Iraq, and giving heft to public diplomacy.[57] Washington and Tehran have common interests in defeating ISIS in Iraq and Afghanistan, an objective Obama suggested in a letter to Ayatollah Khamenei should be pursued together once the nuclear agreement was signed.[58] To be sure, there are also places—Yemen, Israel/Palestine, Libya, and Syria—where the United States and Iran are at odds. But if the nuclear deal moves forward as planned, and termination of sanctions leads to a fruitful economic relationship, the agenda of US-Iran cooperation may expand, and violence by proxy may be greatly reduced. For the United States, an end to one-sided relationships in the Middle East would be a blessing, with positive ramifications for Israel and others, while for Iran, its economy would again thrive, its security sensitivities would be allayed, and its status in the region would rise.

The usefulness of the nuclear agreement showed up in a small but suggestive way in January 2016 when two small US naval patrol boats strayed into Iranian waters. Ten US sailors were taken into custody but then were released after a minimal apology was issued by their commander, not by the US government itself. That was possible because both countries' leaderships did their due political diligence, ensuring that critics in both had no opportunity to garner support for punitive action. Obama did not mention the incident in his State of the Union message, relying instead on quiet diplomacy. The Pentagon admitted that the two boats had violated Iran's territory and that mechanical failure was not the reason. Thus did the incident pass without violence.

Why, therefore, presume the worst, as critics of the nuclear agreement constantly do? The nuclear agreement should be thought of as a foundation for trust building, not a warning to Iran to "comply or die." Why not create a positive road map for normalizing relations between the United States and Iran? American diplomacy should operate on a good faith model, at least until there is reason to conclude otherwise.

The Nuclear Accord after Obama

During his presidential campaign, Donald J. Trump vowed many times to "dismantle" the Iran nuclear accord, which he described as "the worst deal ever negotiated" and an "embarrassment" for the United States. General Joseph Dunford, chairman of the Joint Chiefs of Staff,

Secretary of State Rex Tillerson, and General James Mattis, defense secretary, all favored continued support of the nuclear deal, but that didn't stop Trump from decertifying it in October 2017. Congress was forced either to impose sanctions and new restrictions on Iran or see the United States end its part in the accord. A US pullout would have profound consequences for alliance relations (the European Union was particularly critical of Trump), Middle East policy (except for Netanyahu's cheerleading), and prospects for diplomacy in many other arenas, both bilateral and multilateral. Trump's incoming CIA director, Mike Pompeo, said: "I look forward to rolling back this disastrous deal with the world's largest state sponsor of terrorism." But Pompeo's predecessor, John Brennan, warned against tearing up the deal, arguing that it would be the "height of folly" to take such an "unprecedented" step—one that would cause a new arms race in the Middle East, among other things.[59] John Kerry, in one of his last interviews, said:

> Take Iran. If the US were to decide suddenly that we're not going to pursue this [nuclear agreement], I bet you that our friends and allies who negotiated this with us will get together, and Russia, China, Germany, France and Britain will say "this is a good deal, we're going to keep it." And we'll have done a great injury to ourselves. There are now no longer 19,000 centrifuges spinning and enriching, there are 5,000, which is the agreement. There is no longer a 12,000 kg stockpile that could produce 10 to 12 bombs. There's 300kg, measurable every day. And you can't build a bomb with 300kg.[60]

The new administration did not take this advice, which is not surprising, given that Trump's Iran team in the Central Intelligence Agency (CIA) and the National Security Council (NSC) is dominated by policy hawks, signaling that the United States will be applying pressure to destabilize the regime, denounce its support of terrorism, and discourage US investment in Iran.[61] When Iran conducted a ballistic missile test in February 2017—a test outside the scope of the nuclear agreement, and not in violation of a separate UN Security Council resolution that only banned tests of nuclear-capable missiles—the Trump administration said Iran was "on notice" and was "playing with fire." Such warnings were followed by sanctions against various Iranian individuals and corporations; condemnations of the nuclear accord and Iran's "#1" role (Trump) in supporting terrorism; and Trump's decision to sell Saudi Arabia, Iran's chief competitor, about $110 billion in weapons over ten years. The Iranian leadership, already wary of a Trump presidency, responded by defending the accord and saying that US criticisms revealed "the true face" of Trump's presidency.[62] Visa grants by both countries were discontinued, and Iran tested more missiles.[63]

Several developments might have been taken in Washington as reasons for attempting to improve relations with Tehran. One is that the

Trump administration had twice recertified Iran's compliance with the nuclear agreement prior to October 2017. Another is that Iran reelected Rouhani on a promise to expand human rights. A third is Iran's China card: Beijing is taking advantage of enmity between Iran and the United States to establish a major economic presence in Iran's transportation, mining, construction, and household goods sectors as part of the "One Belt One Road" initiative under Xi Jinping that spans three continents.[64] None of these developments seems to have impacted US policy, however-er. The fundamental lesson when dealing with Iran—proceeding with mutual respect and aiming at mutual gain—was buried.[65]

THE UNITED STATES AND CUBA

Removing Barriers

Every US president since Eisenhower had undertaken contact with Cuba over normalization of relations, and Fidel Castro had long sought recognition of the Cuban revolution's legitimacy, all without success.[66] On occasion hopeful signs emerged; for example, before President John F. Kennedy's assassination, James Donovan negotiated Cuba's release of Bay of Pigs prisoners, American and Cuban, in return for food and medicine.[67] But the legacy of Cuba's dependence on the US sugar market, US interventions early in the twentieth century, US support of the Fulgencio Batista dictatorship in the 1950s, domination of key elements of the Cuba economy by US businesses, and Soviet wooing of Castro pushed aside early State Department proposals for a new US policy of restraint.[68] Then came the Bay of Pigs invasion, Soviet missiles in Cuba and the ensuing missile crisis of 1962, CIA-run assassination attempts on Castro, Cuba's forays in Africa and Latin America, and the US embargo, all of which put Cuban-US relations into a deep freeze—until the Obama administration resurrected them.

Obama evidently had in mind to establish a new relationship with Cuba following his reelection in 2012. He began by removing several restrictions on US-Cuba contact, such as Cuban American remittances and family travel, later adding academic and other people-to-people ex-changes—all while continuing so-called democracy promotion activities designed to encourage dissent and undermine the Cuban regime.[69] Nevertheless, over eighteen months of secret meetings between Obama aides and representatives of President Raúl Castro, variously hosted by Canada and the Vatican, a breakthrough was achieved with an exchange of prisoners, a very prickly subject with domestic political implications for both leaders.[70] On the US side, Senator Patrick Leahy and various Washington NGOs were also instrumental in pushing for a policy change, while in Cuba, Raúl Castro recognized the need to jump-start an economic shift toward a greater role for private enterprise and an end to US sanctions that would permit access to international lines of credit.

Finally, on December 17, 2014, an agreement brokered in the end by Pope Francis, an Argentine with good relations with Cuba, was concluded. It provided for an exchange of alleged spies and Cuba's release of fifty-two people identified by the United States as political prisoners. More important, the agreement stipulated the restoration of diplomatic, commercial, and tourism ties, setting the stage for the reopening of the US embassy in Havana after more than half a century.[71]

The US and Cuban presidents took advantage of several factors in their favor: the change of leadership in Cuba from Fidel Castro to his brother Raúl; the looming end of Obama's second term, which allowed him the space to make a dramatic policy shift with low political risk; generational change in the Cuban community in Miami, which had previously favored a hard line on Cuba; Cuba's need of economic help, coupled with a slow transition to market socialism; the long-standing desire of US businesses to enter the Cuban market; and the clear failure of US policy to produce the political changes in Cuba Washington had long demanded. Announcing the normalization, Obama said: "These 50 years [without official relations] have shown that isolation has not worked. It's time for a new approach." Castro agreed, commending Obama for his "respect and acknowledgment of our people."[72]

At a summit meeting of US and Latin leaders in April 2015, which Cuba attended for the first time, Obama and Castro shook hands. After reviewing a history of grievances against the United States, Castro offered a surprising apology: "I have told President Obama that I get very emotional talking about the revolution. . . . I apologize to him because President Obama had no responsibility for this." And he added: "In my opinion, President Obama is an honest man." Castro praised Obama for his courage in seeking to lift the trade embargo imposed by the US Congress, based on the 1996 Helms-Burton Act and other legislation.[73] Obama responded in kind, noting that differences between the two countries on political systems and human rights should not get in the way of dialogue and the resumption of normal economic and other relations.[74]

Obama was breaking the mold of US policy toward adversarial governments. As he said, that policy was not working, either at the level of government-to-government relations or at the level of public diplomacy. Whereas previous presidents had refused to recognize Cuba because of its official ideology, human rights record, and support of revolutions abroad, Obama made no such moral or political judgments. He took the path of "it is what it is"—better to engage adversaries than try to isolate them—and moved forward, though (with a nod to critics on the right) arguing that transforming Cuba's political system and practices would be easier with recognition than without. Obama's trip to Cuba in March 2016, accompanied by his family and a large entourage of politicians and businesspeople, was a triumph of personal diplomacy of the sort that is essential to successful engagement.[75]

Nevertheless, hard-liners in Havana and anti-Castro forces in and outside of Congress went to great lengths to undermine any prospective deal. Fidel Castro wrote an unusual article in *Granma*, the official newspaper, responding to a *New York Times* editorial that proposed normalizing relations with Cuba.[76] Castro vigorously defended the virtues of the revolution, urging Cubans not to be enticed by Obama's "sweetened words." Though he also suggested avenues of cooperation worth talking about, his influence with the hard-liners would stall Raúl Castro's efforts until Fidel's death on November 25, 2016.[77]

In the United States, the announcement of the restoration of ties between the United States and Cuba drew anger and ridicule from the usual places. Senator Marco Rubio, Republican of Florida, called it "another concession to a tyranny," one that, far from bringing respect for human rights to Cuba, would strengthen Castro's hold on power. Senator Robert Menendez, Democrat of New Jersey, maintained that normalization "vindicated the brutal behavior of the Cuban government." And Jeb Bush, a candidate for the Republican presidential nomination, weighed in that Obama was "rewarding dictators." Of course Obama's action did no such things. It was based on the entirely realistic as well as humanitarian assessment that permanent estrangement deepens enmity, isolates two peoples and separates families, reduces opportunities for improvement in the quality of life in Cuba, inhibits the two-way flow of information, and prevents cooperation on common problems. Rubio, Menendez, and Bush were still fighting the Cold War.

Defying the critics, Obama reinforced his policy direction by issuing a legally binding order—Presidential Policy Directive 43—on October 14, 2016, just months before leaving office.[78] PPD-43 makes the case for normalization of relations with Cuba; recites the extensive diplomatic exchanges that have occurred; outlines cooperation in areas of mutual interest; and expresses the hope of improvement in Cuba's human rights, economy, and regional integration—all while reassuring Cuba that regime change is not US policy. Department by department, the document recites the numerous collaborative ventures ongoing and possible, such as on public health, food security, private investment, environment and ecology protection, immigration, travel, counter-narcotics, and joint scientific projects. One specific step taken by the administration at this time was to remove the ceiling on imports of Cuban rum and cigars. But the one thing Obama could not do was end the embargo, about which right-wing members of Congress have always had their best chance to limit engagement.[79]

After Obama: Trump's Threats

Barack Obama left Donald Trump with a substantial list of new inter-actions with Cuba, some of them—such as money transfers to Cuba and a major increase in tourism—designed to support small businesses and civil society. [80] Obama also left Trump with some unresolved issues with Cuba, such as a sharp increase in Cuban immigration to the United States (in part thanks to the upward pressure on prices due to US tourism), regulatory blockages, and the slow pace of Cuban economic reform. [81] Such problems normally would be resolved over time. Under Trump, however, progress made with Cuba was bound to be set back, just as it was with Iran.

Fidel Castro's death prior to Trump's inauguration ordinarily might have been an opportunity to send a sympathetic note to Havana and to deepen the accords already reached. Instead, Trump tweeted: "If Cuba is unwilling to make a better deal for the Cuban people, the Cuban/American people and the U.S. as a whole, I will terminate deal." The implication was that the United States would demand changes in Cuba's human rights and political system in return for a softening of the embargo.

Trump began the process of dismantling Obama's engagement with Cuba in November 2017 by restricting personal travel and commerce with Cuba's military-owned enterprises. But diplomatic relations remain in place. Reducing contact is more likely to undermine than to promote the slow improvements in Cuban civil society that engagement has produced. Independent journalism and private entrepreneurship are re-emerging there. Limiting US tourism greatly reduces needed interactions between ordinary citizens of the two countries. Maintaining the US embargo, moreover, is highly unlikely to ease Cuban restrictions on human rights, and making the latter a condition for easing the former is sure to arouse official Cuban anger. As one expert in US-Cuba relations observed, negotiating economic and travel arrangements is one thing; sovereignty is another. Cuba's memory of US interference is long, and Cuba will not countenance another such era. [82]

NOTES

1. I rely here mainly on the detailed account by Trita Parsi, *Treacherous Alliance: The Secret Dealings of Israel, Iran, and the United States* (New Haven, CT: Yale University Press, 2007), 243–257, 341–346. A similar account is Connie Bruck, "Exiles," *New Yorker*, March 6, 2006, 46–63. Both accounts note that the Iranians insist the United States, not Iran, initiated the offer for a grand bargain.

2. The text of the proposal is in John W. Limbert, *Negotiating with Iran: Wrestling the Ghosts of History* (Washington, DC: United States Institute of Peace Press, 2009), 203–205.

3. See the declaration issued by Iran and two European foreign ministers in October 2003, in which "the Iranian government has decided to engage in full cooperation

with the I.A.E.A. [the International Atomic Energy Agency] to address and resolve through full transparency all requirements and outstanding issues" concerning its nuclear program. France, Germany, and Iran "believe that this [commitment by Iran] will open the way to a dialogue on a basis for long-term cooperation" (*NYT*, October 22, 2003, A10). About a year later Iran reached agreement with the Europeans to suspend uranium enrichment in exchange for "nuclear, technological, and economic cooperation and firm commitments on security issues." Elaine Sciolino, "Europeans Say Iran Agree to Freeze Uranium Enrichment," *NYT*, November 16, 2004, A3.

4. Parsi, *Treacherous Alliance*, 48.

5. Joby Warrick, "Iran Admits Foreign Help in Nuclear Facility," *Washington Post*, August 29, 2003. Most references to the *Washington Post* in the notes are to the online edition, which omits page numbers; references that include page numbers are to the hard copy edition.

6. David E. Sanger and William J. Broad, "Surprise Word on Nuclear Gains by North Korea and Iran," *NYT*, November 12, 2003, A3.

7. J. Michael McConnell, "Annual Threat Assessment of the Director of National Intelligence for the Senate Select Committee on Intelligence," February 5, 2008, http://fl1.findlaw.com/news.findlaw.com/hdocs/docs/terrorism/nie20805dni.pdf. The *National Intelligence Estimate, Iran: Nuclear Intentions and Capabilities* of November 2007 (https://graphics8.nytimes.com/packages/pdf/international/20071203_release.pdf) had made the same assessment, noting that "Tehran's decision to halt its nuclear weapons program [in 2003] suggests it is less determined to develop nuclear weapons than we have been judging since 2005."

8. Republican members of the House of Representatives intelligence committee echoed the administration's mistrust of the CIA: Dafna Linzer, "U.S. Spy Agencies Criticized on Iran," *Washington Post*, August 24, 2006, A1.

9. "Bush Says Iran Remains a Threat Despite Report," *NYT*, December 5, 2007, A1.

10. President Mahmoud Ahmadinejad sent a lengthy letter—some would say a diatribe—to President Bush in 2006 that, for all its criticisms of the United States and Israel, might have led to a proposal for talks. The letter tried to show the president that US policies were not in accord with religious teachings and revealed only the bankruptcy of Western liberalism. Bush, so far as I know, did not respond. The text of the letter is at www.carnegieendowment.org/publications/indx.cfm?fa=view&id=18317&prog=zgp&proj=znpp, May 9, 2006.

11. Dafna Linzer, "U.S. Uses Drones to Probe Iran for Arms," *Washington Post*, February 13, 2005, A1.

12. Seymour Hersh, "The Coming Wars," *New Yorker*, January 24–31, 2005, 40–47.

13. Douglas Jehl, "Iranian Rebels Urge Pentagon Not to Let Iran Expel Them," *NYT*, December 13, 2003, A9.

14. Steven R. Weisman, "Rice Is Seeking Millions to Prod Changes in Iran," *NYT*, February 16, 2006, 1.

15. A good summary of the Stuxnet story is William J. Broad, John Markoff, and David E. Sanger, "Israeli Test on Worm Called Crucial in Iran Nuclear Delay," *NYT*, January 15, 2011.

16. David E. Sanger, "Rice Says Iran Must Not Be Allowed to Develop Nuclear Arms," *NYT*, August 9, 2004, A3; Seymour Hersh, "The Iran Plans," *New Yorker*, April 17, 2006, 30–37; Seymour Hersh, "The Next Act," *New Yorker*, November 27, 2006, 94–107.

17. Bush said: "The Iranians should not have a nuclear weapon, the capacity to make a nuclear weapon, or the knowledge as to how to make a nuclear weapon." David E. Sanger and Elaine Sciolino, "Iran Strategy: Cold War Echo," *NYT*, April 30, 2006, 4.

18. Sheryl Gay Stolberg, "Nuclear-Armed Iran Risks 'World War III,' Bush Says," *NYT*, October 18, 2007, A6.

19. Sheryl Gay Stolberg, "Cheney, Like President, Has a Warning for Iran," *NYT*, October 22, 2007, A8; Steven R. Weisman, Elaine Sciolino, and David E. Sanger, "Rice Says U.S. Won't Offer Incentives to Halt Nuclear Work," *NYT*, February 4, 2005, A1.

20. Hersh, "The Iran Plans"; Sarah Baxter, "Pentagon 'Three-Day Blitz' Plan for Iran," *Sunday Times* (London), September 2, 2007, 3; David E. Sanger, "Cheney Says Israel Might 'Act First' on Iran," *NYT*, January 21, 2005, A6.

21. "Rice's Remarks on Iran," *NYT*, May 31, 2006.

22. David E. Sanger and Thom Shanker, "Washington Sees an Opportunity on Iran," *NYT*, September 27, 2007. The commander was Admiral William J. Fallon.

23. For example, Ray Takeyh, "Time for Détente with Iran," *Foreign Affairs*, March–April 2007, www.foreignaffairs.com/articles/iran/2007-03-01/time-d-tente-iran. Takeyh wrote that normalization of US-Iranian relations would be a better starting point than the nuclear issue or terrorism. Those subjects could follow on building trust. His idea was to appeal to the young conservative pragmatists in the Iranian leadership: "Washington must strengthen the hands of the pragmatists in Tehran by offering Iran relief from sanctions and diplomatic relations. Washington's recognition of Iran's regional status and deepened economic ties with the West might finally enable the pragmatists to push [Ayatollah] Khamenei to marginalize the radicals who insist that only confrontation with the United States can allow Iran to achieve its national objectives."

24. Helene Cooper and Mark Landler, "For Obama's Iran Plan, Talk and Some Toughness," *NYT*, February 4, 2009, A11.

25. AOL News, "Iranian President Open to Talks with US," http://news.aol.com/article/iran-us-talks/335551.

26. Trita Parsi, *A Single Roll of the Dice* (New Haven, CT: Yale University Press, 2013).

27. Eli Clifton and Ali Gharib, "The Iranophobia Lobby Machine," *Nation*, August 4–11, 2014, 21–24.

28. Jonathan Schell, "Thinking the Unthinkable," *Nation*, April 23, 2012, 20–22.

29. Suzanne Maloney, "How to Contain a Nuclear Iran," Brookings Institution, March 12, 2012, www.brookings.edu/opinions/2012/0305_nuclear_iran_maloney.aspx?p=1.

30. Daniel Wertz, *Track II Diplomacy with Iran and North Korea*, June 2017, National Committee on North Korea, http://www.ncnk.org/sites/default/files/NCNK_Track_II_Conference_Report_0.pdf.

31. "Strategic Options for Iran: Balancing Pressure with Diplomacy," April 2013, www.scribd.com/doc/136389836/Strategic-Options-for-Iran-Balancing-Pressure-with-Diplomacy.

32. Thomas Erdbrink, "Ayatollah Says Iran Will Control Nuclear Aims," *NYT*, February 16, 2013. This was not the first time the ayatollah had spoken against acquiring nuclear weapons. On other occasions he said that nuclear weapons were evil and sinful, as a result of which he issued a fatwa against Iran's acquiring them. See, for example, James Risen, "Seeking Nuclear Insight in Fog of Ayatollah's Utterances," *NYT*, April 14, 2012, A4.

33. Jeff Mason and Louis Charbonneau, "Obama, Iran's Rouhani, Hold Historical Phone Call," *Reuters.com*, September 28, 2013.

34. Limbert, *Negotiating with Iran*, 154–177.

35. Thomas L. Friedman, "Iran and the Obama Doctrine," *NYT*, April 5, 2015.

36. Thomas Erdbrink, "Iranian President Is Sworn In and Presents a New Cabinet of Familiar Faces," *NYT*, August 5, 2013, A4.

37. Robin Wright, "Tehran's Promise," *New Yorker*, July 27, 2015, www.newyorker.com/magazine/2015/07/27/tehrans-promise.

38. The best so far is Trita Parsi's *Losing An Enemy: Obama, Iran, and the Triumph of Diplomacy* (New Haven, CT: Yale University Press, 2017).

39. Keller, "Iran's Hardliners, and Ours," *NYT*, December 11, 2013.

40. The text is at www.niacouncil.org/site/News2?page=NewsArticle&id=10225 (January 14, 2014). Lead organizations in the coalition were the National Iranian American Council, the Friends Committee on National Legislation, and Win Without War.

41. "Public Statement on U.S. Policy Toward the Iran Nuclear Negotiations," June 24, 2015, www.washingtoninstitute.org/policy-analysis/view/public-statement-on-u.s.-policy-toward-the-iran-nuclear-negotiations.

42. David E. Sanger, "Americans and Iranians See Constraints at Home in Nuclear Negotiations," *NYT*, July 13, 2014.

43. For example, Bernadette Meehan, spokeswoman of the National Security Council, said: "If certain members of Congress want the United States to take military action, they should be up front with the American public and say so. Otherwise, it's not clear why any member of Congress would support a bill that possibly closes the door on diplomacy and makes it more likely that the United States will have to choose between military options or allowing Iran's nuclear program to proceed." Quoted in Trita Parsi, "The Illusion of AIPAC's Invincibility," *Huffington Post*, February 8, 2014, www.huffingtonpost.com/trita-parsi/aipac-illusion_b_4751732.html.

44. Thomas Erdbrink, "Iran's Leader Says Obama Has Removed Military Option," *NYT*, June 4, 2014.

45. See Trita Parsi, "Khamenei's Little Helpers in the Senate," January 10, 2014, www.rollcall.com/news/khameneis_little_helpers_in_the_senate_commentary-230056-1.html?pg=1.

46. Robin Wright, "The Adversary," *New Yorker*, May 26, 2014, www.newyorker.com/magazine/2014/05/26/the-adversary-2.

47. Wertz, *Track II Diplomacy with Iran and North Korea*.

48. Mehrdad Balali, "Rouhani Accuses Iranian Hardliners of 'Cheering On' Other Side in Atom Talks," *NYT*, January 31, 2015 (via Reuters).

49. Thomas Erdbrink, "Military Chief in Iran Scolds a Top Official," *NYT*, December 12, 2013, A15.

50. For a comprehensive overview, see Kenneth Katzman and Paul K. Kerr, "Iran Nuclear Agreement," Congressional Research Service, Washington, DC, December 5, 2016, https://fas.org/sgp/crs/nuke/R43333.pdf.

51. The one exception was an offer by the Clinton administration to discuss all issues in dispute without preconditions. Limbert, *Negotiating with Iran*, 192.

52. Richard Garwin et al., "Letter to the President," *NYT*, August 8, 2015.

53. "The Iran Deal Benefits U.S. National Security," *Washington Post*, n.d., http://apps.washingtonpost.com/g/documents/world/read-an-open-letter-from-retired-generals-and-admirals-on-the-iran-nuclear-deal/1689/.

54. Julie Herschfeld Davis, "Obama Denounces Attempts to Derail Nuclear Deal with Iran," *NYT*, April 12, 2015. Sanctions on Iran comprised not only those voted by the US Congress but also UN sanctions, sanctions authorized or limited by the president, and sanctions imposed by each of the other P5+1 (the five permanent members of the UN Security Council plus Germany) countries.

55. Rick Gladstone and Thomas Erdbrink, "As Iran Nuclear Talks Resume, Ayatollah Criticizes U.S.," *NYT*, January 9, 2014.

56. Richard Engel, interview with Mohammad Javad Zarif, foreign minister of Iran, February 19, 2017, http://www.nbcnews.com/video/javad-zarif-foreign-minister-of-iran-full-interview-with-richard-engel-880666691718.

57. Emile Nakhleh, *A Necessary Engagement: Reinventing America's Relations with the Muslim World* (Princeton, NJ: Princeton University Press, 2008), 125.

58. Trita Parsi, "Pen-Palling with the Ayatollah," *Foreign Policy*, November 7, 2014, http://foreignpolicy.com/2014/11/07/pen-palling-with-the-ayatollah/.

59. Dan Bilefsky, "C.I.A. Chief Warns Donald Trump Against Tearing Up Iran Nuclear Deal," *NYT*, November 30, 2016.

60. Larry Elliott and Graeme Wearden, "Xi Jinping Signals China Will Champion Free Trade if Trump Builds Barriers," *Guardian*, January 17, 2017. All references to the *Guardian* are to its online US edition.

61. Matthew Rosenberg and Adam Goldman, "C.I.A. Names New Iran Chief in a Sign of Trump's Hard Line," *NYT*, June 2, 2017.

62. Thomas Erdbrink, "Iran's Supreme Leader Thanks Trump for Showing America's 'True Face,'" *NYT*, February 7, 2017.

63. Karim Sadjadpour, "How America Could Stumble Into War with Iran," *Atlantic*, February 9, 2017, www.theatlantic.com/international/archive/2017/02/iran-trump-nuclear-deal/515979/?utm_source=nl-atlantic-weekly-021017.

64. Thomas Erdbrink, "For China's Global Ambitions, 'Iran Is at the Center of Everything,'" *NYT*, July 25, 2017.

65. Limbert, *Negotiating with Iran*, 159.

66. On the long history of negotiations and the above information, see William M. LeoGrande and Peter Kornbluh, *Back Channel to Cuba: The Hidden History of Negotiations between Washington and Havana* (Chapel Hill: University of North Carolina Press, 2014).

67. Peter Kornbluh, "US-Cuban Diplomacy, *Nation* Style," *Nation*, April 29, 2013, 20–23.

68. The first US ambassador to Cuba after Castro's revolution, Philip Bonsal, later wrote about a January 1960 draft policy paper for the White House that advocated a US policy of nonintervention: "Cuba, Castro and the United States," *Foreign Affairs*, https://www.foreignaffairs.com/articles/cuba/1967-01-01/cuba-castro-and-united-states.

69. William M. LeoGrande, "Cuba: Public Diplomacy as a Battle of Ideas," in *Isolate or Engage: Adversarial States, US Foreign Policy, and Public Diplomacy*, ed. Geoffrey Wiseman (Stanford, CA: Stanford University Press, 2015), 247.

70. Peter Kornbluh and William M. LeoGrande, "Cuba Confidential: Inside the Crazy Back-Channel Negotiations that Revolutionized Our Relationship with Cuba," *Mother Jones*, September–October 2015, www.motherjones.com/politics/2015/07/secret-negotiations-gross-hernandez-kerry-pope-obama-castro-cuba; LeoGrande and Kornbluh, *Back Channel to Cuba*; Peter Kornbluh, "A New Deal with Cuba," *Nation*, January 12–19, 2015, 4–8; and Mark Landler and Michael R. Gordon, "Journey to Reconciliation Visited Worlds of Presidents, Popes and Spies," *NYT*, December 18, 2014.

71. Landler and Gordon, "Journey to Reconciliation."

72. Peter Baker, "U.S. to Restore Full Relations with Cuba, Erasing a Last Trace of Cold War Hostility," *NYT*, December 17, 2014.

73. By the time of the change in US policy, the embargo was highly unpopular in the United States and internationally, with only two countries (the United States and Israel) voting in 2015 against a UN General Assembly resolution to declare the embargo illegal. Joy Gordon, "El Bloqueo," *Harper's*, July 2016, 50.

74. Karen DeYoung and Nick Miroff, "Obama, Castro Hold Historic Meeting, Agree to Foster 'A New Relationship,'" *Washington Post*, April 11, 2015.

75. During his visit, Obama said it "demonstrates you do not need to fear a threat from the United States." And he was clear that change in Cuba would have to come from Cubans themselves. Peter Kornbluh, "Obama in Cuba," *Nation*, April 25–May 2, 2016, 14–18.

76. The Times editorial board added some positive ideas while chronicling a history of abject US failures of sabotage in Cuba in the name of improving conditions there. *NYT*, November 10, 2014.

77. Ernesto Londoño, "Still Pondering U.S.-Cuba Relations, Fidel Castro Responds," *NYT*, October 14, 2014.

78. Presidential Policy Directive on Cuba, *NYT*, October 14, 2016.

79. Gordon, "El Bloqueo."

80. Jorge I. Dominguez, "Can Donald Trump and Raúl Castro Make a Good Deal?" *NYT*, January 10, 2017; Christopher Sabatini, "Trump's Imminent Cuba Problem," *NYT*, June 15, 2017.

81. Michael J. Bustamante, "Obama's Move on Cuba," in *Cuba Libre? U.S.-Cuban Relations from Revolution to Rapprochement*, ed. Gideon Rose (New York: Foreign Affairs, 2016), 304–311.

82. William M. LeoGrande, "What Trump Misses About Cuba," *NYT*, December 1, 2016.

FOUR

Halfway There

US-China Engagement

SAME BED, DIFFERENT DREAMS[1]

In June 2013 President Xi Jinping called for a "new type of great-power relationship" when he met with President Obama. The idea raises important questions about the future of relations between the United States and China. On the surface, it appeared that the two leaders were on the same page. Obama agreed with Xi that "working together cooperatively" and bringing US-China relations "to a new level" were sound ideas.[2] When the G-20 countries convened at St. Petersburg in September, Obama said of Xi's proposed new model: "We agreed to continue to build a new model of great power relations based on practical cooperation and constructively managing our differences." But he added that "significant differences and sources of tension" remain with China, implying that China's "playing a stable and prosperous and peaceful role" in world affairs remained a matter of US concern.[3]

Obama thus endorsed a "new type" of relationship in theory but seemed to want practical results before actually embracing it. Exactly why a new type of relationship remains elusive despite the multitude of contacts and interdependencies between China and the United States and despite the fact that most Chinese and American analysts believe in the central importance of their relations, comes down to mistrust.[4] And beneath the mistrust lie sharp differences in global perspective that stem from the two countries' different self-perceptions and status in the international order. My argument in this chapter is that a number of paths are available to broaden cooperation and thereby reduce mistrust.

US-China Cooperative Engagement

On paper, the relationship between the two countries looks to be solidly moored by extensive transactions, starting with commerce. As table 4.1 shows, official US statistics indicate that total US-China trade in goods and services topped $600 billion in 2016. China is the largest source of US imports and the top US trade partner overall. China is also the third-largest market for US goods and a key customer for certain US industries (e.g., General Motors typically sells more cars a year to Chinese than to Americans, and Boeing expects China shortly to become its largest aircraft buyer). The US and Chinese economies are intertwined in other important ways: China (in 2016) held about $1 trillion in US Treasury securities and $330 billion in stocks and other equities. While China is not one of the top investors in the US economy, its foreign direct investment (FDI) is growing rapidly—cumulatively from 2010 to 2016, about $80 billion. But its growth rate is exceptional, the highest in the world among major economies.[5] The US FDI in China came to about $75 billion in 2015 alone.[6]

As is well known, plenty of contentious issues have emerged over trade and investments, such as the more than $300 billion US trade deficit with China and China's currency valuation, protection of certain industries, restrictions on foreign investment, and inadequate protection of

Table 4.1.   US Merchandise Trade with China: 1980–2016 (US$ billions)

Year	US Export	US Imports	US Trade Balance
1980	3.8	1.1	+2.7
1990	4.8	15.2	−10.4
2000	16.3	100.1	−83.8
2010	91.9	365.0	−273.0
2011	104.1	399.4	−295.3
2012	110.5	425.6	−315.1
2013	121.7	440.4	−318.7
2014	123.6	468.5	−344.9
2015	116.1	483.2	−367.2
2016	115.8	462.8	−347.0
2016 [a]	170.1	479.4	−309.3

Source: Morrison, "China-U.S. Trade Issues," Table 1, p. 3, based on US International Trade Commission (USITC) DataWeb, https://fas.org/sgp/crs/row/RL33536.pdf.
[a]US Bureau of Economic Analysis, www.bea.gov/newsreleases/international/trade/trad_geo_time_series.xls, Tables 1 and 2.

intellectual property rights. Both countries have brought more disputes against each other before the WTO's dispute settlement mechanism than against any other country.[7] And the question of whether more US jobs are being gained than lost to China is a hot political issue in the United States.

Nevertheless, the huge commercial relationship between the United States and China attests to their importance to each other. Other kinds of transactions are also significant: the people-to-people flow, including over 325,000 Chinese students in the United States;[8] US NGOs active in China, particularly on environmental protection; and numerous Track I and Track II meetings that regularly take place on security, trade, the environment, governance, and human rights, such as the US-China Strategic and Economic Dialogue established in 2006 (Track I) and the Council for Security Cooperation in the Asia Pacific (CSCAP; Track II), founded in 1992.

The ties that bind China and the United States underscore the stark contrast between their relationship and the character of US-Russia relations. The global outlook of both Beijing and Moscow is framed by the fundamental structural reality of US global preeminence. But while Chinese leaders chafe at "US hegemony" and resent the United States for seeking to limit China's rise, keeping the relationship stable is a top priority for Beijing, as it is for Washington. China's official defense strategy documents do not, unlike Russia's, label the United States a national security threat. Fairly regular US-China summits and other high-level meetings reflect the priority of diplomacy. So does the wealth of Track II and III interactions that exist between China and the United States, importantly including NGOs, business leaders, academic experts, and Confucius Institutes. The US-Russia conflict map is much larger than the US-China map, embracing Central Europe, the Middle East, and Central Asia as opposed to East Asia. Both Russia and China regularly carry out cyber attacks on US targets, and the United States does likewise against them, but China seeks business, policy, and military secrets, not disruption of US elections and undermining of democratic society. Unlike Russia, China is deeply invested in the global capitalist order, and the huge US-China commercial relationship has no counterpart in US-Russia relations. Indeed, the US international business community has always been a strong advocate of engaging China, whereas many fewer US multinationals see great opportunities in Russia—at least until the Trump administration.[9] In a word, engagement between the United States and Russia rests on a very narrow base compared with the interdependence between the United States and China.

The counterargument to interdependence is that China's rise poses a direct challenge to long-prevailing US hegemony and creates the strong possibility of a direct clash—in the South China Sea or over Taiwan, for instance.[10] This "Thucydides Trap" does not inevitably mean war, but nationalistic leaders such as Donald Trump and Xi Jinping might be disinclined to negotiate differences and seek common ground. Globalization, communication, mutual interests, and other integrating forces, however, argue against falling into the trap, though we can never rule out disastrous miscalculations and localized clashes that escalate.

China's Search for Mutuality

Of late the phrase "new type of great-power relationship" seems to have fallen into disuse, perhaps because since 2013 China's leadership has grown in self-confidence while US influence, at least in Asia, has somewhat receded. Still, exploring the issues behind that phrase may tell us a good deal about the different perspectives and priorities of the United States and China.

What do China's leaders mean by a "new type of great-power relationship" with the United States? One prominent Chinese observer, Zhang Tuosheng, mindful of the Thucydides Trap, has written that a key characteristic of China-US relations should be that it "break[s] the historical cycle in which the rise and fall of great powers inevitably leads to antagonism and war," instead relying on "equality and mutual benefit, and active cooperation."[11] "Equality and mutual benefit" was one of the five principles of peaceful coexistence, a mainstay of China's foreign policy since the establishment of the People's Republic. Its significance today is that the Chinese are not content to be a junior partner of the United States; they believe they have arrived as a great power and want to be treated accordingly. They may not say they want "G-2," codominion with the United States over world affairs. But the Chinese do demand consultation and coordination: "C-2," as the former Chinese state councilor Dai Bingguo put it. Increasingly, however, their leaders and policy analysts speak of a "post-American era" in which China is an alternative to the United States when it comes to defense of sovereign equality, environmental protection, and economic globalization.[12]

There are a least five obstacles to C-2. One is differing notions of international responsibility. In 2005 Robert Zoellick, then a deputy secretary of state in the George W. Bush administration, proposed that China become a "responsible stakeholder" in the international system. Zoellick hoped to attract Chinese leaders with the idea that the United States valued China as a partner in international affairs. But the reception was lukewarm, as a number of Chinese analysts decided that what Zoellick really meant by "responsible stakeholder" was that China should support the US position on key international issues such as North Korea's nuclear weapons, Iran's nuclear plans, and global finance. American policy makers today still use that expression when trying to push China in the US direction.

Chinese leaders and foreign policy specialists prefer to refer to their country as a "responsible great power." They say that their "peaceful development" policy will break the pattern of rising powers challenging the dominant power for top position. They ask how the United States can speak of global responsibility in light of its unilateral interventions in the Middle East and Central Asia, its reliance on sanctions when dealing with North Korea and Iran, its failure to put its financial house in order, and (in response to US accusations of computer hacking) its spying on China and many others. The Americans ask how China can speak of being a "responsible great power" when it acts aggressively in support of its territorial interests in the South China Sea and the Sea of Japan and refuses to put all-out pressure on North Korea to halt its nuclear weapons and ballistic missile testing. On many other international issues, such as global warming and energy, the two countries similarly have widely divergent ideas about what responsibility means. Unless and until the United States and China reach agreement on that question, it is difficult to imagine that a "new type" of US-China relationship can evolve.

A second major stumbling block to creating a "new type of great-power relationship," and perhaps the most important one, is the different self-conceptions of China and the United States. As a rapidly rising power and a "big country," China not only expects to be consulted on all major international questions; it also expects to play a major role in its relations with neighboring countries. "China does not intend to challenge [the United States] as its power grows, but rather seeks to increase its influence within the system," one prominent Chinese analyst has written. It wants to reform the system, not subvert it.[13] While accepting that the United States is a Pacific power, Chinese authorities now resist the notion that the United States has some special claim to predominance in Asia and the western Pacific. More to the point, they see the United States as the chief obstacle to China's rise and as taking actions aimed at "complicating its security environment."[14]

The United States, on the other hand, claims exceptional status in the international community. Historically, US leaders, at least until Trump, have believed the country has universal values and, as the head of the "Free World," is the custodian of freedom and democracy everywhere. Unlike China, the United States believes it has the right and responsibility to speak its mind about every country's internal political affairs. Whereas Chinese leaders give priority to rapid development and preserving internal order, US leaders focus on remaining "number one" in world affairs and maintaining the capability to deploy military power all over the globe. American leaders voice suspicion about China's international ambitions and demand greater transparency on China's military spending and weapons programs. But few in Washington critically examine the wisdom or sustainability of a Cold War–era strategic outlook and military programs.

COLD WAR POLITICS

Indeed, Chinese analysts frequently refer to US "Cold War thinking" as a basic hindrance to better relations—a third major obstacle. Zhang Tuosheng, like many other Chinese analysts, points out that the idea of a new relationship emerged out of a good deal of rethinking among Chinese specialists about the post–Cold War order: the new "international pattern" (*guoji geju*). He observes that the Chinese no longer accept a one-superpower world, though they do accept that the United States is still the most powerful country. They emphasize the multipolar, multidimensional character of the contemporary era and seek a "harmonious world," which requires a "win-win" perspective above all in defining the China-US relationship.[15]

But neither side can claim to have overcome Cold War thinking. Cyber war and computer hacking, Taiwan's status, naval confrontations, and territorial disputes have all been addressed much as they were during the Cold War: with self-justifications, accusations, and occasional shows of force rather than with conflict-prevention institutions or recourse to international adjudication. The handling of the South China Sea dispute (see below) is a case in point. Though analysts on both sides express concern about a confrontation between a rising power and a dominant power, neither country has suggested creating a high-level body, above the level of bilateral dialogue groups, that might adopt new rules in an effort to avoid a direct confrontation.

Actually, the United States and China should have reason for some optimism in this regard, given the ninety or so official bilateral (Track I) forums at which they regularly meet, not to mention all their other points of contact. But finding common ground remains elusive in large part because the ideological dimension of US-China relations contains important Cold War elements. The US side does not accept parity with China any more than it accepted parity with the Soviet Union. Nor are US leaders strong believers in a multipolar world. In China, Mao-era notions of "struggle against (US) imperialism and hegemonism" survive.[16]

Consider, for example, nuclear weapons. China's equivalent to US hawks, speaking through the medium of the nationalistic *Global Times*, had this to say about the possibility, openly discussed by Trump and Putin, of expanding the US and Russian nuclear arsenals:

> China must have "enough" nuclear weapons to the point that the United States would have serious concerns if it wanted to take a tough military stance against China, "enough" that the United States will be convinced that, once it engaged in military provocation against China, the PLA [People's Liberation Army] would not hesitate to counter and counterattack. For the Chinese, the biggest threat from the United States today is still a military threat. Such a threat will cause chronic erosion of China's social confidence. The fundamental reason that the

United States is even more arrogant toward China than it is toward Russia is because China's nuclear deterrent is far weaker than Russia's. Only when China's strategic nuclear deterrent can forcefully suppress the U.S.'s attitude towards China can the situation change.

Even the United States and Russia feel that their strategic nuclear weapons are "not enough." Therefore how can China's nuclear weapons be "enough"? China has to accelerate the development of the Dongfeng-41 and other strategic nuclear missiles. The work is an urgent need. We must not worry too much about the consequences in this issue or be overly concerned about the attitude of the United States and the reaction of the Western public opinion. China is already a country standing in the global geopolitical cusp. In this major issue of nuclear deterrence, we should not have the slightest hesitation. [17]

A fourth obstacle is that a number of problematic communication issues between the two countries persist. Defining international "responsibility" has already been mentioned. "Containment," "hegemony," "cooperation," and "consultation" are fraught with political ambiguity. Chinese notions of sovereignty, particularly on the high seas, are challenged by US notions of "freedom of the seas." Protection of human rights means very different things to Beijing and Washington, as does freedom of the press. Media reports of the other's politics and foreign policy views are often distorted. Journalists working in China have to be careful what they say if they want a visa for their next visit, [18] just as Chinese news outlets and journalists have to weigh conformity with the unwritten rules of criticism or face silencing by the great Chinese firewall. Confucius Institutes in the United States, part of Chinese efforts to enhance their soft power, have sometimes been attacked by US academics as propaganda platforms. [19]

The fifth obstacle in US-China relations is the military imbalance. Simply put, by nearly every indicator of military power, the United States has huge advantages over China. Military spending in the United States, at well over $600 billion today, is roughly three times China's by most outside estimates (shown in table 4.2[20]). The United States has a huge lead over China in nuclear weapons (about 5,400 to 270[21]), air and naval capability (e.g., China has one deployed aircraft carrier against eleven for the United States), and military technology innovation that takes place in a deeply structured military-industrial complex. Whereas China has no security treaty allies and only one overseas base (in Djibouti, Africa), the United States has security treaties and military partnerships—involving bases, aid, and access arrangements—with several of China's neighbors. Altogether, the United States has around eight hundred bases in seventy countries and territories, giving it the potential to deploy forces virtually anywhere. The United States is also far and away the world leader in arms sales—another form of leverage on security partners—typically accounting for a third to 40 percent of global sales, compared with about 6 percent for China. And while it is sometimes said that China's substantial year-to-year increases in military spending will eventually yield a military equal or superior to that of the United States, such a prediction neglects two considerations: the United States is not standing still while China modernizes its military, regardless of US budget woes, and Chinese leaders seem determined not to follow the Soviet Union's destructive path of trying to match US military spending or weapons.

China has demonstrated that it is a regional military power, particularly when it comes to contingencies that involve Taiwan and Japan. But when its leaders protest US containment of China, or when its hawkish press calls for more nuclear weapons (as quoted above), they are acknowledging that China once again is ringed by a huge array of US firepower and basing options that put it at a great strategic disadvantage in the event of an armed conflict with the United States and its allies. China would find itself alone in such a conflict, for despite closer ties with Russia in recent years, they are not allies and have differing views on a number of economic and Asia-related issues.[22]

In sum, talk of a "new type of great-power relationship" is premature. Xi Jinping's idea has not generated serious official interest in the US government.[23] American policy toward China remains a combination of competition, cooperation, and containment (or "constrainment"), unchanged from previous recent US administrations and more laden with mistrust than before. For US leaders to accept President Xi's invitation would mean (in *their* view) conceding comparable status and influence to China and acknowledgment of China's "core interests" in Taiwan, Tibet, and Xinjiang—a remarkable concession, one that would be politically very risky at home. These days, no US political leader would contemplate sharing leadership with China, since that would be tantamount to acknowledging that the era of US leadership in Asia, in the Pacific, and worldwide was over. Chinese analysts surely understand that, for they know that no Chinese leader could survive if he argued that China should abide by US notions of "responsible stakeholder." Nationalism, in a word, is alive and well in both countries.

Table 4.2. China's Military Spending, 2009–2017 (US$ billions)

	2009	2010	2011	2012	2013	2014	2015	2016	2017
Official China Budget	70.2	75.8	88.8	103.1	114.8	131.3	144.2	146.6	148.3
US Dept. of Defense	150.0	160.0	120.0	135.0	145.0	163.0	180.0	NA	NA
IISS[a]	98.4	111.3	136.7	146.3	162.2	180.1	193.0	NA	NA
SIPRI-1[b]	137.5	144.5	156.0	169.4	185.2	200.9	214.1	225.7	NA
SIPRI-2[c]	105.6	115.7	138.0	157.4	179.9	200.8	214.1	215.2	NA

Source: "What Does China Really Spend on Its Military?," Center for Strategic and International Studies, http://chinapower.csis.org/military-spending/,2017.

[a] International Institute for Strategic Studies, Great Britain.

[b] Stockholm International Peace Research Institute, Sweden. Constant 2015 dollars.

[c] Current year dollars.

CHINA'S WEAK LINKS

Who would have imagined that in January 2017, during the week of Donald Trump's inauguration, Xi Jinping would tell an international audience that while one major country was ready to engage in trade protectionism and perhaps bring on a trade war, China remained deeply committed to globalization, not only with respect to trade and investment but also to fighting climate change.[24] In truth, that claim is weak.[25] Nevertheless, it reflects the unusual opportunity China believes it has to exert global leadership now that the Trump administration has rejected the Trans-Pacific Partnership free-trade agreement and the Paris accord on climate change but has continued US military involvement throughout the Middle East and escalated tensions with Russia. Beijing's party elite can also claim that China's political stability and steady economic growth measure up well against America's unpredictable new president, fracturing democracy, gridlock in Congress, health-care crisis, racial violence, and high crime rate. What more perfect scenario could there be for China to claim international leadership as a globally "responsible power?"

But the bigger picture is China's own very serious problems at home. Like leaders in Mao's time, today's leaders believe the key to international status and power—and to their own legitimacy and longevity—is domestic stability and prosperity. While Beijing can boast of several major domestic accomplishments in recent years—consistently high economic growth figures, reduction of the poverty rate, ending of the one-child policy, modest legal reforms, and substantial investments in renewable energy—its leaders have reason to feel insecure about the future.

Politics and Leadership

- Xi Jinping has been amassing personal power by acquiring new titles and concentrating real authority in various special groups rather than in the cabinet and ministries. He has abandoned the supposedly established principle of collective leadership in favor of personalized rule as "core" leader, inspiring charges of Mao-style cultism. This tendency culminated at a party congress in November 2017 at which "Xi Jinping Thought on Socialism with Chinese Characteristics in a New Era" was incorporated in the party constitution, making Xi the third Chinese leader (besides Mao and Deng) to be so designated. The honor further cements Xi's place as supreme leader until 2023.
- Communist Party rule has been further cemented by the issuance of guidelines for lawyers and media designed to ensure conformity with the party line.
- China's promise to maintain Hong Kong's open political system has eroded ever since the quashing of the Umbrella Movement in

2014. The selection rather than popular election of a pro-Beijing chief executive in March 2017 demonstrated anew just how limited is Hong Kong's promised "high degree of autonomy."

Law and Society

- Human rights and civil society are under assault. The Xi Jinping leadership is jailing lawyers and labor leaders, and abducting and repressing journalists, historians who defame Mao, book sellers in Hong Kong, and publishers.
- Prospects are dim for deeper legal reform that would embrace the principle of an independent judiciary.
- Corruption is a fact of life at every level of Chinese society and a major reason for wealth inequality.[26] To at least one astute observer, corruption is so entrenched that it may prove the undoing of the Chinese Communist Party.[27] Xi's anticorruption campaign has netted numerous violators; but it also clearly has a political purpose as well, inasmuch as the campaign has not targeted the families of the party elite, the so-called princelings, of whom Xi is one.
- Crime and punishment are heavily politicized. The harshest sentences are reserved for the least powerful in society.
- "Rule by law" is often something of a farce considering the Orwellian charges used to jail dissidents and activists, such as "subverting state power," "picking quarrels and provoking troubles," and "improper discussion of the Center's policies."
- Labor strikes and protests doubled in 2015 over 2014 as troubled state-owned businesses in manufacturing, mining, and construction either closed down or denied workers promised benefits.
- Official warnings about the dangers of "foreign influences" remind some of the Cultural Revolution. NGOs and nonprofit organizations have come under new restrictions, and universities are undergoing political surveillance to ensure conformity with the party line. Foreign journalists are often followed and harassed.[28]

The Economy

- Capital flight is becoming a serious problem; outflow from overseas investment and individuals' movement of their money abroad significantly exceeds inflow from foreign investment.
- The gap between rich and poor in China now exceeds the gap in the United States. The top 20 percent of Chinese earners have received nearly half of total income, while the poorest 20 percent of earners account for 5 percent of total income.[29]
- The economy's extraordinary rise masks serious weaknesses that raise questions about its long-term sustainability. High growth

rates are a thing of the past; "the new normal" is more moderate growth. The weaknesses are of long standing, and include resistance to deeper reforms at the top as well as at the grassroots; the lack of financial viability of state-owned enterprises, which contribute very little to the overall economy despite state protection; lack of employment for well-educated young people; a looming debt crisis that threatens the banking system;[30] overvalued and overbuilt real estate; a new materialism linked to very unsocialist values; large-scale internal migration; and a rapidly aging society.

- To avoid what leaders fear most—"instability"—party leaders will have to address the rapidly rising cost of internal security, as well as significant annual increases in the military budget.

Energy and the Environment

- Greenpeace reports that China, while promising to draw 20 percent of its energy from renewable sources, is in fact continuing to construct coal-fired plants—on average, one plant *a week* until 2020.[31] Coal burning caused toxic smog in over twenty cities at the end of 2016. Reliance on coal, especially at local levels, is undermining wind farms, in which China is a world leader. Chinese energy companies are also leaders in exporting coal-fired plants to developing countries, compromising China's commitment to fight climate change.[32]

- China faces a water crisis: "Four hundred Chinese cities now face a water shortage. One hundred and ten cities face a severe water shortage. This is a very serious problem," says Liu Changming, a retired hydrologist with the Chinese Academy of Sciences in Beijing. One small Chinese city in Gansu Province, out in the northwest, has actually run out of water.[33]

- Serious problems in China's nuclear power industry have come to light: sixteen safety incidents at eight plants in 2016. (China will soon have thirty-five nuclear plants in operation.) Chinese experts say that the problems are ultimately political: too much pressure from party officials on too few well-trained nuclear technicians, resulting in lack of transparency on safety matters and inadequate inspection of plants.[34]

In short, China is not setting an example of superior governance or sustainable economics at home; quite the opposite. In fact, in some respects—such as wealth and income inequality, ethnic repression, climate change, destruction or waste of natural resources, and now especially the meaning and future of democracy—China faces problems similar to those faced by the United States and other Western countries. But given China's population, the scale of the problems is less manageable, and given its closed, top-down political system, popular pressure for change is seldom effective. As Francis Fukuyama writes, China has a strong state but lacks two other major ingredients for effective governance: rule of law and democratic accountability.[35] It also lacks a value system that might promote social cohesion, as Wang Jisi writes.[36] The country is therefore quite a distance away from realizing the "China dream," becoming a development model for Third World countries, or practicing humane governance. Chinese analysts such as Wang recognize that the country falls short in some areas of diplomacy—such as creating alliances, overcoming historical grievances with neighboring countries, and abiding by international legal norms (as in the case study below)—but the chief obstacles to acceptance as a great power lie within. Demonstrating not just high gross domestic product (GDP) but also growth with social justice, and not just smooth leadership transitions but also accountable, transparent, and lawful governance, are some of the ways China can elevate its international stature as a "responsible great power."

DEALING WITH CONFLICT: THE CASE OF THE SOUTH CHINA SEA[37]

The US and Chinese Positions

The foreign policy views of Chinese and American experts diverge on a fundamental point: how to characterize the state of China-US relations. One major conference of think tank experts in China concluded that the best description is "simultaneous increases in cooperation and competition." This "new normal" means that "Sino-US confrontation can make a situation very bad, whereas cooperation can be a big deal."[38] But in the United States the debate these days is about the "China challenge" and whether or not it will eventuate in war. Cooperative possibilities are less studied than is the question of how to meet "the challenge," which often is cast in military terms. Experts in and out of government in both countries would probably agree that war is not inevitable. But that conclusion depends on whether or not US and Chinese leaders clearly understand each other's and their own core interests and will commit to not fighting over nonessential matters. The South China Sea (SCS) dispute falls precisely in that category.

In the SCS, six nations—China, Taiwan, Malaysia, Philippines, Brunei, and Vietnam—have claims to tiny islands in the Spratly and Paracel groups (called Xisha and Nansha by China) that sit astride important gas and oil reserves and fisheries. On the surface the dispute concerns sovereignty, resting on claims based on either history or international law: 200 nautical miles of exclusive economic zones (EEZ) and territorial waters that a country may legally claim under the 1982 United Nations Convention on the Law of the Sea (UNCLOS). But in recent years, such claims have masked deeper conflict over larger strategic interests, propelled by nationalism, a level of conflict that brings China face to face with the United States. If the dispute merely concerned tiny islands not on most maps, it would stand a good chance of being quietly resolved through diplomacy or legal adjudication; but with regional influence and energy needs on the line, the dispute stands a good chance of leading to violent conflict.

The United States has no territorial claim in the SCS. Nor has it ratified the UNCLOS, though it has recognized the convention as customary international law. But Washington cannot serve as an honest broker, though it has made the offer. Simply put, the reason is that since the end of World War II the United States, far from being an innocent bystander, has acted on the basis that the Pacific is an American lake (as General Douglas MacArthur once put it).[39] Officially, the US position is framed in terms of freedom of navigation and the consequent right to sail or fly anywhere, anytime "that international law permits," which includes the Chinese-claimed islands. In 2015 US ships and planes carried out some seven hundred patrols in the SCS area.[40] That presumed right requires a "rules-based regional order," as Secretary of State John Kerry put it in 2014.[41] China, on the other hand, ratified UNCLOS in 1996 and in more recent times has referred to the SCS as a major strategic (and possibly a "core") interest. In 2006 Beijing declared that it had sovereignty over all the disputed islands, not only in the SCS (which it defines by an expansive so-called nine-dash line) but also in the East China Sea (ECS), where it is in dispute with Japan over islands known variously as Diaoyudao or Senkaku.

Bridging Chinese-US differences is especially difficult because China regards its sovereignty claims as nonnegotiable, not subject to legal argument, and not a matter for discussion with outside parties such as the United States. China sees the United States as meddling in its backyard, where China believes it has license to exploit the SCS islands in any way it chooses, including seizing land, creating artificial islands, and deploying weapons and troops. The backyard also has strategic significance for China: its missile-capable submarine base in Hainan enhances its nuclear deterrent. Any talks on the SCS, Beijing insists, can only be among the six parties and preferably on a bilateral rather than multilateral basis. The talks, it says, should neither "internationalize" nor "ASEAN-ize" the dispute. ASEAN does not have a common position on the SCS dispute, but it does have a code of conduct, drafted with China in 2002—the Declaration of Conduct of Parties to the South China Sea—that could form the basis for dispute resolution. Completion of the code of conduct has proven very difficult, however, despite an agreement between China and ASEAN in July 2011 on guidelines for implementation. Foreign ministers of all the parties were unable to reach agreement on a legally binding code proposed by Vietnam in August 2017. The declaration itself calls for peaceful settlement of disputes and "restraint" on any action that would disturb the status quo. But the declaration is nonbinding, does not clarify "restraint," and only discusses confidence-building measures rather than conflict prevention or resolution. The United States is not a party to the declaration.

The United States insists that freedom of navigation conveys an interest in regional stability. On that basis, it seeks to constrain Chinese expansion through an ongoing naval presence; calls for China to freeze its activities in the SCS; spying on Chinese naval activities in and around Hainan; and, especially since Obama's announcement in 2009 of a "pivot" to Asia, rotation of US forces to Australia, Singapore, Guam, and (for the time being) Philippines. The United States has also strengthened its security alliance with Japan; the Obama administration determined that the security treaty covers the Senkaku/Diaoyudao area. While Obama did not support Japan's sovereignty claim, his action essentially linked the two East Asia territorial disputes and lent credence to Chinese concerns about US intentions.

If this duel sounds like a Cold War scenario, it just might be, though at a meeting in 2014 in Beijing Kerry, with Xi Jinping at his side, sought to reassure the Chinese that US policy was not to "push back against or be in conflict with China." Trouble is, the Chinese do not seem reassured by US involvement and *are* prepared to push back.[42] Quite a few Chinese analysts see the renewed US military attention to Asia as a return to a containment strategy and not an innocent call for talking. On the US side, the real worry seems to be that China's steady undermining of the territorial interests of the other parties adds up to an effort gradually to erode the US alliance system. Some experts think China's eventual goal is to push the United States out of East Asia altogether.

Escalation

The territorial dispute has been escalating. Prior to 2015 there were occasional firefights involving Chinese, Filipino, and Vietnamese vessels; landings of personnel on particular islands (e.g., China took Scarborough Shoal from the Philippines in 2012); competing contracts with international oil companies; detention of fishermen; deployments of ships; and interference with other parties' vessels. In 2014 China forcibly sought to remove Vietnamese vessels from the contested areas. Large anti-Chinese demonstrations took place in Vietnam, and the Philippines defied Chinese warnings and took its case against Chinese territorial claims before the UNCLOS Permanent Court of Arbitration. But since 2015 the dispute has taken on a distinctly military dimension. China's strategy papers refer to an expanded strategic role for its navy; it has constructed ports, airfields, barracks, and storage areas in three of the SCS islands, reclaiming land to create artificial islands; and it has emplaced mobile artillery on one SCS island as well as antiship and antimissile weapons in the Paracels—all in violation of President Xi's promise to President Obama not to "militarize" the SCS.[43]

Not to be outdone, US surveillance and show-the-flag naval maneuvers in the SCS area have all intensified. At least two close encounters between US spy planes and Chinese jets occurred in 2015. The United States and Vietnam have normalized relations: the US Navy is visiting Cam Ranh Bay for resupply, major US corporations are investing in Vietnam, and Obama ended the US embargo on arms to Vietnam. India is also being courted as a strategic partner. Cooperative military ties are being forged, cemented by Prime Minister Nahendra Modi's visit to Washington in June 2016, during which he spoke of mutual security concerns such as "freedom of navigation on seas." The two countries' navies are following up, discussing cooperation options that include antisubmarine warfare directed at China.[44] American diplomats have also been successful at generating support for their stance at various international forums, such as the G7 meeting in Japan in May 2016 and the International Institute for Strategic Studies Shangri-La Dialogue in June 2016.

The SCS dispute came to a head in a stunning ruling by the five-member UNCLOS arbitral court in July 2016. Both the decision and China's response had been determined months ahead of time. The court ruled against China's boundary claims under the "nine-dash line" and therefore declared illegal China's land reclamation and construction projects in the SCS islands. The islands, said the court, count as rocks, not land extensions or part of China's EEZ. China was therefore encroaching on the Philippines' EEZ. (The ruling did not extend to the issue of sovereignty over the islands.) The court also found China guilty of harming the marine environment by building artificial islands and of illegally interfering with Filipinos' fishing and oil exploration.[45] China's response was to declare the arbitration court's decision "null and void and without binding force." A foreign ministry statement repeated China's sovereignty claim over the SCS islands and asserted that it is consistent with international law, a view that hardly squares with its denial of the arbitration court's jurisdiction, much less its decision. China, the statement says, is committed to direct negotiations with the interested parties and to peaceful settlement of disputes; but "regarding territorial issues and maritime delimitation disputes, China does not accept any means of third party dispute settlement or any solution imposed on China."[46]

But the SCS dispute has hardly been put to bed. China turned defeat into victory when the new Philippines president, Rodrigo Duterte, angry with the Obama administration's criticism of his violent methods of dealing with drug users and dealers, chose to ignore the court case and attempt a reconciliation with Beijing. During a trip to Beijing in October 2016, Duterte received China's approval for resumption of Filipino fishing in areas cut off by Chinese boats, along with about $24 billion in economic development loans and investments. He may also seek to bury the territorial dispute by declaring the Scarborough Shoal a marine sanctuary and avoiding forceful challenges to Chinese claims. The Philippines, while not abrogating its 1951 defense treaty with the United States, apparently decided to downgrade some activities, such as joint exercises. Yet in spring 2017 US Special Forces assisted the Philippines army in operations against Islamic militants who seized a southern city. And oil drilling in the area remains an unresolved issue between China and the Philippines.

Although the sudden warming to China of a longtime US ally unnerved Washington, China, in its self-proclaimed role of "responsible great power," also suffered a stinging setback to its ambitious territorial claims. Any further expansion of reclamation and construction in the SCS will come at the expense of its claim to lawfulness—and conceivably will run up against US freedom-of-navigation patrols.

A Shared Responsibility and a Shared Opportunity

Both the United States and China must bear responsibility for the ratcheting up of tension in the SCS and ECS. Washington clings to "freedom of navigation" even though various Chinese officials have issued reassurances about navigation and pledged to protect shipping in conformity with international law. American show-the-flag maneuvers in and around Chinese-claimed territory may be lawful, but they are a clear provocation, especially when they venture close to the southern end of Hainan, where Yulin nuclear submarines and other submarines and surface ships are based. One day the Chinese navy, with more advanced capabilities than it currently has, may challenge these US ships; China is already conducting periodic naval and air exercises around the disputed islands and near Taiwan, including a joint exercise with Russia. When the next close encounter occurs, will the US commander or the president see it as a challenge to predominance in the Pacific? China has issued warnings to Japan, India, and Singapore not to support US activities in the SCS.[47] We thus have two camps engaged in the quarrel, adding to its Cold War profile.

On the Chinese side, the stubborn insistence on an unassailable historic right to the islands and an absolute refusal to adhere to whatever decision the arbitration court reaches are weak positions at best. China's strategic purpose for building runways, ports, and supply facilities in the SCS is said to be defensive, no doubt referring to Hainan Island. Since there is no direct threat to Hainan, we are left with the question of how far China intends to go with its SCS buildup. What we are witnessing, and what is distressing to China's neighbors, is a buildup that appears to be aimed at creating permanent bases with increasingly long-range weapons. Beijing should be consistent in recognizing that a legitimate territorial dispute exists, just as it demands that Japan acknowledge a dispute over the Diaoyutai/Senkaku islands. China should give up its insistence on bilateral talks with the ASEAN countries as the only acceptable format for peaceful resolution. And China should recognize the contradiction in its argument that it protects freedom of navigation but insists that continued land reclamation and military construction are perfectly legitimate.

The cat-and-mouse game now being played is dangerous. A firefight—whether by accident, design, a collision of aircraft or ships, or the impetuous action of a military commander on the scene—is increasingly possible, regardless of the intentions of national leaders. An incident such as the one that occurred in December 2016, in which a Chinese vessel retrieved a US ship's unmanned underwater vehicle (UUV), used for military as well as nonmilitary purposes,[48] could have triggered a serious confrontation. (The Chinese returned the UUV in a few days.) Some US analysts think China's expanding military presence there is worth a confrontation, and some members of the US Congress want to see Chinese claims challenged by sending ships inside the twelve-mile limit of the artificial islands.[49] Other specialists, however, think the United States and ASEAN should adjust to the reality of China's predominance there.[50] In the latter case, that means ongoing friction between the United States and China short of a firefight, underscoring the urgent need for channels of communication to bring about conflict management.

Direct talks between senior military and political leaders, such as the Security and Economic Dialogue meetings, are necessary and desirable and have resulted in improved communications at sea. There are several other more far-reaching options, such as no close-in US surveillance flybys or ship passage, in return for cessation of Chinese air and sea maneuvers near the disputed islands. China should also reduce military personnel there and freeze military-related construction, as should all other parties. China should stop plans to begin new construction, and it should make permanent the right of Filipinos and all others to fish in the disputed area. Finally, China should drop any plans for declaring an air defense identification zone (ADIZ) over the SCS. China tried this tactic in 2013 when it declared an ADIZ over the ECS. The United States, Japan, and South Korea protested, and the United States sent bombers over the ADIZ. It would be unfortunate to see that scenario repeated in the SCS.

China and the United States must also tackle the longer term challenge, which is to allow the rule of law to prevail in this as in any other dispute. All sides, starting with China, should abandon the useless historical arguments over sovereignty—useless, because they persuade no one outside their country of origin. The UNCLOS court's involvement is an opportunity for China to demonstrate that it is a "responsible great power," while for the United States, in keeping with a "rules-based" approach, it is an incentive for Senate ratification of the UNCLOS and perhaps for becoming an outside party to the Declaration of Conduct of Parties. Implementing a binding code of conduct is a very important assurance to ASEAN that its giant neighbor prefers negotiating to use of threats or force. Agreement should be reached on prior notification of military exercises or other significant movements of personnel or equipment. Some formula for joint or clearly demarcated exploitation of undersea resources would need to be devised—as China proposed in 1992 and Taiwan's former president endorsed a few years ago—and, when carried out, monitored, such as by joint patrolling of ships and planes. But exploration must take into account the fragile undersea ecology and overfishing, both of which already threaten to make the SCS an environmental disaster.

As I point out in the next section, the new US president may make Taiwan and trade bargaining chips in dealing with China over the SCS, presenting a whole new set of obstacles in the way of conflict management and US-China engagement.

TRUMP AND CHINA[51]

The Trump administration represents the new wild card in US-China relations. During his presidential campaign, Donald Trump had highly negative and one-sided views of China, a stark contrast to his exceedingly friendly view of Russia. "These are not our friends," he said of the Chinese. "These are our enemies."[52] Yet Trump insisted that he "likes" and "loves" China, though the only positive statement he made was admiration for the crackdown at Tiananmen in 1989. What he said revealed very limited understanding of Chinese views, sensitivities, and motivations and a strong inclination to always assume the worst about China. This bad-faith model, as political scientists call it, accounts for wildly inaccurate statements, such as the claim that global warming is a "hoax" created by the Chinese or the charge that China is guilty of currency manipulation even after it changed the yuan-dollar rate to US advantage.

To be clear, Donald Trump doesn't know much about China. He hadn't been there until a visit in November 2017, certainly hasn't studied it, and tends to rely for advice on people with conspiratorial views about China. During his campaign, Trump frequently said he believes China is "raping" the United States through unfair trade practices. "China has gotten rich off us. China has rebuilt itself with the money it's sucked out of the United States and the jobs that it's sucked out of the United States."[53] This is false posturing; Trump himself profits from Chinese investors in his properties and from Trump products made in China.[54]

Yet Trump believes that China's rise will falter—a trade war "will cause a depression in China," he said—unless it gives in to US demands.[55]

During his campaign, Trump's team produced a program that was notable for its oversimplifications and emphasis on bullying tactics.[56] It called for imposing a 25 percent tax on Chinese imports if China did not stop currency manipulation, reclaiming US manufacturing by rejecting Chinese export subsidies and "sweatshops" and lowering the US corporate tax rate, and "bolstering the U.S. military presence in the East and South China Seas to discourage Chinese adventurism." But as president, Trump has been far less confrontational on all these issues. He has acknowledged that China was not a currency manipulator, for example, and the Pentagon has reduced "freedom of navigation" operations in the SCS. Those steps were largely due to his belief that China holds the key to reining in North Korea's nuclear weapons program—a mistake that he acknowledged in mid-2017.[57]

Taiwan is another example of Trump's inconsistency. Several weeks before taking office, Trump broke with long-standing precedent and held a telephone conversation with Taiwan's president Tsai Ing-wen. It was the first conversation between US and Taiwanese leaders since the 1979 US recognition of the People's Republic of China (PRC) as the sole government of China. As with his trade threats, Trump's idea apparently was to use the One China pledge as leverage to move China on other issues, such as its currency policy and North Korea. But before long that strategy backfired, and Trump told Xi Jinping in a telephone conversation that the US One China policy was still in place. Months later, Trump said he would not have another conversation with President Tsai, since that would cause Xi discomfort.[58] Once Trump decided that China could not deliver on North Korea, however, he did cause China discomfort. The administration resumed arms sales to Taiwan (a $1.4 billion sale was announced in June 2017), sanctioned a Chinese bank and shipping company that does business with North Korea, and again raised the issue of China's unfairness on trade. Chinese sources reacted angrily to these moves. On the SCS dispute, moreover, the United States has moved closer to Vietnam, which has been the most resistant to Chinese oil drilling. A joint statement of Trump and Vietnamese prime minister Nguyen Xuan Phuc on May 31, 2017, took a common position on "unlawful restrictions to freedom of the seas" and "peaceful resolution of disputes"—essentially, Hanoi's argument for a binding code of conduct.[59]

Trump had an opportunity to mend fences with China and even define a "new great power relationship" when he visited Beijing in November 2017.[60] But what emerged from his time with Xi Jinping was a clear indication of just how much the balance of influence in US-China relations had shifted in China's favor. While Trump complimented Xi Jinping on his leadership and clever trade policy, Xi gave Trump neither ironclad agreements on trade and investments nor better access to Chinese financial markets. Trump said nothing about human rights in China, letting Xi believe it's no longer an American priority; and his search for stronger Chinese sanctions on North Korea proved fruitless. Publicly, at least, Trump did not offer a forceful message on the South China Sea dispute or relations with Russia. And since Trump had pulled the United States out of the Trans-Pacific Partnership and the Paris accord on climate change, he had nothing to say about multilateral trade arrangements or global warming, not to mention some of the other pressing global issues of our time, such as nuclear weapons, poverty alleviation, military spending, migration, and alternative energy. Xi obliged by not offering the United States a role in a few signature Chinese economic development projects, such as One Belt One Road and the Asian Infrastructure Investment Bank.

In short, Trump emerged looking like a supplicant, whereas Xi came off looking like the head of a coequal great power. Trump's failure in Beijing mirrored his weak political position back home, in stark contrast with Xi's consolidation of power. Trump's very legitimacy is in question, due not only to the Russia election meddling charges but also to legislative defeats, inner-Republican Party turmoil, and serious criticisms of the president's moral compass, psychological stability, and governing experience. Xi on the other hand has no challenger in sight and may even rule beyond his second term ending in 2022. That Xi conceded so little in his meeting with Trump surely related to his American counterpart's weaknesses.

US friends in Asia expected that Trump would use the visit to recommit the United States to Asian security and economic growth. For them, the central issue is being able to take advantage of positive US-China relations rather than, as in Cold War days, having to choose between Washington and Beijing. Trump let Asian leaders down, enabling Xi to credibly lay claim to China being the foremost economic power in Asia and a "responsible great power" when it comes to addressing urgent global issues.

SEEKING COMMON GROUND[61]

Halfway engagement between China and the United States amounts to coexistence. But not necessarily *peaceful* coexistence; that depends on how much leaders are willing to bend to ensure that inevitable frictions do not lead to a collision. Regular dialogue at multiple levels certainly helps ensure a nonviolent future, though dialogue in turn depends on both sides understanding each other's frame of reference.

President Xi's proposal for a new type of US-China relationship may start a useful dialogue with the United States and others about alternatives to a world dominated by a single hegemon. As both countries face serious domestic problems, they may be more motivated than before to establish a strategic partnership on issues of vital mutual importance. Contrary to the view of some political scientists, the world does not have to rely on a hegemonic power to operate peacefully and productively. Leadership can, and should, be a shared responsibility. So far as Asia is concerned, that means a US-China relationship that is cooperative and mutually respectful: C-2, in short. The benefits of US-China cooperation should be self-evident: for example, on global issues such as the demilitarization and exploration of space, international financial stability, environmental protection, peacekeeping missions, humanitarian assistance, military action against terrorist groups,[62] and prevention of cyber attacks.

American cooperation with China will not be possible on all issues and may even be undesirable in a few instances. The "war on terror" was an example of misplaced and exaggerated common interest that China's leaders used to justify a crackdown on ethnic "separatists." A common policy on murderous dictatorships will always be very difficult to craft, as Libya and Syria most recently demonstrate. But as we witness more frequent national and regional crises that have global implications and major human consequences—the Asian financial crisis of 1997–1998, Southeast Asia's tsunami in 2008, the US financial crisis of 2008–2010, Japan's nuclear plant disasters of 2011, mass hunger and civil wars in developing countries, and uncontrollable global warming—we come to understand the imperative of a cooperative approach to real security. Asian countries would be among the greatest beneficiaries of a system in which they were not squeezed by two competing giants as happened during the Cold War. And a cooperative US-China relationship would have one more crucial payoff: the opportunity for both countries to shift attention and resources away from each other and into environmental challenges and support for impoverished, crisis-prone areas of the world.

The United States cannot afford to be on a negative trajectory with China, and the reverse is equally if not more true. Seeking (or being reasonably perceived as seeking) to contain China, and pretending that US (or Western) superiority will endure indefinitely, are not sound ideas in a world that is increasingly integrated economically and ecologically and in which China is playing ever larger geopolitical and economic roles. Nor will worrying about the "China challenge" improve the US economic or political situation, no more than Chinese worries about "US hegemony" will solve China's internal problems. In neither case is the challenge primarily military, anyway.[63] The United States needs to take care of its own affairs, with a sense of purpose that springs from its professed values and enormous material advantages. Let China's people and leaders worry about their country's domestic affairs. They do; and as I have shown, they have plenty to worry about. As one prominent Chinese specialist on the United States has written, Chinese leaders recognize that "a more aggressive foreign policy or holding a tougher position vis-à-vis the US would solve none of [China's domestic] problems." But, he added, that position only holds if a US-China crisis, such as over Taiwan, can be avoided.[64]

An Agenda for Better US-China Relations

The history of US-China relations shows that when they are positive, meaning mutually productive and based on consultation, the consequences for regional security in Northeast Asia are likewise positive. When, on the other hand, those relations are marked by tension and competitive tit-for-tat actions, regional security in Northeast Asia suffers. Take the matter of security and stability on the Korean peninsula. A cooperative US-China relationship, marked by regular military and civilian engagement, can go a long way toward promoting improved inter-Korean communication, laying the basis for productive multiparty dialogue on security issues (whether a resumption of the Six Party Talks or a successor group, as discussed below), and minimizing dangerous miscalculations from occurring in the wake of a sudden crisis such as North Korea's collapse. China's support of escalating UN sanctions against North Korea since 2013, though well short of measures that would undermine the regime, is an example of what can happen when high-level US-China dialogue takes place.

Or take cybersecurity. In contrast with discord between the United States and Russia over computer hacking, the United States and China reached agreement at a summit meeting in September 2015 to create a bilateral "dialogue mechanism" to fight cyber crime following a major occurrence of commercial espionage by a unit attached to the People's Liberation Army.[65] More specifically, Obama and Xi agreed that "neither country's government will conduct or knowingly support cyber-enabled theft of IP, including trade secrets or other confidential business information, with the intent of providing competitive advantages to companies or commercial sectors." They agreed to set up a cyber hotline, which became operational in August 2016.

What further steps can be taken by the United States and China to reduce tensions, promote trust, and widen the basis for cooperation?

First, US forward deployment of forces and extended nuclear deterrence should be reconsidered. The THAAD system in South Korea should either be withdrawn or demobilized, a step that would also help smooth China-ROK relations. American arms sales to Taiwan should be reduced. The United States and Japan should resist the temptation to become more active security partners, lest either one be drawn into a clash stemming from US security commitments to Japan. Unfortunately, change seems unlikely on any of these issues. Although the "rebalancing" of US forces to Asia under Obama has apparently halted, the Pentagon has retained an "Air-Sea Battle Plan" explicitly designed to counter what it calls China's "anti-access, area-denial" strategy aimed at Taiwan.[66] Under Trump, major arms sales to Taiwan are continuing, as mentioned, as is security cooperation with Japan. Only in South Korea, where a new president halted further deployment of THAAD by agreement with China and questioned Trump's threats against North Korea, is there a slim prospect of realignment of US military plans in East Asia.

But China has also acted to reduce confidence in its proclamations of a "harmonious world" and a "peaceful rise." Its naval expansion in support of claims to Diaoyudao and the SCS islands is alienating neighboring countries and risking open conflict with Japan as well as the United States. China's assertiveness also invites precisely the response it wants to avoid, namely, an increased US military commitment to Asian allies, particularly Japan. Active patrolling of disputed waters also raises questions of trust in Southeast Asia, inasmuch as China has supported promises regarding the nonuse of force.

The continuing emphasis by both China and the United States on military power in support of diplomacy suggests the need to go beyond bilateral forums when seeking to build confidence. Regular Track I and Track II dialogues involving the ROK, Japan, and other interested parties should take place under joint China-US chairmanship. Direct, regular channels of communication between top-level officials below the presidents need to be established, especially between military leaders.[67] If the Trump administration fulfills the early promise of its secretary of state to deny China "access" to the SCS islands and prevent any further Chinese military buildup, the need for a direct military channel will become acute.[68] The good news is that US-PRC military-to-military contacts have become more frequent, including participation in joint exercises and regular dialogues.[69] These activities gain all the more importance for the United States in light of reports of growing convergence between China and Russia in conventional weapons transfers and nuclear weapons modernization.[70]

Second, China and the United States should lead the way toward creating a new security dialogue mechanism (SDM) for Northeast Asia, discussed in detail in chapter 5.[71] Formats such as the Six Party Talks on North Korea's nuclear weapons, writes one Chinese specialist, might "gradually become a more regular and systematic mechanism" for regional security.[72] Rather than wait for another round of the Six Party Talks, Beijing and Washington might do better to focus on the SDM idea, since that would create a permanent institution devoted to many other regional security issues, including environmental and territorial disputes—issues that are more amenable to diplomacy than North Korea's denuclearization and might produce enough trust to eventually reach a verifiable agreement on it. The SDM would have the authority to convene on the call of any member. It would be "an early warning and crisis management system," as the Chinese specialist said. His comment suggests a larger point: as China becomes increasingly comfortable working within multilateral groups, US diplomacy with China might profit from doing the same in order to arrive at a common position on regional security issues.[73]

Third, a US-PRC code of conduct that prevents the kinds of dangerous confrontations that have occurred at sea and in the air, such as the December 2013 near-collision between US and PRC ships, would be enormously beneficial. Reducing and redeploying US forces involved in close surveillance of the Chinese coast around Hainan would be an essential element of any such negotiation, as would agreement on "rules of the road" to prevent confrontations at sea or in the air.

Fourth, the United States and China should cooperate more closely on development financing and trade rather than continue to engage in competitive organizing. Washington has relied on the IMF and World Bank, in which it has always held the greatest voting power, and until Trump's arrival had hoped to launch the Trans-Pacific Partnership without Chinese participation in addition to various bilateral free-trade agreements (FTAs). China has been even more active than the United States in forming FTAs. In addition, it is part of several multilateral organizations that conspicuously do not include the United States: the BRICS (Brazil-Russia-India-China-South Africa), the Shanghai Cooperation Organization with Russia and the Central Asian countries, the Regional Comprehensive Economic Partnership, and the Asian Infrastructure Investment Bank (AIIB). Under an ambitious initiative called "One Belt One Road," moreover, China has launched a strategy of economic integration across Eurasia. Though Chinese officials do not cast it as a challenge to the postwar Bretton Woods system, the initiative seeks to put a fair share of trade and financial resources to work for China's development while promising other countries advantages denied them under liberal Western development models.

There is no reason that China and the United States should not be participants in some of each other's large-scale economic initiatives, such as the AIIB. Chinese officials have in fact invited US investments in those initiatives, so long as Chinese investments are allowed in US energy and other projects.[74] That such mutuality has not happened may be attributed to internal politics, not to questions of efficacy or differences in development philosophy.[75]

The key question that US and Chinese leaders must address is how they can create a legitimate and effective framework for cooperative security, one that lays the groundwork for alleviating the most serious *human* security problems. For the United States and China, as for other countries with regional and global reach, the answer is to embrace *common* security as the touchstone of *national* security. They must recognize that the greatest security challenges of our time are poverty—and violence in response to poverty—climate change and destruction of the global commons generally, and nuclear weapons. These challenges can only be effectively met if they are the highest priorities of all countries.

If China and the United States, which together command exceptional resources, can find common ground on cooperative security, both can truly lay claim to being responsible great powers. Shifting their focus to climate change, global poverty, and nuclear weapons would lay a new foundation for building trust—for example, by cooperatively developing and exporting wind and solar energy technologies—and move the spotlight away from their bilateral disagreements on territorial disputes, trade, and human rights. Otherwise, the two countries will be hard put to avoid being trapped into direct conflict, whether by past commitments, mutual fear, or strategic miscalculation.

NOTES

1. Portions of this chapter are adapted from my article, "The Uncertain Future of US-China Relations," *Asia-Pacific Journal—Japan Focus*, December 27, 2013, http://apjjf.org/2013/11/52/Mel-Gurtov/4052/article.html.

2. See their press conference remarks of June 8, 2013 at www.whitehouse.gov/the-press-office/2013/06/08/remarks-president-obama-and-president-xi-jinping-peoples-republic-china-.

3. "Remarks by President Obama and President Xi of the People's Republic of China Before Bilateral Meeting," September 6, 2013, www.whitehouse.gov/the-press-office/2013/09/06/remarks-president-obama-and-president-xi-peoples-republic-china-bilatera.

4. "Strategic distrust" (*zhanlue huyi*) is also the chief finding of a unique joint study by two senior US and Chinese analysts. See Kenneth Lieberthal and Wang Jisi, "Addressing U.S.-China Strategic Distrust," Brookings Institution, John L. Thornton China Center Report No. 4 (March, 2012). See also David Shambaugh, ed., *Tangled Titans: The United States and China* (Lanham, MD: Rowman & Littlefield, 2013).

5. Organization for International Investment, *Foreign Direct Investment in the United States*, Washington, DC, September 2016, appendix A.

6. Wayne M. Morrison, "China-U.S. Trade Issues," Congressional Research Service, Washington, DC, February 9, 2017, 1–20; https://fas.org/sgp/crs/row/RL33536.pdf.

7. Morrison, "China-U.S. Trade Issues," 1–2.

8. In 2016 those Chinese students constituted around a third of all international students in the United States and also roughly a third of all Chinese students studying abroad. Data from the Chinese education ministry also show that about four million students have studied abroad since 1978, that China is the leading country for sending students abroad for study, and that around three-quarters of Chinese students abroad return home. ICEF Monitor, "A Record Number of Chinese Students Abroad in 2015," April 6, 2016, http://monitor.icef.com/2016/04/a-record-number-of-chinese-students-abroad-in-2015-but-growth-is-slowing/.

9. President Trump has long-standing ambitions to expand his hotel chain into Russia, and Rex Tillerson, the secretary of state, previously headed Exxon Mobil, whose oil drilling plans in Russia were put on hold by US sanctions.

10. Graham Allison, "How Trump and China's Xi Could Stumble into War," *Washington Post*, March 31, 2017; and www.belfercenter.org/publication/how-trump-and-chinas-xi-could-stumble-war. Allison links the possibility of war to the parallel personalities of Trump and Xi.

11. Zhang Tuosheng, *"Ruhe goujian Zhong-Mei xin xing daguo guanxi"* [How to construct a new China-US great power relationship], Nautilus Institute Special Report, July 23, 2013, www.nautilus.org.

12. Mel Gurtov, "Are We in a 'Post-American Era'?" *China-US Focus*, November 1, 2017, https://www.chinausfocus.com/foreign-policy/2017/1101/15635.html.

13. Wu Xinbo, "Chinese Visions of the Future of U.S.-China Relations," in Shambaugh, *Tangled Titans*, 377.

14. Wu, "Chinese Visions," 376. Dai Bingguo is quoted by Wu (p. 376) as saying, with obvious reference to the United States: "We hope that what they say and do at our gate or in this region where the Chinese people have lived for thousands of years is also well intentioned and transparent." See also Wang Jisi's section on Chinese perceptions in Lieberthal and Jisi, "Addressing U.S.-China Strategic Distrust."

15. Zhang Tuosheng, *"Ruhe goujian Zhong-Mei xin xing daguo guanxi."*

16. Zhang Tuosheng (*"Ruhe goujian Zhong-Mei xin xing daguo guanxi"*) acknowledges the obstacle posed by Cold War thinking on both sides, particularly their military establishments, as exemplified by worst-case scenarios (*zui huai qianjing*). But he insists that such thinking poses a more serious problem in the United States.

17. *Global Times*, December 24, 2016. Thanks to Joe Parker for sending me this editorial.

18. The *New York Times* reported that a PRC government spokesman, Hong Lei, said: "As for foreign correspondents' living and working environments in China, I think as long as you hold an objective and impartial attitude, you will arrive at the right conclusion"—a statement right out of *1984*. Mark Landler and David E. Sanger, "China Pressures U.S. Journalists, Prompting Warning from Biden," *New York Times*, December 4, 2013.

19. Marshall Sahlins, "China U.," *Nation*, October 30, 2013, https://www.thenation.com/article/china-u/.

20. There has always been a large discrepancy between China's officially reported military spending and the various (but more reliable) estimates of its actual spending by non-Chinese governmental and think tank sources.

21. These are either stockpiled or deployed nuclear warheads. See Arms Control Association, "Nuclear Weapons: Who Has What at a Glance," July 2017, https://www.armscontrol.org/factsheets/Nuclearweaponswhohaswhat.

22. China's military ties with Russia, which include joint training exercises and Russian military sales to China, are well short of constituting an alliance with mutual defense obligations. Russian sales to China of major weapons systems in fact have declined since 2012. Sources of friction remain important, such as Russia's closeness with Vietnam and India, two countries with difficult relations with China. China and Russia also have different foreign policy priorities: China's is with the United States, Russia's with Europe. Ethan Meick, "China-Russia Military-to-Military Relations: Moving Toward a Higher Level of Cooperation," U.S.-China Economic and Security Review Commission Report, Washington, DC, March 20, 2017; Lora Saalman, ed., *China-Russia Relations and Regional Dynamics: From Pivots to Peripheral Diplomacy* (Stockholm: Stockholm International Peace Research Institute, 2017).

23. When Rex Tillerson made his initial visit to China in March 2017, the Chinese press reported that he had proposed, word-for-word, Xi Jinping's definition of a "new type of great-power relationship," with the accent on respect for mutual interests. Since Tillerson did not allow the US press corps to accompany him, these reports are probably exaggerated.

24. The speech was presented at the annual Davos World Economic Forum of the rich and powerful; see Larry Elliott and Graeme Wearden, "Xi Jinping Signals China Will Champion Free Trade if Trump Builds Barriers," *Guardian*, January 17, 2017.

25. Elizabeth C. Economy demonstrates in a survey that China's embrace of globalization actually is very partial: "Beijing Is No Champion of Globalization," *Foreign Affairs*, January 22, 2017, www.foreignaffairs.com/articles/china/2017-01-22/beijing-no-champion-globalization.

26. As for income inequality in China, see the study cited by Ana Swanson, "China's Economic Miracle Has an Ugly Underbelly," *Washington Post*, May 1, 2017.

27. Minxin Pei, *China's Crony Capitalism: The Dynamics of Regime Decay* (Cambridge, MA: Harvard University Press, 2016).

28. Melissa K. Chan, "Reporting from China: 400 Reports, on 1.4 Billion People, in One Authoritarian State," *International Journal of Communication*, no. 11 (2017), http://ijoc.org/index.php/ijoc/article/view/5155/1976.

29. Ian Talley, "China Is One of the Most Unequal Countries in the World, IMF Paper Says," *Wall Street Journal*, March 26, 2016, online ed.

30. China's debt load continues to be high because of borrowing by state-run enterprises and others to maintain high growth rates. Banks seem unwilling to rein in loans to inefficient and failing corporations. China's debt profile is not the same as that of Western countries, however, where the system collapsed in 2008 and a deep recession occurred. Keith Bradsher, "Moody's Downgrades China Over Worries About Its Growing Debt," *NYT*, May 23, 2017.

31. Edward Wong, "China Pledge to Curb Coal Plants, Greenpeace Says It's Still Adding Them," *NYT*, July 14, 2016.

32. Hiroko Tabuchi, "As Beijing Joins Climate Fight, Chinese Companies Build Coal Plants," *NYT*, July 1, 2017.

33. Rob Schmidt, "A Warning for Parched China," *NYT*, April 21, 2016; and www.marketplace.org/2016/04/21/world/warning-parched-china-city-runs-out-water.

34. Radio Free Asia, "China Nuclear Power Plant Incidents Highlight 'Systemic' Safety Concerns," January 9, 2017, www.rfa.org/english/news/china/concerns-01092017121057.html.

35. Center on Democracy, Development, and the Rule of Law, "Reflections on Chinese Governance," February 2016, http://fsi.stanford.edu/sites/default/files/fukuyama_feb.16_wp_0.pdf).

36. Wang, "Inside China," *Global Asia* 5, no. 2 (Summer 2010): 8.

37. This section draws from some of my previous publications, including "Trouble at Sea," http://apjjf.org/-Mel-Gurtov/4795/article.html; and "Rules and Rocks: The US-China Standoff Over the South China Sea," http://apjjf.org/2015/13/23/Mel-Gurtov/4330.html. I am also indebted to the work of Mark J. Valencia.

38. "China-US Relations Have Entered a 'New Normal' of Simultaneous Increases in Cooperation and Conflict," *Renmin wang*, May 26, 2017, http://world.people.com.cn/n1/2017/0526/c1002-29301699.html.

39. A more recent expression of that view occurred when President Clinton sent two aircraft carriers into the Taiwan Strait in response to Chinese missile tests in 1996. Then defense secretary William J. Perry said: "China should know [that] the premier, the strongest military power in the western Pacific is the United States." Keith Johnson and Dan De Luce, "U.S. Gears Up to Challenge Beijing's 'Great Wall of Sand,'" *Foreign Policy*, September 22, 2015, http://foreignpolicy.com/2015/09/22/u-s-gears-up-to-challenge-beijings-great-wall-of-sand-obama-xi-south-china-sea/.

40. Mark J. Valencia, "Toe to Toe: The China-US Struggle Over the South China Sea Grows," *Global Asia* 11, no. 4 (Winter 2016): 86.

41. John Kerry, "U.S. Vision for Asia-Pacific Engagement," August 13, 2014, www.state.gov/secretary/remarks/2014/08/230597.htm.

42. "China today is no longer susceptible to U.S. coercion or bullying. Under President Xi Jinping, the more confrontational stance Washington takes, the more assertive Beijing will become in response. That's the new reality of Chinese foreign policy." Feng Zhang, "Provoking Beijing in the South China Sea Will Only Backfire on Washington," *Foreign Policy*, May 21, 2015, http://foreignpolicy.com/2015/05/21/united-states-provoke-beijing-south-china-sea-air-defense-identification-zone/.

43. Thomas Shugart, "China's Artificial Islands Are Bigger (and a Bigger Deal) Than You Think," https://warontherocks.com/2016/09/chinas-artificial-islands-are-bigger-and-a-bigger-deal-than-you-think/.

44. Nilanthi Samaranayake, Michael Connell, and Satu Limaye, "The Future of U.S.-India Naval Relations," Center for Naval Analyses, February 2017, www.cna.org/cna_files/pdf/DRM-2016-U-013938-Final2.pdf, 41–42.

45. The text of the ruling is at Permanent Court of Arbitration on the West Philippine Sea, Press Release, July 12, 2016, https://www.scribd.com/document/318075282/Permanent-Court-of-Arbitration-PCA-on-the-West-Philippine-Sea-Arbitration#download.

46. Xinhua, "Full Statement," July 12, 2016, http://www.xinhuanet.com/english/.

47. Valencia, "Toe to Toe." As Valencia points out, Vietnam and Indonesia, both of which have fishing interests in and near the SCS, have been seeking military assistance to protect them.

48. The US contention at the time was that the UUV was being used for an oceanographic survey. But the US Navy lists a variety of military purposes for UUVs, such as antisubmarine warfare, intelligence, and surveillance. Mark Pomerleau, "DoD Plans to Invest $600M in Unmanned Underwater Vehicles," *Defense Systems*, February 4, 2016, https://defensesystems.com/articles/2016/02/04/dod-navy-uuv-investments.aspx.

49. Johnson and De Luce, "U.S. Gears Up."

50. Mark J. Valencia, "Beijing Now Calls the Shots in the South China Sea, and the US and ASEAN Must Accept This for Lasting Peace," *South China Morning Post*, July 9, 2017, http://m.scmp.com/comment/insight-opinion/article/2101696/beijing-now-calls-shots-south-china-sea-and-us-and-asean?amp=1.

51. This section is adapted from my essay, "Trump Faces China: Some Unsettling Thoughts," *China-US Focus*, December 22, 2016, http://www.chinausfocus.com/foreign-policy/trump-faces-china-some-unsettling-thoughts.

52. Interview with Wolf Blitzer, CNN, January 20, 2011, http://cnnpressroom.blogs.cnn.com/2011/01/20/the-situation-room-with-wolf-blitzer-donald-trump-on-china-these-are-not-our-friends-these-are-our-enemies/.

53. Julia Glum, "Beijing Dismisses Trump China Comments," September 1, 2015, www.ibtimes.com/beijing-dismisses-donald-trump-china-comments-disturbances-because-most-americans-2077141.

54. John Kell, "Trump Tower Funded by Rich Chinese Who Wanted Visas," *Fortune*, March 7, 2016, http://fortune.com/2016/03/07/trump-tower-chinese-visas/.

55. Jack Perkowski, "Trump on China," *Forbes*, April 5, 2011, www.forbes.com/sites/jackperkowski/2011/04/05/trump-on-china/#153401d040ca.

56. www.donaldjtrump.com/positions/us-china-trade-reform.

57. On June 20, Trump tweeted: "While I greatly appreciate the efforts of President Xi & China to help with North Korea, it has not worked out. At least I know China tried!"

58. "My problem is that I have established a very good personal relationship with President Xi," said Trump. "I really feel that he is doing everything in his power to help us with a big situation [with North Korea]. So I wouldn't want to be causing difficulty right now for him. So I certainly would want to speak to him first." Stephen J. Adler, Steve Holland, and Jeff Mason, "Trump Says 'Major, Major' Conflict with North Korea Possible, But Seeks Diplomacy," Thomson Reuters, April 27, 2017, https://www.reuters.com/article/us-usa-trump-exclusive/exclusive-trump-says-major-major-conflict-with-north-korea-possible-but-seeks-diplomacy-idUSKBN17U04E.

59. See Hunter Marston, "Why Tensions Are Rising Between Vietnam and China," *Foreign Affairs*, August 15, 2017, www.foreignaffairs.com/articles/asia/2017-08-15/why-tensions-are-rising-between-vietnam-and-china.

60. See my "Trump and Xi in Beijing: A Snapshot," China-US Focus, November 17, 2017, https://www.chinausfocus.com/foreign-policy/trump-and-xi-in-beijing-a-snapshot.

61. This section draws on the final chapter of my book *Will This Be China's Century? A Skeptic's View* (Boulder, CO: Lynne Rienner Publishers, 2013).

62. For example, a report in 2017 indicated joint Chinese-Afghan patrols along the narrow Afghanistan-China border, though against which terror organization these are

directed is not clear. As US forces draw down in Afghanistan, Chinese forces may help replace them. Shawn Snow, *Military Times*, March 5, 2017, www.militarytimes.com.

63. As the American Chamber of Commerce in China suggests, the real China challenge is economic—specifically, future technologies (Fred Hiatt, "China Is Bent on World Domination, But Not in the Way You Think," *Washington Post*, May 7, 2017). Trump administration officials are reportedly concerned about the huge state investment and state protection China is providing for robotics, driverless cars, electric cars, and other advanced technologies that will challenge US exports. Keith Bradsher, "Trump Administration Said to Open Broad Inquiry into China's Trade Practices," *NYT*, August 1, 2017.

64. Wang Jisi, "America in Asia: How Much Does China Care?" *Global Asia* 2, no. 2 (Summer 2007): 24–28.

65. Morrison, "China-U.S. Trade Issues," 43–44.

66. See Michael O'Hanlon and James Steinberg, "Going Beyond Air-Sea Battle," *Washington Post*, August 23, 2012.

67. See Michael D. Swaine, "Conclusion: Implications, Questions, and Recommendations," in Swaine and Zhang Tuosheng, eds., *Managing Sino-American Crises: Case Studies and Analysis* (Washington, DC: Carnegie Endowment for International Peace, 2006), 425.

68. At his confirmation hearing, Rex Tillerson said: "We're going to have to send China a clear signal that, first, the island-building stops. And, second, your access to those islands is also not going to be allowed." Michael Forsythe, "Rex Tillerson's South China Sea Remarks Foreshadow Possible Foreign Policy Crisis," *NYT*, January 12, 2017. Tillerson likened China's policy to Russia's seizure of Crimea—a rather inapt comparison, but one that certainly got China's attention.

69. Examples are the Chinese navy's participation in the US Pacific Fleet's 2016 RIMPAC exercise, joint disaster and humanitarian relief exercises, port calls, exchanges of high-level visits, and use of the Maritime Management Consultation Agreement to avoid air and sea accidents. A full list of military-to-military exchanges in 2016 is in Office of the Secretary of Defense, *Annual Report to Congress: Military and Security Developments Involving the People's Republic of China 2017*, Washington, DC, May 2017, 85–90 and appendix 1. See also Yao Yunzhu, "The 'New Normal' in China-U.S. Military Relations," *China-US Focus Digest* 12 (December 2016): 25–28.

70. Saalman, ed., *China-Russia Relations and Regional Dynamics*.

71. See my "Averting War in Northeast Asia: A Proposal," *Asia-Pacific Journal* 9, no. 2 (January 10, 2011), http://japanfocus.org/-Mel-Gurtov/3467.

72. Wang Yizhou, "China's Path: Growing and Learning," *Global Asia* 5, no. 1 (Spring 2010): 12–16.

73. In agreement on that point, see Zhang Tuosheng, "The Shifting US-China Balance of Power in the Western Pacific: Getting the Transition Right," *Global Asia* 11, no. 1 (Spring 2016): 18–22.

74. See, for example, He Weiwen, "What's Next After Beef?," *China-US Focus Digest* 14 (June 2017): 34–38.

75. Amitai Etzioni, "The Asian Intrastructure Investment Bank: A Case Study of Multifaceted Containment," *Asian Perspective* 40, no. 2 (2016): 173–196. Etzioni argues that the failed US effort to persuade allies not to join China's AIIB was a form ("multifaceted") of containment.

FIVE

Disengagement

Failures in US-Russia and US–North Korea Relations

THE RESET THAT WASN'T: RUSSIA AND THE UNITED STATES

The Brief End of the Cold War

Relations between the United States and Russia demonstrate how quickly different interests and perceptions can upend an attempt at engagement. President Obama had spoken optimistically about "resetting" relations soon after he took office in 2009, and in a presidential campaign debate with Mitt Romney in 2012, during which Romney said Russia was the "number one geopolitical foe" of the United States, Obama countered that "the Cold War's been over for 20 years." But that remark, which set aside Russia's intervention in Georgia in 2008 to secure the "independence" of Abkhazia and South Ossetia, proved premature.

At first a reset seemed to be moving along just fine. The two countries worked together to make possible Russia's entry into the WTO and the G-8 economic group. They cooperated to allow US military overflights into Afghanistan to supply troops. They signed arms control treaties and joined in crafting the nuclear deal with Iran following implementation of sanctions. Russia refrained from exercising its veto in the UN Security Council (UNSC) in 2011 when US-led forces helped overthrow Libya's leader, Mu'ammar Gadhafi. Cooperation between Russia and the United States facilitated Assad's seeming agreement to remove chemical weapons munitions and components from Syria in 2013. The United States and Russia recognized the rise of ISIS (the Islamic State) as a national security threat. And starting in late 2015, US-Russia negotiators attempted to bring about a cease-fire in Syria and formation of a transitional Syrian government.

But some of the more positive efforts did not stay that way for long. Putin evidently regretted not vetoing the intervention in Libya. He had watched with trepidation as the United States supported the Arab Spring, which to Russia seemed like a lead-up to regime change in the same way the "color revolutions" in Eastern Europe had ousted pro-Russian leaders. Prodemocracy demonstrations followed in Moscow, which—according to Tom Donilon, Obama's adviser on national security—pushed Putin fully into "a posture of pretty active hostility toward the United States and the West."[1] In Syria, Assad defied Obama's "red line" on chemical weapons, not only preserving the capability to produce them but using them several times on the battlefield.[2] Russia surely was aware of that. But apparently to preserve the possibility of Russian cooperation on a peace agreement in Syria, Obama rejected military action there.[3]

The Unraveling: From Ukraine to Syria

By 2012 Putin was determined to push back against the West, which he did by abandoning arms control and intensifying attacks on dissenters at home.[4] But the crunch point, according to observers who blamed Russia exclusively, was the thinly disguised Russian intervention in Ukraine's civil war in support of pro-Russian separatists. In 2014 Russia annexed Crimea and supplied the Ukraine opposition with a missile (as determined by a Dutch investigation) that shot down a Malaysian airliner, with the loss of 298 lives. The intervention in Ukraine resulted in substantial US sanctions on members of the Russian elite and various Russian institutions that surely hurt Russia's economy and plunged relations into a deep Cold War–like freeze. In the new post-Ukraine environment, hostile rhetoric, tension over military movements, and the continuing modernization of nuclear weapons came to dominate the US-Russia relationship, as they had during the Cold War.[5] Events in Syria fed the mutual hostility, which found its way into public opinion.[6] Once Russia intervened with air power on Assad's side, cooperation with the United States directed at ISIS became sporadic, as the Russia-Syria alliance focused mainly on eliminating the local forces resisting Assad.

Putin blamed US interference in Ukraine's presidential election, which resulted in a pro-Western leader replacing one friendly to Russia, for Russia's subsequent actions, arguing (with some credibility) that the United States was trying to squeeze Russia in its "near abroad" and deny it a proper senior role in world affairs. As a prominent Russian analyst describes Moscow's view, "Russia's subordinate position [in the liberal international order] is the illegitimate result of a never-ending U.S. campaign to keep Russia down and prevent it from regaining its proper status."[7] In 2016 Putin signed off on a strategic assessment that viewed Russia's national security as threatened by US efforts to retain global domination.[8]

The consensus of many observers seems to be that for Russia, and for Putin in particular, the overarching aim is to regain great power status in a one-superpower world order.[9] Lacking the domestic and international economic resources that China possesses to be a country whose interests must consistently be taken into account by the United States and others, Russia has deployed its military might to make the point—which it did in Syria—that it must be treated as a power of equivalent rank and with special security interests in bordering countries. Putin clearly rejects what he sees as the West's presumption that with the collapse of the Soviet Union, "Russia would forever . . . play a fundamentally diminished role in the world."[10] By the same token, he also rejects the post–Cold War American presumption that US hegemony, exemplified by unilateral interventions in the former Yugoslavia and the Middle East starting in the 1990s, is a permanent fixture in world affairs. Restoring Russian pride of place, so damaged by the way the Cold War ended in Europe, seems to figure prominently in the country's international outlook. By the end of 2016 Putin could claim important victories, with Russian influence at its height in Syria and Iran.

The United States and its allies may not be entirely innocent in the deterioration of relations with Russia. Stephen F. Cohen and Katrina van-den Heuvel deplore the demonization of Putin in the Western media and insist that addressing US national security interests should mean putting the threat posed by ISIS ahead of collision with Russia.[11] On one key point, however—that US officials in the Bill Clinton and George W. Bush administrations failed to honor a pledge to Russia in 1990 not to expand the North Atlantic Treaty Organization (NATO) in return for Russian acceptance of German reunification—the most recent evidence suggests otherwise.[12] Still, some of Putin's actions may indeed have been in response to the West's. Ukraine was considered a potential NATO member, along with Georgia. Then, in February 2014, the United States helped overturn an elected pro-Russian government in Ukraine, taking advantage of popular protests that turned violent. A tape recording surfaced of a four-minute conversation between two US diplomats about how to orchestrate the Ukraine situation.[13] In Syria, would the Russians have intervened had the United States, France, Great Britain, Turkey, and Saudi Arabia not sought the overthrow of Assad, whom Putin seems to regard as a bulwark against Islamic fundamentalism *and* generalized instability nearby? Cohen and vanden Heuvel are sometimes myopic in their treatment of Putin, neglecting the fact that Russian intervention in Ukraine and Syria has had large human costs—high civilian casualties, the destruction of cities such as Aleppo, hundreds of thousands of desperate immigrants—that simply cannot be justified on the basis of national interest. But they and other critics do make a sensible point about demonization of Russia and the desirability of cooperation with it on Syria and Ukraine.

Some scholars have made the argument that NATO had no intention of admitting Ukraine anytime soon, that Russian leaders never raised the issue of NATO expansion in talks with Obama, and that Putin's seizure of Crimea "appears to have been an improvised gambit" chiefly motivated by fear of losing the Black Sea Fleet's base at Sevastopol.[14] Perhaps so, but the Pentagon used the growing discord to successfully lobby for investing in "smaller," more precise nuclear weapons.[15] It also quadrupled weapons and equipment transfers to NATO, including antitank weapons and artillery. NATO's defense ministers voted in February 2016 to expand the troop presence and military exercises near Russia's borders, specifically with an eye to protecting Hungary, Romania, Ukraine, and the Baltic states against Russian "aggression." Later in the year NATO members—mainly Britain, Germany, France, Canada, and Denmark—followed up the exercises by sending troops to Poland and the Baltic states.[16] Russia thereupon withdrew from a 2000 treaty on plutonium disposal. To at least one critic of US policy, Washington was again raising the "red scare" to arouse anti-Russian feelings and feed the military-industrial complex.[17]

But the most volatile ingredient in the US-Russia disengagement, discussed below, was US accusations of Russian interference in the 2016 presidential election.

The New Cold War

The public debate over US-Russia relations was now about how strongly to press Putin, especially after the Obama administration charged that "senior-most" Russian officials had authorized hacking of the Democratic Party's e-mail system, "intended to interfere with the US election process" on Donald Trump's behalf.[18] The trigger for the hacking may have been the barely concealed feud between Putin and Hillary Clinton. She had a well-established reputation of contempt for Putin's domestic and foreign policies, and in 2011 she had made disparaging remarks about Russia's parliamentary election process that Putin regarded as interference.[19] As secretary of state until 2013, Clinton reportedly was skeptical of Obama's reset idea, partly because she viewed Putin, a former KGB agent and prime minister at the time, with great suspicion.[20] When she left office, she advised Obama not to be too eager to get together with him. Putin, she argued, only understands "strength and resolve"—a striking statement reminiscent of Clark Clifford's advice to Harry Truman on dealing with Stalin's Russia only from a position of strength. During a campaign debate with Senator Bernie Sanders in February 2016, Clinton said that Russia was the biggest threat to the United

States, using Cold War language to make the point.[21] Russia's leader had every reason to view the possibility of a Clinton presidency with apprehension.

The influential *New York Times* columnist Thomas L. Friedman was among the liberal commentators who were ready to draw the line:

> Obama believed that a combination of pressure and engagement would moderate Putin's behavior. That is the right approach, in theory, but it is now clear that we have underestimated the pressure needed to produce effective engagement, and we're going to have to step it up. This is not just about the politics of Syria and Ukraine anymore. It's now also about America, Europe, basic civilized norms and the integrity of our democratic institutions.[22]

Echoing that view, Leon Panetta, who had served as Obama's CIA director, said: "Let's not kid anybody. Putin's main interest is to try to restore the old Soviet Union. I mean that's what drives him." In Panetta's view, the Cold War lineup was being revived: Russia against NATO, with central Europe a contested zone.[23] Tough talk like that echoed the views of a considerable number of US State Department specialists, who publicly urged deeper US military involvement in Syria as the human toll, in lives and refugees, mounted.[24]

Obama, his term in office ending, was not about to intervene further in the Middle East. Though he did deploy an additional 200 Special Forces to Syria, his preeminent concern was to avoid involvement in which US forces might come into direct conflict with Russia. Nevertheless, Putin was not about to stand still. He contributed to these threat perceptions by undertaking a major rebuilding of his armed forces, with emphasis on the nuclear component and large-scale exercises evidently geared to a potential confrontation with NATO. The rebuilding is taking place even as the Russian economy plunges due to collapsing oil prices, capital flight, sharp depreciation of the ruble, and Western sanctions. But Putin's popularity remains sky high, and he has used it to proclaim success in elevating Russia's international standing even as the quality of life for the average Russian declines and human rights conditions deteriorate, especially repression (including assassination of and planting of false stories about) journalists, ethnic groups, and critics of the regime. As noted in the previous chapter, Putin has found partnership with China in opposition to US hegemony.

Trump's Failure at Reset II

The rapid downward spiraling of US relations with Russia showed the exceptional difficulty of changing Cold War patterns of behavior and establishing a new basis for partnership between a superpower that still is and a country that once was. Obama's failed attempt to reset US-Russia relations raised the question of whether or not engaging Russia in the fullest sense would be possible in the near future. Most cooperative ventures between Russia and the United States had fallen by the wayside, replaced by competition and the potential for confrontation. For the balance to swing back to attempting a reset would require leaders in Moscow and Washington who believe engagement is a worthy objective—and publics sufficiently trusting of the other side to support it.[25]

Donald Trump said during his presidential campaign that he was the man to fix US-Russia relations. He consistently praised Russia's leader (stronger than Obama, Trump said of Putin) and displayed an uncritical attitude toward Russia's foreign policy. Perhaps motivated by prospects for expanding his hotel brand in Russia,[26] Trump displayed indifference to repression in Russia, the annexation of Crimea, or the civilian casualties resulting from Russia's bombing in Syria. He talked confidently about being able to work out a common front with Russia against ISIS. Putin responded with similar praise for Trump and hopes for improved relations with the United States. Russians tied to the Kremlin made a number of contacts with the Trump campaign—contacts the Trump officials tried to hide—supposedly to promote better relations but surely with the specific goal of ending US sanctions. Clearly, in Putin's view a Trump administration held out much greater prospect than Obama's or Hillary Clinton's that Russia would be treated as an equal, without US interference in its internal politics or challenges to its strategic interests.[27]

But once elected, Trump would have to overcome a major battle on the home front: accusations that hackers working for Russian official entities were responsible for revealing hundreds of thousands of e-mails in the computers of the Democratic National Committee and Hillary Clinton.[28] The e-mails, which WikiLeaks published, embarrassed and harmed Clinton's campaign and clearly benefited Trump's. The actual hackers were said to be associated with the Federal Security Bureau, successor to the KGB, and the military intelligence unit GRU. Trump was defiant in insisting, like Putin, that there was no evidence to support the charge of Russian involvement, saying it was "ridiculous" and even suggesting (as he had during the campaign) that China "or some guy in New Jersey" could have been responsible.

But there was plenty of evidence of Putin's direct involvement in Russian interference in the US election, and not just by hacking e-mails. Obama was made aware of the evidence as early as August 2016, but he reportedly decided that before the election he could not accuse Russia directly and take serious countermeasures. Among his reasons was not wanting to appear to be using intelligence for partisan political purposes.[29] Once past the election, however, the accusations reached a crescendo, especially after the CIA, in a formal briefing to senators late in 2016, expressed certainty about Russian hacking and said it was orchestrated to help Trump's campaign.[30] The FBI and all sixteen of the other

US intelligence agencies concurred. With the evidence overwhelming, Obama, just a month before Trump's inauguration, ordered a "full review" in order to consider "lessons learned."[31]

The US intelligence community did not stop there; it further asserted at year's end that Putin himself probably directly ordered the hacking, initially as a "vendetta" against Hillary Clinton but later as "an effort to show corruption in American politics and to 'split off' key American allies by creating the image that [other countries] couldn't depend on the U.S. to be a credible global leader anymore."[32] Trump, in refusing to accept either the intelligence community's conclusions or even the report that the Republican National Committee was also hacked, probably had political reasons; Russian interference cast a shadow over the legitimacy of his (and other Republican candidates') election and undermined his numerous endorsements of Putin as a great leader. But this time the Republican congressional leadership would not follow his lead. They joined with Democratic leaders in pushing for hearings and denouncing Putin in advance of them. This put Trump and his incoming team in a bind. For while Trump insisted that the intelligence agencies "have no idea" about the source of the hacking, Admiral Michael S. Rogers, director of the National Security Agency (NSA) and commander of the US Cyber Command, said: "There shouldn't be any doubt in anybody's mind. . . . This was a conscious effort by a nation-state to attempt to achieve a specific effect."[33]

Even before the report on Russian hacking came out on January 6, 2017, Obama promised retaliation, citing in addition persistent claims of harassment of diplomatic personnel in Moscow, such as illegal entry into their homes and stalking of them on the streets. The first step was sanctioning both Russian intelligence services, three companies accused of supporting the cyber attacks, and several individuals. In all, thirty-five Russians were declared persona non grata and forced to leave the country. Partisan politics intruded despite general agreement among Republicans and Democrats that Russia needed to be punished. Some Republican leaders claimed the sanctions came too late, after US policy had already "failed." But Donald Trump remained unconvinced, saying "we all ought to get on with our lives."[34]

To everyone's surprise, Putin did not retaliate immediately. Instead, he decided that waiting for Trump to take office was wiser than engaging in tit-for-tat with Obama. About this Trump tweeted: "Great move on delay (by V. Putin)—I always knew he was very smart!" Not until February 2017 did it become clear why Putin was so generous. Prior to Trump's inauguration, his national security special assistant, General Michael Flynn, had told (or strongly hinted to) Russia's ambassador, Sergey Kislyak, in a wiretapped telephone conversation that a soft Russian response to Obama's action would help the cause of removing sanctions on Russia. Flynn was forced to resign, but important questions remained: Who else besides Flynn was in touch with Russian officials before Trump took office? What did they discuss, and promise? And did they speak for Trump? People in his administration knew of Flynn's lying about his conversation with Kislyak *a month earlier.* Why didn't Trump act then? (A fair guess is that Trump was committed to protecting Flynn and his Russia connection—until the Flynn case could no longer be covered up.) Trump kept insisting he "had nothing to do with Russia" and knew of no one who did, but that assertion proved completely untrue. The dangling question was whether or not contacts with Russians constituted collusion, a serious crime.

These dramatic events were not Trump's only headache as he pondered a new relationship with Russia. Russia was discovered to have deployed a land-based, nuclear-weapon-capable cruise missile, which is specifically banned in a Reagan-Gorbachev arms control agreement. Russian jets buzzed US ships in the Baltic and Black Seas. And members of Russia's parliament said that Flynn's resignation showed the bad turn relations had taken with the United States. The harsh reaction in Congress, with several investigations begun into reported contacts between Trump's campaign and Russians, and a law passed by the Republican-controlled Senate to expand sanctions on Russia and insulate them from a Trump veto, narrowed Trump's options for befriending Putin while also changing the Russians' strategy for engaging the Trump administration. Then came Assad's chemical weapon attack on the town of Khan Sheikhoun via a Russian aircraft that killed eighty civilians, including many women and children. The United States responded with a cruise missile strike that disabled the military airport from which the aircraft carrying the chemical weapons was believed to have been launched. Russia-US relations went from bad to worse, with Prime Minister Dmitry Medvedev saying the US strike had "completely ruined" relations and warning that the United States was "one step away from military clashes with Russia." [35]

Less than one hundred days into Trump's presidency, he said relations with Russia were at "an all-time low." The Russians didn't disagree with that assessment. But a burning question remained: What explains Trump's avoidance of criticism of Russia? While his cabinet appointees occasionally said critical things about Russia, Trump never criticized Putin's authoritarianism, and he said that American democracy is really no different from Russia's. [36] Trump never acknowledged Russian meddling in the election (a "hoax," he said) or discussed ways to prevent its reoccurrence. [37] One area of official investigation that might yield an answer to the question centers on Trump's real estate financing. He is in debt to Deutsche Bank for over $300 million and was able to draw lines of credit from that bank when no other bank would loan his real estate empire money. Could it be that $10 billion in Russian money was laundered through Deutsche Bank by Vnesheconombank, a "bank" controlled entirely by Russian officials, to benefit Trump as well as his son-in-law, the senior adviser Jared Kushner?

"Now it is time to move forward constructively with Russia!" Trump said following his first meeting with Putin at the Hamburg G-20 summit. He supposedly pressed Putin on meddling in the US election but accepted Putin's disclaimer of Russian involvement. Putin, however, said Trump "agreed" with his denial, and Putin's foreign minister added that Trump said US news organizations had "exaggerated" the Russian role. The two leaders did reach agreement on two matters—setting up a "cyber security unit" and reaching a cease-fire in Syria—but few observers saw merit in either one.[38]

The upshot is that Putin's gambit was a short-term success but probably a failure in the long term. New sanctions on the Russian economy passed by an unusually bipartisan Congress in July 2017 defied the president and literally forced him to accede. How much pain the sanctions will actually cause Russia is less significant than the message it sends—a message of disengagement opposite the one Obama sent when he eased sanctions on Iran as part of the nuclear deal. Trump should therefore have learned a lesson about the art of engagement: attempting to ease sanctions on an adversary will always have difficulty getting over domestic political hurdles. Even though US intelligence analysts and members of Congress disagreed over Russia's objective in the 2016 election—whether it was intended to collude with the Trump campaign to help him win or to destabilize American politics—they were convinced that Russia represented a serious national security threat. Trump chose secret back-door dealings with the Russians and ignored that sentiment—and paid the price.

Options for US-Russia Relations

That Trump's and Putin's inner circles might share a preference for nationalism over globalism and an antipathy to human rights and other "politically correct" values will not be sufficient to overcome US-Russia differences in the near future. Nevertheless, we should consider other possibilities. Russia, after all, is still a nuclear-weapon state with a powerful military, a member of the UN Security Council Perm-5, and a major player in its periphery that now includes the Middle East. What might a new US-Russia compact look like? One alternative is described by a former US ambassador to Russia and longtime diplomat, William J. Burns. Very much in the mold of George Kennan's advice on how to contain the Soviet Union, Burns writes that with regard to NATO, Ukraine, Syria, and other issues, a policy of "firmness and vigilance [is] . . . the best way to deal with the combustible combination of grievance and insecurity that Vladimir Putin embodies."[39] Burns also said that Trump must be aware that "Putin believes the way to restore Russia's great power status is at the expense of an American-led order."[40] That view, probably the sort of realism Hillary Clinton would have embraced, would probably only widen the gap between the United States and Russia, perpetuating a competitive and volatile relationship.

It may take a new US administration, headed by a president more in the mold of Obama than either Trump or Hillary Clinton, as well as a less provocative and ambitious Vladimir Putin, to get US-Russia relations back on track. From the perspective of engagement, we have to consider how a restoration of Russia's status might be accomplished *without* clashing with legitimate US interests or further destabilizing prospects for peace. A new basis for relations might be the following. Washington (in coordination with the EU) promises an end to troop deployments and exercises on Russia's western borders (notably the four thousand troops deployed early in 2017 to Poland), agrees with Russia to cease mutually demonizing language, assures Russia that no additional Eastern European countries will be allowed into NATO, and unofficially accepts the seizure of Crimea. In return, Russia withdraws military forces and equipment from eastern Ukraine; pledges not to send them back; and further pledges to respect the territorial integrity of Ukraine, Georgia, and the Baltic states. Russia further agrees to end efforts to divide NATO by engaging in hacking and disinformation campaigns in the United States and Europe.[41] Specifically in Syria, a new agreement exchanges Russian assurances against a repetition of chemical weapons use in return for US acceptance of Assad's rule pending a final political settlement. As Russian compliance with all these terms is verified, the West gradually eliminates economic sanctions on Russia, Western investment in Russia resumes, and high-level summitry on nuclear weapons is restored.[42]

That package is a tall order for both countries. But it contains several enticing incentives, including a new opportunity for Ukraine to achieve political and economic stability, a way to resolve US and European anguish over Russian hacking, avoidance of a direct clash in Syria, and a path to removal of sanctions on Russia. Most important, it might bring the West's interaction with Russia back to discussion of common ground, starting with acceptance of Mikhail Gorbachev's idea of mutual security.

STICKS BEFORE CARROTS: THE UNITED STATES AND NORTH KOREA

Since the Korean War, North Korea (the DPRK) has been one of the foremost outliers in international politics. Its Stalinist political system, complete with gulags and omnipresent surveillance of class enemies; its isolation from several regional and international organizations that might assist its development; its periodic provocations against South Korea; its proliferation of missile and nuclear technology; and its resistance to any kind of reform that would disrupt the Kim dynasty's domination all confound the North's friends and foes alike. They also gravely undermine the quality of life for most North Koreans, who pay the price for heavy government investment in "military-first" politics, starting with poor agricultural performance that has caused major food shortages and helped push North Korea's economic development far behind South Korea's.

In recent years under the third member of the Kim dynasty (Kim Jong-un), North Korea has continued to rattle the cages of both friend and foe. He has defiantly disregarded the major powers (China included) and ever more stringent UN sanctions, forging ahead with developing new and improved weapons. I ask why Kim Jong-un is willing to accept international isolation and punishment, but also why, on the other side of the coin, the United States has not made North Korea a foreign policy priority and advanced meaningful proposals to address its nuclear weapons ambitions.

My argument is that US-DPRK engagement, though seemingly a remote prospect and (to some critics) much less attractive than punishment and pressure, is the only practical way to get the North Koreans' attention and, in the extreme, avoid a second Korean war.

The Case for Engaging North Korea

For a number of years, I and many other specialists on North Korea, notably including former US officials concerned with Korean affairs, have urged the United States and other governments to carry out sustained engagement with that country. Despite various confrontations with the DPRK over nuclear weapons and missile tests, name-calling, and on-again, off-again talks in both multilateral and bilateral settings, we have clung to the view that only engagement holds out hope of eliminating or at least freezing North Korea's nuclear weapons and preserving some degree of access to the beleaguered North Korean people. We are well aware of and condemn the North Korean gulag: the secret network of camps, the arbitrary arrests, the heroic efforts to escape the country, and the stories of torture and killings of both ordinary people and those who run afoul of Kim Jong-un, notably, his uncle and number-two person in the leadership, Jang Song-thaek, along with some of Jang's top assistants, all executed in December 2013. And we are naturally disturbed by the draconian nature of the Kim dynasty's rule—disturbed enough to be fairly confident that it is going to be around for a long time, despite the expectations in Washington and elsewhere of the regime's imminent demise.

We have watched as Kim Jong-un has followed in the footsteps of his grandfather (Kim Il-sung) and father (Kim Jong-il) in forging ahead on development of nuclear weapons and delivery systems. Under Kim Jong-un since 2011, the DPRK has conducted four nuclear weapons tests (a total of six since 2006 and the last, in September 2017, possibly being a hydrogen bomb) and more than eighty full-flight missile launches as of July 2017.[43] As Sigfried Hecker, former director of the Los Alamos National Laboratory and a regular visitor to the North, pointed out in 2016, the North Koreans "may have enough bomb fuel for 18 bombs, with a capacity to make 6 to 7 more annually. That, combined with the increased sophistication they surely achieved with this test [in January 2016], paints a troublesome picture."[44] Sanctions, threats, and "half-hearted diplomacy," Hecker observes, have failed to stifle North Korea's nuclear weapons program.

North Korean leaders have also been dismissive about unprecedentedly harsh international criticism of the country's human rights abuses. In a report of February 2014 that took a year to compose, the UN Commission of Inquiry on Human Rights in North Korea, comprised of nationals of Australia, Serbia, and Indonesia, examined nine areas of human rights violations.[45] These include the right to food, inhuman treatment, arbitrary arrest and detention, freedom of expression, and freedom of movement. The report is a searing indictment, not merely of those who perpetrated these crimes against humanity (individuals are not named, but the state agencies are), but also of the supreme leader. Predictably, North Korean sources unequivocally rejected the report both before and after it was published, and its findings had no immediate consequences for the regime's leaders. Nor did the report alter North Korea's human rights situation, in particular the existence of political prison camps employing what amounts to slave labor.[46] The Chinese and Russian UN delegates on the Security Council did not allow the report to be referred to the International Criminal Court.

Understanding North Korea

My study of North Korea leads me to four fundamental insights about the forces that drive its leadership:

- Militant nationalism—a fierce determination to maintain independence, practice self-reliance to the extent possible, and reject external interference in its decision making.
- Mistrust of the outside world, which consists of implacable enemies and faithless friends.
- Insecurity, born of a pervasive sense of threats inside and outside the country.
- A need for international attention to its interests, security guarantees from the great powers, and respect for regime legitimacy.

These forces should not be interpreted—though they often have been interpreted—as meaning that North Korea is immune to policy shifts or unwilling to respond to gestures from its enemies. Its conclusion of a denuclearization accord with South Korea in 1992 suggested a willingness to bury the nuclear option, but clearly on the assumption that the United States, Japan, and others would conclude diplomatic relations with it just as China and Russia had established diplomatic relations with the ROK. That assumption proved wrong and may have paved the way for the nuclear crisis during the Bill Clinton administration in 1993–1994. North Korea was then found to have a nuclear weapons program and withdrew from the Nuclear Nonproliferation Treaty. But in 1994 an Agreed Framework was crafted under which North Korea froze its nuclear weapons program in exchange for promised energy assistance. That trade-off restrained North Korea from producing fissile material for bomb making for roughly a decade.

When Kim Dae-jung was in office in South Korea (1998–2003), the so-called Sunshine policy toward North Korea led to a sharp reduction in hostile propaganda exchanges and the opening of an industrial zone (the Kaesong Industrial Zone) and a tourist facility (the Mt. Kumgang Tourist Region) in the eastern and western areas of North Korea, just across the demilitarized zone from South Korea. Though Kim was a realist who recognized that military power might sometimes be a necessary tool in dealing with Pyongyang, "Sunshine" was forged with the national interest firmly in mind.[47] What made the policy revolutionary is that it accepted the North Koreans' need for security and legitimacy, rejected a hegemonic approach ("we will not absorb you"), and searched for common ground. Kim was convinced that his policy would do more to secure South Korea and eventual national unification than would endless confrontation. He also reminded critics—who included top officials in the George W. Bush administration—of the costs of *non*-engagement with North Korea: an ongoing nuclear crisis and periodic provocative behavior by the North. Both Kim Dae-jung and his successor, Roh Moo-hyun, found North Korea receptive to summit meetings, in 2000 and 2007, that produced expressions of a common nationalism: the desire of all Koreans to be free from foreign interference.

Kim Dae-jung's efforts facilitated international diplomacy with North Korea: the Six Party Talks (the United States, China, Russia, Japan, and the two Koreas), which began in 2003 and led to two agreements on pathways to resolving the nuclear issue. But they fell short, in no small measure thanks to US opposition—underscored by George W. Bush's pronouncement in January 2002 that North Korea was part of an "axis of evil" and his administration's pointed warnings to the DPRK to learn from the US invasion of Iraq.[48] To be sure, US representatives have met numerous times with North Korean diplomats since then, as discussed below, and occasionally have made progress in defining terms of a rapprochement. But even when openings for engagement have seemed to appear, they have gotten nowhere.

As just one example, on October 20, 2014, the DPRK's UN ambassa-dor, Jang Il-hun, made an unusual appearance at the Council of Foreign Relations to defend against the Commission of Inquiry's charges. Al-though he made the expected denials that North Korea has political pris-oner camps, Jang did say Pyongyang was willing to "have a human rights dialogue" with the European Union and "enter into technical coop-eration with the UN Office for Human Rights Commission."[49] The next month, North Korea released three Americans held prisoner there, in two stages. Kim Jong-un, according to North Korean sources, personally or-dered the initial release of the Americans, and no doubt also the second release after James R. Clapper Jr., President Obama's director for national intelligence, traveled to Pyongyang. But the door to further contact closed quickly. Obama dismissed the prisoner release as a "small ges-ture" and gave no indication that he would reciprocate. Yet the available evidence suggests that North Korea was sending a message, not reacting to foreign pressure.[50] Here again, whether or not the North Koreans were planning to have a coming-out party needed to be explored and wasn't.

Unofficial diplomacy with North Korea belies the popular notion that North Korea is still the "hermit kingdom," a pejorative widely in use by media. Increasing numbers of North Koreans are going abroad for train-ing, touring, and exchanges of ideas. North Korean diplomats and government analysts have been participating in Track II discussions since the end of the Cold War, in recent years attending multilateral security talks such as meetings under the Council for Security Cooperation in the Asia Pacific, gatherings sponsored by the Korea Society in New York to promote people-to-people exchanges, and behind-the-scenes meetings with US officials using the "New York channel."[51] The National Commit-tee on North Korea, an organization that supports engaging the DPRK, regularly sponsors Track II dialogue. Track II contacts are often especially fruitful means of exchanging views when official diplomacy has broken down or when policy positions require clarification.[52]

Inside North Korea, foreign educators are leading medical and science and technology training; Chinese are helping start businesses; and a va-riety of international and national NGOs—from the UN, the United States, South Korea, Germany, and many other countries—are operating more than one thousand projects involving business, professional train-ing, and economic development.[53] Small and large privately run markets have become important parts of the economy, and food production is slowly improving. People's access to the outside world is increasing in spite of intensive official surveillance thanks to "a motley crew of foreign nongovernmental organizations, defectors, smugglers, middlemen, busi-nessmen, and bribable North Korea soldiers and officials [who] have cobbled together a surprisingly robust network that links ordinary citi-zens to the outside world through contraband cell phones, laptops, tablet computers, and data drives."[54] North Koreans live under dictatorship, but they have carved out space, often at great personal risk, for learning about the outside world.

Yet US officials continue to operate in the dark when it comes to North Korea. American officials are not ordinarily allowed to visit the North—the Clapper assignment was a special case—nor are North Korean officials allowed outside a twenty-five-mile perimeter from UN Headquarters in New York. What this means is an analytical deficit and a gratuitous insult to North Korean sovereignty. The analytical deficit must somehow be remedied by defectors' and satellite observations, useful sources but hardly the best for understanding North Korean political, economic, or social policy. Limiting North Koreans' travel not only deprives them of opportunities to interact with US audiences; it tells them that they are justified in their jaundiced view of the US government. And restricting travel to the DPRK by Americans, as the State Department decided to do in July 2017, is likewise shortsighted.

Understanding US Policy

On the US side, what are the policy implications of my four observations for dealing with North Korea?

First, continued nuclear testing by North Korea is its way of demonstrating independence of action—in other words, having a reliable deterrent. Nuclear weapons are the DPRK's "insurance policy," David Sanger has written[55] —its last best hope for regime survival and legitimacy and the most dramatic way to insist that the North's interests should not be neglected. Aidan Foster-Carter offers the same view: "Just as in Jerusalem—which gets away with this—unlike North Korea—the view from the Pyongyang bunker is that, in a dangerous world, nuclear weapons are the only sure guarantee of security and survival."[56] Former US defense secretary William J. Perry adds:

> I believe that North Korea has three key goals. First is the security of the Kim dynasty. Second, they want international respect. Third is improving their economy. They are willing to subordinate the third goal for the other two goals. The evidence of that is what they've done with nuclear weapons, despite sanctions. It's very clear that they've prioritized the first two goals over improving their economy. The North Korean regime believes correctly, that their conventional capabilities are not as good as those of South Korea and the U.S., so they compensate for this with their nuclear forces.[57]

All one has to do is see, through North Korean blinkers, what has happened in Iraq, Iran, and Libya, where dictators did not have a nuclear deterrent. The United States attacked two of them, and two had to surrender their nuclear weapons capability. The frequent official North Korean insistence that it "was forced to develop its nuclear arsenal because of the US's hostile policy against North Korea"—or the proposal that if the US "stops the nuclear war exercises in the Korean peninsula, then we should also cease our nuclear tests"[58] —may seem incredible to Americans, but it has logic and experience behind it. When North Korea conducted another missile test in April 2017 and the Trump administration announced it was dispatching a flotilla to Korean waters, Pyongyang recited the defensive logic behind having nuclear weapons so that, unlike those other countries, it would be able to strike back.

Second, the long-standing US approach to dealing with North Korea's nuclear weapons has failed. The Obama administration's strategy of "strategic patience" was different in form but not really in substance from the US strategy under George W. Bush that saw North Korea as part of an "axis of evil."[59] Both approaches showed little sensitivity to North Korean motivations; on the contrary, they were based in part on "patiently" awaiting the collapse of the Kim regime. Worse still, both administrations disparaged the DPRK's supreme leader. George W. Bush's demeaning references to Kim Jong-il, calling him a "pygmy" and a "tyrant," were not taken lightly by the North Koreans. Nor were John Kerry's comments on Kim Jong-un and his regime following the execution of Kim's uncle.[60]

A third conclusion is that the United States will not get far by constantly demanding that China step up and use its relationship with North Korea as leverage to force it to agree to denuclearize. To be sure, Chinese leaders, and some prominent Chinese intellectuals,[61] have made plain that North Korea's nuclear and missile testing endangers China's as well as Korean peninsula security. Beijing has shown its displeasure by resuming trilateral Japan-South Korea-China security dialogue after a three-year hiatus, by condemning North Korea's nuclear tests, and by going along with UN sanctions up to a point. But with all that, the Chinese are not about to dump Kim Jong-un. Political distancing, yes; economic sanctions, yes; but no drastic action, such as a complete cutoff of food or oil, that would destabilize the North Korean regime and leave China open to the accusation that it, like the United States, undermines an ally when that suits its interests.

Fourth, neither US nor international sanctions will bring North Korea to its knees. They are more likely to stiffen the North's resistance and defiance of international norms, as I argue in the following section. Similarly, US and South Korean air and ground military exercises, which take place regularly and are stepped up each time a North Korean nuclear or missile test occurs, only seem to provoke intensified military preparations by the North—as was demonstrated yet again in March 2017 when the DPRK carried out four missile tests while the annual Foal Eagle joint exercises were underway. These US-ROK activities in the name of "extended deterrence" are an important obstacle, real and symbolic, to engagement.

Fifth, attacking North Korea in retaliation for its nuclear and missile tests, or to prevent further tests or other provocative acts, is not feasible.

Although US strategists have long debated the option of using force, they have invariably wound up rejecting it, mainly because of the probable costs in lives and economies—often estimated at one million dead and $1 trillion in damage—resulting from both a US attack and a North Korean counterattack. A further reason is that North Korean long-range weapons are well hidden; an attack could never hope to destroy enough of them to prevent the North from launching a devastating retaliation on Seoul, US bases in South Korea, and Japan. A Pentagon report to Congress acknowledged that it would take a US ground invasion to secure North Korea's nuclear weapons.[62] In short, as James Mattis, the defense secretary, said in 2017, "If this goes to a military solution"—referring to another confrontation over a North Korean missile test—"it's going to be tragic on an unbelievable scale."[63]

Sanctions: A Failed Strategy

Between 2006 and September 2017, North Korea was sanctioned ten times by the UN Security Council (UNSC) for its nuclear and missile tests.[64] Each resolution is a bit more targeted than the previous one, spelling out in great detail the proscribed goods and requiring that all parties neither import them from nor export them to North Korea. (Resolutions 2321 and 2371 in 2016 and 2017, for example, significantly restrict North Korean coal and other mineral exports, limit petroleum and natural gas sales to North Korea, prohibit its textile and seafood exports, stop North Korea's sending of workers abroad, and prohibit "the opening of new joint ventures or cooperative entities with DPRK entities or individuals," putting a major crimp in the North's hard currency earnings.[65]) Each resolution obliges the members to carry out the terms of the sanctions, emphasizes the search for "a peaceful and comprehensive solution through dialogue," and the most recent ones refer to the Iran nuclear deal as a model of peacemaking through diplomacy. But the Security Council's task is wearisome; North Korean nuclear and missile tests have prompted numerous emergency meetings and bargaining over the extent of the sanctions.

This is a case of mission impossible for two fundamental reasons: the sanctions will not cause North Korea to change course—North Korea is actually busily modernizing its weapons arsenal, as described below—and sanctions impede any chance for a "peaceful and comprehensive solution." The typical pattern begins with a new North Korean weapons test that violates a UN sanction, followed by additional sanctions, North Korean protests, and a further distancing of all sides from direct talks.[66]

Aside from North Korea's stubborn nationalism, the two main obstacles to an effective sanctions regime against it are poor implementation and North Korean ingenuity. As to the first, a UN special report in March 2017 found that despite all the sanctions, "implementation remains insufficient and highly inconsistent."[67] The problems start with smuggling along the China-DPRK border. Military items disguised as ordinary goods seem easily able to evade detection thanks to inconsistent inspection by border guards, bribery, false declarations, and North Korean firms based in China that actually belong to military-run trading companies.[68] Since these practices are surely well known to the Chinese authorities, it seems fair to assume they have no strong interest in preventing or at least substantially reducing it—something they could accomplish with a more intensive border inspection process. That China is not doing so no doubt reflects its oft-stated position that the North Korean nuclear issue is the result of other countries' policies, not China's; hence resolving it is others' responsibility, mainly the United States'.

This is not to say that China is refusing to follow the UNSC's resolutions. Beijing's criticism of North Korea's nuclear and missile tests has become increasingly harsh and open over the last few years, and voting to approve UN sanctions is one way to underscore its criticism. Reports in 2016, for example, indicate that China did close its ports to North Korean coal and iron ore exports.[69] In September 2017 China's central bank ordered all banks to stop doing business with North Korea and close all accounts. But the Chinese have created a large loophole. At their insistence, the resolutions allow for humanitarian trade affecting people's "livelihood." Thus, as China's foreign ministry spokesperson said on March 4, 2016, "We will earnestly observe the UNSCR 2270. The resolution prohibits the DPRK's export of coal, iron ore and iron, but those that are deemed essential for people's livelihood and have no connection with the funding of the DPRK's nuclear and missile programs will not be affected."[70] As a result, China's exports to North Korea actually rose about 15 percent in the first three months of 2016 compared with 2015, and Chinese imports rose nearly 11 percent.[71] Reports from the main bridge at Dandong that connects the two countries suggest a thriving through slightly reduced trade. North Korean coal exports to China, virtually its sole customer, were at record levels until early in 2017, when new UN sanctions pushed China to stop exporting coal.[72] But overall China-DPRK trade still went up, and the impact of the coal cutoff on North Korean earnings was estimated to be fairly minimal.[73]

The DPRK has now mastered "evasion techniques that are increasing in scale, scope and sophistication," according to the same UNSC report in March 2017. North Korea has numerous entities and agents that do business abroad in illicit goods, including weapons; Namibia, Iran, Egypt, and Russia are usually mentioned. These North Korean firms have access to international banking, mainly via China, and thus the ability to launder money and obtain US dollars.[74] Two specialists call these trading entities "North Korea, Inc." Their research concludes that "sanctions have actually improved North Korea's ability to procure components for its nuclear and missile programs."[75] The reason is that the trading firms, based mainly in China and Hong Kong, have been willing and able to pay a higher price for these goods to middlemen, who in turn are willing to take greater risks to sell. The writers acknowledge the great difficulty in getting ahead of the curve when it comes to identifying the North Korean firms and finding ways to put them out of business. In the end, they say, only diplomacy will resolve the fundamental problem, which is the weapons tests themselves.

Reflagging and renaming North Korean ships is another common tactic, as is falsely claiming a ship's destination as (for example) China rather than the DPRK.[76] For example, an unpublished UN report describes how the North Koreans used a Singapore branch of a Chinese bank to pay for their ships to transport weapons through the Panama Canal.[77] Then there is the story of a British banker who set up a front company in Pyongyang, registered in the British Virgin Islands, to sell and procure arms.[78]

North Korea's military program also benefits from the fine line that often exists between civilian and military items. Commercial trucks, for example, can be used to mount a variety of weapons. A Chinese-made truck used in both China and North Korea for mining operations has reportedly been adapted by the North Korean military for its new mobile-rocket-propelled artillery system.[79] Six mobile intercontinental missiles (possibly fakes or mock-ups) paraded in Pyongyang in April 2012 likewise were mounted on Chinese-made trucks.[80]

When all is said and done, the most likely scenario is that new sanctions will produce no better results than previous rounds. This is so not only because North Korea has many ways to procure items needed for its military purposes and plenty of willing private sellers. China, as mentioned, is not going to watch the North disintegrate in spite of Beijing's discomfort over Pyongyang's nuclear and missile programs. China's leaders will do more than previously to enforce sanctions, such as inspection of cargo bound for and incoming from North Korea, but they will do a good deal less than the United States wants, especially when it comes to border inspections. For just as US presidents have hawkish advisers who want to turn the screws on North Korea even tighter in hopes of regime change, President Xi has people around him who think resisting US pressure is strategically more important to China than undermining Kim Jong-un. Secretary of State John Kerry once commented that China's approach "has not worked, and we cannot continue business as usual." Donald Trump's top foreign policy advisers said the same. But the Chinese have a perfectly good comeback, namely, that Washington and Pyongyang must find a way back to the negotiating table.

The Kim regime has proven remarkably resilient in responding to international sanctions. Its *byungjin* (simultaneous advancement) policy, announced early in 2013, couples rapid military modernization with modest market-oriented reforms and continued repression. To one veteran observer, *byungjin* has defied predictions of North Korea's demise and instead seems increasingly likely to sustain the regime for the foreseeable future.[81] North Korea's economic path is not emulating China's "reform and openness" (*kaifang*) approach initiated under Deng Xiaoping, but it is showing signs of growth and expansion of private initiative. The clear implication of this "developmental dictatorship" (as Andrei Lankov calls it) for the foreign policy of the United States and others is that they will have to abandon the notion of regime implosion and grapple with a Kim Jong-un who will be around for some time to come.

North Korea's New Weapons: Full Speed Ahead

North Korea is on a military procurement and development tear. In response to UN sanctions and the annual month-long US-ROK military exercises, starting in 2016 the DPRK diverged from its usual practice by openly drawing attention to a number of new weapons. It paraded a road-mobile intercontinental-range missile, launched five short-range missiles into the East or Japan Sea, claimed to have an indigenously produced engine that would enable an ICBM to reach the United States with a nuclear weapon, claimed to have tested a miniature nuclear weapon, test-fired an intermediate-range missile, and tested a missile launched from a submarine.

How and when any of the weapons the North claims to have might actually be operational is open to speculation. The North's two tests of an intercontinental ballistic missile in 2017 suggest that it is one step away from being able to reach US shores with an ICBM fitted with a nuclear warhead. South Korean sources are convinced the North can already put a nuclear warhead on a medium-range (eight hundred miles) Rodong missile capable of reaching all of the ROK and Japan. This is the type of missile the North launched in a test in March 2017.[82] What does seem clear is that Kim Jong-un is pressing his weapons specialists to produce a reliable deterrent that will force the issue of direct talks with the United States. Meeting with nuclear specialists in early March, he praised their work and, according to the North Korean press, specifically cited "research conducted to tip various type tactical and strategic ballistic missiles with nuclear warheads," meaning a miniaturized nuclear weapon. Kim is quoted as saying that it "is very gratifying to see the nuclear warheads with the structure of mixed charge adequate for prompt thermo-nuclear reaction. The nuclear warheads have been standardized to be fit for ballistic missiles by miniaturizing them. . . . [T]his can be called [a] true nuclear deterrent. . . . Koreans can do anything if they have a will."[83]

One thing is certain: North Korea's long history of militant nationalism means that it is not going to take orders from foreign powers on national security matters, and that it will treat international sanctions as incentives to push ahead with development and production of new weapons *for deterrence*. Kim Jong-un, like his father and grandfather, is ever mindful of the fact that North Korea is surrounded by the overwhelming military power of the United States and its South Korean and Japanese partners. He is no doubt aware that the United States has used cyber and electronic warfare to disable or destroy North Korean missiles on the launch pad or shortly after launch.[84] He also has to consider that the US military is significantly upgrading its nuclear weapons inventory, which includes miniaturization. From one angle—the one most likely to have the North Korean military's attention—miniaturization increases the possible use of a nuclear weapon in warfare. North Korea's evident work on miniaturization may hardly be coincidental.

The Obstacle Course

American administrations have consistently regarded engagement as *a reward* for North Korea's good behavior rather than a strategy for finding common ground.[85] The US insistence that negotiations are not worthwhile unless and until North Korea agrees to denuclearize ensures continuing tension, more North Korean nuclear weapons and improved means of delivering them, and the danger of a disastrous miscalculation. Increased tensions and more nuclear weapons and missiles have already come to pass; only a miscalculation remains.

Making the case for engaging North Korea, however, truly amounts to swimming against the tide. Given North Korea's crimes against its own people and its investment of scarce resources in a military buildup, engaging the North hasn't a ghost of a chance of gaining acceptance in the White House or the Congress in the current US political climate. Engaging Iran and Cuba is one thing—and those success stories may be overturned by the Trump administration—but when it comes to North Korea, there is no constituency such as Iran and Cuba have for direct talks and perhaps another package deal. Nevertheless, the alternative approaches—ignoring North Korea, banking on the Kim regime's implosion, confronting it with threats, or combining a few carrots with big sticks—carry far greater risks than engagement.

Further complicating the case for US-DPRK engagement is its sensitivity to unmet expectations and unpredictable events. An example of the first is the nuclear crisis in the early 1990s. It may have had its roots at least partly in dissatisfaction among the DPRK leadership over lack of rewards for signing the nuclear and exchange accords with South Korea, such as US diplomatic recognition of Pyongyang, an end to the trade embargo, and the start of economic aid. As for unpredictability, two events may be cited. One was Sony Corporation's plan to release a film, *The Interview*, whose supposedly comic plot was the assassination of Kim Jong-un by two Americans. Hackers calling themselves Guardians of

Peace, said by the United States to be North Korean, succeeded at getting into Sony's computers and releasing numerous embarrassing company e-mails and other documents. And in 2017, when an American student who had been imprisoned was released seventeen months later after suffering a fatal illness, the US State Department drastically limited travel to North Korea by US citizens.[86] What incidents of these kinds do is reinforce the worst stereotypes each government has of the other, undermining trust that already hangs by a thread.

Of the four policy alternatives cited above, the last one—carrots with sticks—seems to be most popular among analysts who believe North Korea, and perhaps China as well, need to be provided with incentives to return to the bargaining table, with nuclear disarmament of North Korea the goal. But they also believe North Korea must be punished if it rejects the bargain the United States would offer, lest it become an unmanageable threat to its neighbors and eventually to the US homeland. Retired Joint Chiefs chair Admiral Mike Mullen and former senator Sam Nunn, for example, offer a four-point plan: dialogue with China to avert a crisis on the Korean peninsula; a new diplomatic initiative to North Korea that would look toward "a peace agreement that would finally end the Korean War and gradually normalize relations in exchange for complete nuclear disarmament and progress on human rights"; strengthening of economic sanctions on the DPRK; and expanded US deterrent capabilities to "enforce sanctions and impede North Korean missile programs."[87] The Mullen-Nunn plan advocates a military response if North Korea causes trouble: "Future North Korean aggression would be met with an active and proportionate self-defense response, including inside North Korea," and interception of long-range North Korean missiles.[88]

These ideas are an improvement over the Obama administration's policy of "strategic patience." Kim Jong-un evidently is amenable to denuclearization talks, based on a North Korean statement of July 6, 2016. But adding a few carrots to the sticks is very unlikely to interest Kim, for the simple reason that he and his military leaders will see the formula as *sticks now, carrots later.* They will need to see real carrots from the United States, South Korea, and Japan up front before they put their own sticks down. What they are seeing now is commentary from experts that stresses the North Korean nuclear *threat* and the urgency of a multilateral effort to halt it.[89] When North Korean leaders read such remarks or are confronted with shows of force, they tend to react by demonstrating their military might, thus playing into US threat perceptions.

Calling for North Korea's complete denuclearization as a condition of an agreement puts the cart before the horse. Its nuclear weapons, as the North's leaders see it, are the only thing standing between survival and regime change—and probably also between China's support and abandonment. North Korean leaders are not about to surrender those weapons at the outset or during negotiations, and even if a new agreement is arranged, it seems doubtful at this point that they would surrender them at all. We have to believe Kim Jong-un when he says the DPRK will never give them up. No doubt the Chinese believe him; they understand that many years of living under the shadow of US nuclear superiority requires a credible deterrent, and the North is clearly bent on having one of its own.

Denuclearization should therefore be the *last* item on a negotiating agenda, not the first. It should follow on other agreements that build trust and convince the North that regime change is not US or South Korean policy, as Mullen and Nunn say. If the North Koreans are given incentives that are meaningful and reliably delivered, nuclear weapons—and weapons modernization in general—will be useless to them except as the ultimate deterrent and a prod to the great powers to accept them as negotiating partners. A package of incentives should be put before Kim Jong-un that would include security assurances and economic help. North Korea would have to reciprocate; *mutual* threat reduction is essential. But even then, timing is everything. The "North Korean nuclear issue" is much more than that, for it is embedded in larger, interlinked issues of peace and security in Northeast Asia: strategic mistrust between the United States and China, discord between China and South Korea, territorial disputes, increasing military spending and basing agreements, cross-border environmental problems, and the actual and potential nuclear weapons of other countries (China, the United States, and Russia today; perhaps Japan and South Korea tomorrow). Decision makers in Washington, though overwhelmed by problems in the Middle East, need to pay attention to the Korean peninsula and think outside the box.

Determining the proper mix of incentives to engage is one part of the formula for jump-starting talks with North Korea. The other is acknowledgment that resort to force is unacceptably risky. When the George H. W. Bush administration took steps to bring about a nuclear-free Korean peninsula, starting with the unilateral withdrawal of US tactical nuclear weapons, it cautioned South Korea and Japan not to resort to force against Pyongyang.[90] President Clinton rejected an attack on North Korea's nuclear facility in 1994 at a time when it had the capacity to produce only a few nuclear weapons. Now, quite apart from the difficulties in locating North Korea's weapons, it has built up a substantial arsenal of nuclear, missile, conventional, and chemical and biological weapons that, in response to attack, would surely result in hundreds of thousands of deaths in the South as well as in Japan, which is in easy range of North Korean missiles. Some years ago a high-level war game was conducted that dramatized the fallacy of going to war with North Korea. Diplomacy was, and still is, the only realistic alternative, even if (as Robert Gallucci, Clinton's chief negotiator with North Korea, noted) the DPRK should cheat on an agreement.[91]

Persisting in finding engagement opportunities with North Korea comes down to six other situation-specific considerations. First, of course, is its ongoing nuclear weapons and long-range missile programs, which can only add to instability on the Korean peninsula and the danger of a terrible miscalculation that would affect all of Asia. Second, every time North Korean leaders feel threatened or ignored, they undertake a weapons test or other provocative action. Third, China's view of North Korea has changed; it has come to regard the Kim regime as a strategic liability, though not to the extent of dumping it altogether or consistently carrying out UN-approved sanctions. But China's changed attitude does present an opportunity for creative multilateral diplomacy that would forestall a nuclear confrontation on its border, as well as a US-engineered strategy that amounts to regime change, which Beijing evidently regards as *more* dangerous than North Korean nuclear weapons. Differences between the United States and China have created a contentious relationship, however, and even in the best of circumstances, China could never be expected to undermine Kim's rule and risk a chaotic border situation that ultimately would redound to the benefit of South Korea and its ally.[92]

Fourth, as former South Korean president Kim Dae-jung argued in crafting his Sunshine policy, greater security for the North really promotes greater security for the South. That means providing the North with security assurances and economic assistance rather than driving it into a corner or ignoring it altogether. Fifth, engagement increases opportunities for direct contact with the North Korean people and lower-level officials. We do have concrete examples of how appreciative these Koreans are when they receive meaningful help, such as medical supplies and training, wind power generation, fisheries, apple orchards, and scientific and academic exchanges. Someday, that help will facilitate peaceful Korean unification.

Sixth, talking with North Korea has been productive, belying the notion of not negotiating with "evil."[93] Among the most important understandings reached between the United States and the DPRK are the Agreed Framework (October 1994) to freeze North Korea's entire nuclear program (both uranium enrichment and plutonium production) under international inspection in exchange for energy assistance (heavy oil and two light-water reactors); an exchange of visits between US Secretary of State Madeleine Albright and DPRK Vice Marshal Jo Myong-nok (October 2000) that produced agreement "to undertake a new direction in their relations" and not to show "hostile intent" in their actions; and establishment of the Six Party Talks, which led to agreement in September 2005 on common principles, including North Korea's right to peaceful uses of nuclear energy, normalization of relations between the DPRK and the United States and Japan, verifiable denuclearization of the Korean peninsula, and US assurances of "no intention to attack or invade the DPRK."

A Stanford University study in 2008 found that North Korea had a pretty good record of compliance with those and other agreements.[94]

On the other hand, consider what it means when the United States, along with the European Union, Japan, and South Korea, rejects engagement and continues to insist that North Korea must first denuclearize in some fashion before serious negotiations can get under way. North Korea will add to its nuclear weapons arsenal, carry out more nuclear and missile tests, and keep selling weapons components to militant groups and governments. In addition to armed provocations, the DPRK will continue to make use of its cyberwarfare capabilities, creating incidents short of war that will force difficult US decisions on how to respond. It will crack down even harder on its population, in search of "enemies of the state" who have cell phones or listen to South Korean broadcasts. It will bar or greatly limit foreign NGOs that offer economic or other assistance. It will embolden the most hawkish elements in the North Korean leadership, providing them with evidence that more nukes provide the only real security.

Step by Step

The first step is to reach out to North Korea. When the White House press secretary to Obama said that the US goal of defanging North Korea had not been reached but that "we have succeeded in making North Korea more isolated than ever before," he was actually acknowledging a policy failure. The task is, or should be, not to further isolate North Korea but rather to *bring it out of its isolation*, starting by accepting the seriousness of its security concerns. The more isolated the regime is and the more it is driven into a corner, the more likely it is to resort to provocations and shows of strength. Isolating and punishing Pyongyang may seem perfectly logical responses to its missile and nuclear tests and other actions, but they are very unlikely to promote dialogue. On the other hand, if US diplomats were to place denuclearization in the context of fulfilling Kim Il-sung's and Kim Jong-il's "last wishes," that might be the kind of face-saving approach that would appeal to Kim Jong-un.[95]

By replacing threats with high-level direct dialogue, negotiators can also indicate sensitivity to issues of face and status. As two distinguished South Korean experts on North Korea have written, one serious deficiency of most Western writing on the DPRK is that it completely ignores its "obsession" with "supreme dignity" and national pride. Saving face and gaining status recognition are quite important explanations of the North's provocative behavior and search for a deterrent.[96] Jimmy Carter's visit to Kim Il-sung in 1994 paved the way for the Agreed Framework. Madeleine Albright's visit to Pyongyang in 2000, noted above, produced an importantly symbolic joint statement of "no hostile intent." Former president Bill Clinton's visit in June 2009, which resulted in the pardoning and freeing of two American journalists, also reflected respect. Former New Mexico governor and UN ambassador Bill Richardson's mission in 2007 recovered the remains of US servicemen killed during the Korean War. He has since visited North Korea several more times as head of a center for humanitarian assistance. Richardson makes a strong case that building trust through personal relationships is central to effective engagement and negotiations.[97]

The Bill Clinton administration was particularly effective at using personal diplomacy in 1999–2000 to create high-level contact with North Korea.[98] The exchanges then resulted in US recognition of the DPRK's legitimate security concerns, the conviction that the leadership could be addressed through diplomacy, and the conclusion that the endgame should be verifiable denuclearization of the Korean peninsula and normalization of US-DPRK relations. In the midst of those exchanges, the United States demanded and received permission to inspect what was wrongly believed to be an underground nuclear facility at Kumchang-ni. If Clinton's term had not ended in January 2001, he might have been able to reach a new deal with North Korea that would have dramatically reduced its weapons inventory in exchange for a large US aid package. Kim Jong-il apparently also thought so.[99] But time ran out, complicated by the disputed 2000 presidential election results.[100]

American diplomats have been resistant to a new package deal with North Korea, arguing that they are tired of talk for talk's sake and determined not to "buy the same horse twice." But the North Koreans surely feel the same way. The challenge, in any case, is not about buying but about selling: how to reach agreement on the "horse's" fair selling price. For the United States, engagement should be seen not as guaranteeing immediate results, but as creating "opportunities to build momentum and trust." Pyongyang must see engagement as strengthening regime and state survival. North Korean officials have long insisted that if the United States abandons its "hostile policy," "assures the DPRK of nonaggression," and shows "good faith," the DPRK will respond in kind and the nuclear issue and much else can be resolved.[101] Washington should test that view, one step (and one incentive) at a time—even as it supports international condemnation of the Kim regime's human rights record.

The immediate focus of US policy, therefore, should be on trust building, not on the nuclear issue.

How might engagement be undertaken?[102] The first step is *revival of the Six Party Talks without preconditions* and with faithfulness to previous six-party and North-South Korea joint declarations—in particular, the principle contained in the Six-Party Joint Statement of September 2005: "commitment for commitment, action for action." At a new round of talks, the United States and its partners might present a package that, in return for verifiable steps to freeze North Korea's nuclear arsenal (since elimination of its nuclear weapons seems increasingly remote), provides the North with security assurances, a proposal for a peace treaty to end the Korean War, a nonaggression pact with big power guarantees (with China on board), and meaningful economic development assistance from both NGOs and governments. The peace treaty, guaranteed by the United States, China, Russia, South Korea, and Japan, would provide security assurances to the DPRK by acknowledging the legitimacy of the North Korean state, pledging not to attack it, and establishing diplomatic relations. These steps would respond to Kim Jong-il's secret message to President George W. Bush in November 2002: "If the United States recognizes our sovereignty and assures nonaggression, it is our view that we should be able to find a way to resolve the nuclear issue in compliance with the demands of a new century. . . . If the United States makes a bold decision, we will respond accordingly."[103]

As for North Korea's stockpile of nuclear weapons and the increasing capability to deliver them across the Pacific, the best deal might be to freeze and *warehouse* those weapons under strict supervision by the IAEA. That might satisfy the DPRK's military and undermine the case for a South Korean or Japanese nuclear weapon option. But as Andrew Nathan writes, such a new deal may require US recognition of North Korea as a nuclear weapon state, thus granting it the status it craves as a matter of national identity.[104]

The second step is *creation of the Northeast Asia Security Dialogue Mechanism* (NEASDM), an idea that was anticipated in the final statements of the Six Party Talks and that South Korea's president Park Geun-hye also proposed.[105] In the absence of honest brokers for disputes in Northeast Asia, the NEASDM can function as a "circuit breaker," able to interrupt patterns of escalating confrontation when tensions in the region increase. But the NEASDM would not focus exclusively on North Korean denuclearization. It would be open to a wide range of issues related to security, such as environmental, labor, poverty, and public health problems; a code of conduct to govern territorial and boundary disputes; military budget transparency, weapons transfers, and deployments; measures to combat terrorism and piracy; creation of a nuclear-weapon-free zone (NWFZ) in all or part of Northeast Asia; and ways to support confidence building and trust in the dialogue process itself. North Korea's participation would be most likely if the United States and Japan normalized relations with it.

All six countries in the Six Party Talks should be members of NEASDM, but no others, although other countries or organizations might be invited to participate for a specific session. If North Korea rejects membership, the group should nevertheless go on with its work, keeping the door open to Pyongyang's later participation. The NEASDM should be institutionalized, perhaps situated in Beijing, with a commitment to meet several times a year at regular intervals regardless of the state of affairs in the region and with an open agenda—but with the provision that any of the parties can convene a meeting in a crisis. There should be an understanding among the member states that the NEASDM meets whether or not all parties are willing to participate, so that a boycott by one party cannot prevent the group from meeting.

An NEASDM would bring decided advantages to each party. For example, North Korea would gain diplomatic recognition (and thus added legitimacy); access to long-term economic development assistance; and the potential for security guarantees by the major powers sufficient for it to eliminate its nuclear weapons, if not immediately then later. The other parties would also gain from security and stability on the Korean peninsula—for example China, which would presumably want the United States and South Korea to agree on removal or at least indefinitely delayed full deployment of the THAAD antimissile system in return for Beijing's assistance in dealing with the DPRK.[106] And a successful regional institution would provide a much-needed boost to development of a regional identity.

The third step toward engagement is *significant new humanitarian and development assistance to North Korea*. The US and South Korean emphasis on sanctions punishes too many of the wrong people. The United States provided virtually no aid from 2009 on; humanitarian assistance came almost entirely from NGOs and the United Nations World Food Program. Obama made a surprise gift of humanitarian aid for flood relief just before leaving office, although it was sent via the UN and not government to government.[107] Kim Jong-un's complete disregard for human rights should not affect humanitarian aid to North Korea—food, medicine, medical equipment, educational exchanges, and technical and business training—which at least helps some portion of its population and sends the message that the international community cares about the North Korean people. While it is impossible to say how many North Koreans are positively affected by contacts with Western, Chinese, and other foreigners who run these activities, surely a considerable number do see the benefits of exposure to the outside world. As the Under Secretary-General of the UN, Jeffrey Feltman, said in December 2015, even though the Commission of Inquiry concluded that "the gravity, scale and nature of the [human rights] violations reveal a State that does not have any parallel in the contemporary world," the North Korean people deserve better. But international humanitarian assistance to the DPRK is pitifully little—under $50 million in 2014 and declining every year.[108]

Prospects after US and South Korean Elections

American policy on North Korea hardened in the first year of the Trump administration. It rejected direct negotiations with North Korea,[109] pushed through harsh new sanctions at the UN, hyped North Korea's missile threat to the continental United States, and pressed China to do more to rein in the North.[110] In the absence of a new US overture—and Tillerson's announced policy of "peaceful pressure" was not much different from Obama's "strategic patience"—no change occurred in the behavior of the players, with the exception of South Korea, which elected a new president (Moon Jae-in) in the mold of Kim Dae-jung and Roh Moo-hyun. Moon's version of the Sunshine policy—negotiating with the North on a nuclear and missile freeze and eventual denuclearization while maintaining sanctions; offering North Korea increased contacts, including family reunions and military-to-military talks; and reevaluating the THAAD deployment—raised the possibility of a warming relationship with China and a distancing from the United States.

Meanwhile, North Korea's nuclear and missile program proceeds ahead, each test bringing it a step closer to a nuclear-armed intercontinental missile but also closer to a US preemptive strike that would mean war. The Trump administration has to confront the same realities preceding administrations have confronted: Kim Jong-un is determined to have the ultimate deterrent unless he is offered incentives that suggest a moderation of the US "hostile policy";[111] US and allied countermeasures, such as development of missile interceptors, cannot keep pace with the North's missile advances;[112] and China cannot be relied on to divert North Korea from its course. Making matters worse, these realities are cemented by exchanges of threats that have reached a personal level between Trump and Kim, significantly increasing the risk of war.[113] In fact, Trump has consistently indicated a preference for strategic surprise—a decapitation of the North Korean leadership or attempted elimination of a missile complex that might include use of nuclear weapons. While that possibility may seem incredible, it would fit with the longstanding actual US nuclear policy of *first use*, as described by one of its early architects.[114]

But the policy debate in Washington remains ossified, focused on North Korea's military capabilities and what combination of sanctions and threats will bring Pyongyang to heel. No one can provide a persuasive argument that force and pressure will produce different results, yet few are willing to talk the language of diplomacy, such as by sending a special emissary to Pyongyang. People seem to have forgotten, or refuse to acknowledge, that Iran was not forced into a nuclear agreement by sanctions and military threats. That agreement was *negotiated*, with concessions on both sides.

NOTES

1. Quoted in Evan Osnos, David Remnick, and Joshua Yaffa, "Active Measures," *New Yorker*, March 6, 2017, 47.

2. Amy E. Smithson, "Assad's Phony Farewell to Arms," *Foreign Affairs*, October 26, 2016, www.foreignaffairs.com/articles/syria/2016-10-26/assads-phony-farewell-arms.

3. Colum Lynch, "To Assuage Russia, Obama Administration Backed Off Syria Chemical Weapons Plan," *Foreign Policy*, May 19, 2017, http://foreignpolicy.com/2017/05/19/to-assuage-russia-obama-administration-backed-off-syria-chemical-weapons-plan/.

4. Joby Warrick and Karen DeYoung, "From 'Reset' to 'Pause': The Real Story Behind Hillary Clinton's Feud with Vladimir Putin," *Washington Post*, November 3, 2016.

5. As Robert Legvold argues, today's US-Russia relationship may not be exactly like relations during the earlier Cold War years, but there are enough parallels to make the current period a new Cold War. *Return to Cold War* (Cambridge, UK: Polity, 2016).

6. A Pew Research Center opinion poll conducted in December 2015 on perceived threats to US national security found that while ISIS and the Iran nuclear program ranked highest among seven threats listed, Russia scored on the low end. Some 50 percent of Republicans, 40 percent of Democrats, and 40 percent of independents polled regard "growing authoritarianism in Russia" as a threat. China and North Korea ranked slightly higher. Mona Chalabi, "Could Foreign Policy Be Bernie Sanders' Undoing?," *Guardian*, February 5, 2016.

7. Fyodor Lukyanov, "Putin's Foreign Policy: The Quest to Restore Russia's Rightful Place," *Foreign Affairs* 95, no. 3 (May–June 2016): 31.

8. Reuters, "Russia Security Strategy," *NYT*, January 2, 2016.

9. Stephen Kotkin, "Russia's Perpetual Geopolitics," *Foreign Affairs* 93, no. 3 (May–June 2016): 2–9.

10. Lukyanov, "Putin's Foreign Policy," 31.

11. "Coalition or Cold War?," *Nation*, December 21–28, 2015, www.thenation.com/article/coalition-or-cold-war-with-russia-2/.

12. For the argument that such a promise was made, see Joshua R. Itzkowitz Shifrinson, "Russia's Got a Point: U.S. Broke a NATO Promise," *Los Angeles Times*, May 30, 2016, online ed. The counterargument, based on new Russian and German archival material, is by Mark Kramer, "The Myth of a No-NATO-Enlargement Pledge to Russia," *Washington Quarterly* 32, no. 2 (April 2009): 39–61.

13. The conversation (www.youtube.com/watch?v=MSxaa-67yGM#t=89) showed disdain for the European Union as a relevant partner in piecing together a new Ukrainian government and the arrogance of a superpower in believing it has the right and responsibility to orchestrate a change in another country's government. The Russians, who probably did the taping, naturally were upset about US "meddling" in their backyard, and Germany's Angela Merkel came out with a blistering attack on the diplomats.

14. Daniel Treisman, "Why Putin Took Crimea," *Foreign Affairs* 95, no. 3 (May–June 2016): 47–54.

15. William J. Broad and David E. Sanger, "As U.S. Modernizes Nuclear Weapons, 'Smaller' Leaves Some Uneasy," *NYT*, January 11, 2016.

16. Thomas Gibbons-Neff, "Russian Warships to Bypass Spanish Refueling Port," *Washington Post*, October 26, 2016.

17. Andrew Cockburn, "The New Red Scare," *Harper's*, December 2016, 25–31.

18. David E. Sanger and Charlie Savage, "U.S. Says Russia Directed Hacks to Influence Elections," *NYT*, October 7, 2016.

19. After the election, Clinton said that Putin's "personal beef" against her for those remarks was directly responsible for Russian interference on Trump's behalf in the US election. Amy Chozick, "Hillary Clinton Ties Loss to Russian Hacking and Comey Letter," *NYT*, December 16, 2016.

20. Warrick and DeYoung, "From 'Reset' to 'Pause.'"

21. Clinton said: "Russia is trying to move the boundaries of the post–World War II Europe. The way that [Putin] is trying to set European countries against one another,

seizing territory, holding it in Crimea. Beginning to explore whether they could make some inroads in the Baltics. . . . We've got to do more to support our partners in NATO, and we have to send a very clear message to Putin that this kind of belligerence, that this kind of testing of boundaries will have to be responded to. The best way to do that is to put more armor in, put more money from the Europeans in so they're actually contributing more to their own defense." Transcript at www.nytimes.com/2016/02/05/us/politics/transcript-of-the-democratic-presidential-debate.html. On Syria, during debates with Donald Trump Clinton advocated establishing a free zone to protect civilians in the besieged Aleppo area, even though she acknowledged potential problems such a zone would create.

22. Friedman, "Let's Get Putin's Attention," *NYT*, October 5, 2016.

23. Curt Mills, "Vladimir Putin Wants to Restore the Soviet Union, Former Secretary of Defense Says," December 3, 2016, www.aol.com/article/news/2016/12/03/vladimir-putin-wants-to-restore-the-soviet-union-former-secreta/21619534/.

24. Mark Landler, "51 U.S. Diplomats Urge Strike Against Assad in Syria," *NYT*, June 17, 2016.

25. Opinion polls in the United States and Russia show public wariness, though Russian criticism of US sanctions and interventions (precisely in keeping with Putin's view) is stronger than US criticism of Russian actions. Interestingly, US public support of engaging Russia, especially among Democrats, was running ahead of the views of public officials and policy wonks. See the report by Dina Smeltz, Stepan Goncharov, and Lily Woitowicz, "US and Russia: Insecurity and Mistrust Shape Mutual Perceptions," November 4, 2016, www.thechicagocouncil.org/publication/us-and-russia-insecurity-and-mistrust-shape-mutual-perceptions.

26. Tom Hamburger, Rosalind S. Helderman, and Michael Birnbaum, "Inside Trump's Financial Ties to Russia and His Unusual Flattery of Vladimir Putin," *Washington Post*, June 17, 2016.

27. Andrew Higgins, "A Subdued Vladimir Putin Calls for 'Mutually Beneficial' Ties with the U.S.," *NYT*, December 1, 2016.

28. The best and most concise summary of events between the last days of the Obama administration and the tumultuous early months of Trump's administration is by Osnos, Remnick, and Yaffa, "Active Measures."

29. The fullest accounting to date is by Greg Miller, Ellen Nakashima, and Adam Entous, "Obama's Secret Struggle to Punish Russia for Putin's Election Assault," *Washington Post*, June 23, 2017.

30. Adam Entous, Ellen Nakashima, and Greg Miller, "Secret CIA Assessment: Russia Tried to Help Trump Win," *Washington Post*, December 9, 2016; David E. Sanger and Scott Shane, "Russian Hackers Acted to Aid Trump in Election, U.S. Says," *NYT*, December 9, 2016.

31. The report of the FBI and Department of Homeland Security that followed is at www.nytimes.com/interactive/2016/12/29/us/politics/document-Report-on-Russian-Hacking.html.

32. NBC News broke the story: "Two senior officials with direct access to the information say new intelligence shows that Putin personally directed how hacked material from Democrats was leaked and otherwise used. The intelligence came from diplomatic sources and spies working for U.S. allies, the officials said." (William M. Arkin, Ken Dilanian, and Cynthia McFadden, "U.S. Official: Putin Personally Involved in U.S. Election Hack," NBC News, December 15, 2016, www.nbcnews.com/news/us-news/u-s-officials-putin-personally-involved-u-s-election-hack-n696146?cid=sm_fb.) Michael McFaul, a former US ambassador to Russia, found the evidence of Putin's involvement credible and "not surprising," since such a major operation would have needed the highest level of approval. MSNBC, evening broadcast, December 14, 2016.

33. Eric Lipton, David E. Sanger, and Scott Shane, "The Perfect Weapon: How Russian Cyberpower Invaded the U.S.," *NYT*, December 13, 2016.

34. Missy Ryan and Ellen Nakashima, "Obama Administration Announced Measure to Punish Russia," *Washington Post*, December 29, 2016.

35. Rhys Blakely, "Russia and US 'One Step' from Clash," *Times* (London), April 8, 2017, www.thetimes.co.uk/edition/news/russia-and-us-close-to-clash-bt8qq8sg0. Even though Trump, in August 2017, called the Senate's sanctions bill "seriously flawed," Medvedev said the US sanctions package "ends hopes for improving our relations with the new administration." Merrit Kennedy, "Russian Prime Minister Slams Trump Administration 'Weakness' Over U.S. Sanctions," National Public Radio, August 3, 2017, www.npr.org/2017/08/03/541333270/after-new-sanctions-russian-prime-minis ter-slams-trump-administration-s-weakness.

36. Michael McFaul, "Trump Has Given Putin the Best Gift He Could Ask For," *Washington Post*, May 17, 2017.

37. Russian interference in US and other countries' political affairs is multipronged and technically sophisticated, making extensive use of social media. Such "active measures" originate in the Cold War but now deploy information warfare in new ways, such as by using bots and trolls. Of course we need to be mindful that the US CIA also has carried out disinformation campaigns abroad for many years. But what is new is the lackadaisical US response to Russian interference, with no sense of alarm or major government-led effort to counter it through defensive measures and strengthening of electoral machinery. James N. Ludes and Mark R. Jacobson, "Shatter the House of Mirrors: A Conference Report on Russian Influence Operations," Salve Regina University, Pell Center for International Relations and Public Policy, October 2017, http://pellcenter.org/wp-content/uploads/2017/09/Shatter-the-House-of-Mirrors-FINAL-WEB.pdf.

38. Julie Hirschfeld Davis, "'Time to Move Forward,' Trump Says After Putin Denies Election Hacking," *NYT*, July 9, 2017.

39. Burns, "How to Fool Ourselves on Russia," *NYT*, January 7, 2017. A similar view was offered in a Carnegie Endowment for International Peace report, which urged against attempting another reset in relations with Russia: "There should be no illusions that pursuing a full-scale rapprochement with Putin would not entail a major retreat from core U.S. principles, inflict enduring damage to transatlantic relations, undermine U.S. global influence, and threaten the survival of the international order." Eugene Rumer, Richard Sokolsky, and Andrew S. Weiss, "Guiding Principles for a Sustainable U.S. Policy Toward Russia, Ukraine, and Eurasia: Key Judgments from a Joint Task Force," Carnegie Endowment, February 9, 2017, http://carnegieendowment. org/2017/02/09/guiding-principles-for-sustainable-u.s.-policy-toward-russia-ukraine-and-eurasia-key-judgments-from-joint-task-force-pub-67893.

40. Quoted in Roger Cohen, "Trump's Pivotal Russian Test," *NYT*, January 13, 2017.

41. Germany became a specific focus of Russian-backed fake news and other efforts aimed at disrupting the election of the chancellor in 2017. Reuters, "Germany Investigating Unprecedented Spread of Fake News Online," *Guardian*, January 9, 2017. Some in France also charged Russian with hacking in its presidential election campaign in 2017.

42. For other arguments in favor of engagement, see Legvold, *Return to Cold War.*

43. Ian Williams, "North Korean Missile Launches: 1984–Present," Center for Strategic and International Studies, Washington, DC, April 20, 2017, https://missilethreat. csis.org/north-korea-missile-launches-1984-present/; CNN, "North Korea Missile Tests," May 29, 2017, www.cnn.com/2017/05/29/asia/north-korea-missile-tests/index. html.

44. Steve Fyffe, "Hecker Assesses North Korean Hydrogen Bomb Claims," *Bulletin of the Atomic Scientists*, January 7, 2016, http://thebulletin.org/hecker-assesses-north-korean-hydrogen-bomb-claims9046#.

45. A thirty-six-page summary and the full report are available at United Nations Human Rights, Office of the High Commissioner, *Report of the Commission of Inquiry on Human Rights in the Democratic People's Republic of Korea*, February 7, 2014, www.ohchr. org/EN/HRBodies/HRC/CoIDPRK/Pages/ReportoftheCommissionofInquiryDPRK. aspx.

46. See, for example, the report based on satellite imagery by Joseph S. Bermudez Jr., Andy Dinville, and Mike Eley, "North Korea Camp No. 25—Update 2," November 29, 2016, The Committee for Human Rights in North Korea, www.hrnk.org/uploads/pdfs/ASA_HRNK_Camp25_Update2.pdf.

47. Chung-in Moon, *The Sunshine Policy: In Defense of Engagement as a Path to Peace in Korea* (Seoul: Yonsei University Press, 2012).

48. Mike Chinoy, "How Washington Hard-liners Helped to Create the North Korean Crisis," *Washington Post*, April 19, 2017.

49. "Ambassador Jang Il Hun on Human Rights in North Korea," October 20, 2014, www.cfr.org/north-korea/ambassador-jang-il-hun-human-rights-north-korea/p33642.

50. See Frank Jannuzi, "Roadblocks Removed: Can the US Travel the Diplomatic Path with the DPRK?," November 9, 2014, http://38north.org/2014/11/fjannuzi110914/.

51. The "New York channel" refers to meetings with the North Korean UN delegation. These have even gone on when US and DPRK leaders exchanged very public threats, as happened in the summer of 2017. See Matthew Pennington, "Beyond Bluster, US, NKorea in Regular Contact," *Seattle Times*, August 11, 2017, www.seattletimes.com/nation-world/nation-politics/apnewsbreak-beyond-bluster-us-nkorea-in-regular-contact/.

52. Daniel Wertz, *Track II Diplomacy with Iran and North Korea*, June 2017, National Committee on North Korea, www.ncnk.org/sites/default/files/NCNK_Track_II_Conference_Report_0.pdf.

53. Among the most active NGOs with long-term involvement in North Korea are Mercy Corps, Nautilus, American Friends Service Committee, and World Vision. United Nations agencies include the World Food Program and UNESCO. See Andrew I. Yeo, "Evaluating the Scope of People-to-People Engagement in North Korea, 1995–2012," *Asian Perspective* 41, no. 2 (2017): 309–339. Yeo used a mapping initiative called Engage DPRK, which "identifies over a thousand projects and approximately 4,000 activities implemented by 480 bilateral, multilateral, nongovernmental, nonprofit, and for-profit organizations between 1995 and 2012" in North Korea.

54. Jieun Baek, "The Opening of the North Korean Mind: Pyongyang Versus the Digital Underground," *Foreign Affairs* 96, no. 1 (January–February 2017): 107.

55. David E. Sanger, "North Korea Blast Revives Question: How Do You Contain Pyongyang?" *NYT*, January 6, 2016.

56. Aidan Foster-Carter, "In a Dangerous World, North Korea's Latest Nuclear Test Makes a Kind of Sense," *Guardian*, January 6, 2016.

57. "Interview: Former US Secretary of Defense Favors 'Three Noes' on North Korean Nukes," *Hankyoreh* (Seoul), October 3, 2016, http://english.hani.co.kr/arti/english_edition/e_northkorea/763863.html.

58. The DPRK foreign minister, Ri Su-yong, gave the Associated Press that proposal on April 23, 2016, shortly after North Korea carried out a test of a submarine-launched ballistic missile. President Obama rejected the proposal immediately. Eric Talmadge, "Obama Dismisses NKorea Proposal on Halting Nuke Tests," April 24, 2016, http://bigstory.ap.org/article/20c4cf71589542a2858a2b885d9de2bc/nkorea-ready-halt-nuke-tests-if-us-stops-skorea-exercises.

59. John Delury, "The Disappointments of Disengagement: Assessing Obama's North Korea Policy," *Asian Perspective* 37 (2013): 149–182.

60. On the North Korean reaction to Bush's remarks, see Michael Hersh, "North Korea's Kim Jong Il," *Newsweek*, October 21, 2006, www.newsweek.com/north-koreas-kim-jong-il-111871. In a televised interview, Kerry said: "It tells us a lot about, first of all, how ruthless and reckless he is, and it also tells us a lot about how insecure he is." He characterized Kim Jong-un as "spontaneous, erratic, still worried about his place in the power structure and maneuvering to eliminate any potential kind of a adversary or competitor." Choe Sang-hun, "Kim Jong-un's Aunt Appear[s] to Survive Husband's Purge," *NYT*, December 15, 2013.

61. For example, Shen Zhihua, China's top historian on relations with Korea, called North Korea a "latent enemy" of China in a speech in 2017. He said: "Putting it

objectively, the fundamental interests of China and North Korea are at odds. China's fundamental interest lies in achieving stability on its borders and developing outward. But since North Korea acquired nuclear weapons, that periphery has never been stable, so inevitably Chinese and North Korean interests are at odds. The spokespeople for our Foreign Ministry claim that the North Korean nuclear crisis was triggered by antagonism between the United States and North Korea, and that's entirely understandable as diplomatic language. But, as scholars, we must see clearly that North Korea's shift to a policy of holding nuclear weapons was triggered by the shifts in its relationship with China." The more tensions there are between North Korea and the United States, Shen believes, the worse the situation is for China. Chris Buckley, "Excerpts from a Chinese Historian's Speech on North Korea," *NYT*, April 18, 2017.

62. Dan Lamothe and Carol Morello, "Securing North Korean Nuclear Sites Would Require a Ground Invasion, Pentagon Says," *Washington Post*, November 4, 2017.

63. Thomson Reuters, "Jim Mattis: Any North Korea Military Solution Would Be 'Tragic on an Unbelievable Scale,'" May 19, 2017, https://www.reuters.com/article/us-usa-northkorea-mattis/u-s-military-solution-to-north-korea-would-be-tragic-on-an-unbelievable-scale-idUSKCN18F26M.

64. Texts of the resolutions are available at United Nations Security Council, "Security Council Resolutions," www.un.org/en/sc/documents/resolutions/2016.shtml.

65. Text at United Nations Security Council, SC Resolution 2321/2016, www.un.org/ga/search/view_doc.asp?symbol=S/RES/2321(2016); United Nations Security Council, SC Resolution 2371, August 4, 2017, www.un.org/en/ga/search/view_doc.asp?symbol=S/RES/2371(2017).

66. See Delury, "The Disappointments of Disengagement."

67. UN Security Council, "Report of the Panel of Experts Established Pursuant to Resolution 1874 (2009), Summary,"http://undocs.org/S/2017/150.

68. Choi Song Min, "Military Items Smuggled Through Chinese Customs Despite Sanctions," *Daily NK*, April 4, 2016, www.dailynk.com/english/read.php?cataId=nk01500&num=13839.

69. Choi Song Min, "Coal-Laden Ships in Limbo Out at Sea," *Daily NK*, March 24, 2016, www.dailynk.com/english/read.php?cataId=nk0500&num=13819; Seol Song Ah, "Trucks Loaded with Mineral Extracts Block From Entering China," *Daily NK*, March 7, 2016, www.dailynk.com/english/read.php?cataId=nk01500&num=13784.

70. Ministry of Foreign Affairs of the PRC, "Foreign Ministry Spokesperson Hong Lei's Regular Press Conference on March 4, 2016," www.fmprc.gov.cn/mfa_eng/xwfw_665399/s2510_665401/2511_665403/t1345253.shtml.

71. "China's Q1 Trade with North Korea Up Despite Sanctions," *Straits Times* (Singapore), April 13, 2016, www.straitstimes.com/asia/east-asia/chinas-q1-trade-with-north-korea-up-despite-sanctions. These figures come from a Chinese customs official. They may underplay the actual trade figures, which are said to have been deleted from official PRC trade reports in order to hide the volume and character of the trade. See Leo Byrne, "China Cuts Online Access to North Korean Trade Data," *NK News*, April 4, 2016, www.nknews.org/2016/04/china-cuts-online-access-to-north-korean-trade-data/.

72. Two events in February 2017 may also account for China's cutoff of coal imports from North Korea for the remainder of the year: another North Korean mid-range missile test and the assassination in Malaysia of Kim Jong-un's elder half brother, a man who sometimes made his home in China and was under China's protection.

73. Susan V. Lawrence and Mark E. Manyin, "China's February 2017 Suspension of North Korean Coal Imports," Congressional Research Service, Washington, DC, April 25, 2017, https://fas.org/sgp/crs/row/IN10659.pdf.

74. North Korean front companies in China bank with Chinese banks that do business in the United States. David S. Cohen, "One Powerful Weapon to Use Against North Korea," *Washington Post*, April 21, 2017.

75. Jim Walsh and John Park, "To Stop the Missiles, Stop North Korea, Inc.," *NYT*, March 10, 2016.

76. Andrea Berger provides a comprehensive picture of the sanctions issues. See "The New UNSC Sanctions Resolution on North Korea: A Deep Dive Assessment," 38 North, March 2, 2016, http://38north.org/2016/03/aberger030216/.

77. Colum Lynch, "U.N. Panel: North Korea Used Chinese Bank to Evade Nuclear Sanctions," *Foreign Policy*, March 7, 2016, http://foreignpolicy.com/2016/03/07/u-n-panel-north-korea-used-chinese-bank-to-evade-nuclear-sanctions/?wp_login_redirect=0.

78. Nigel Cowie, "British Banker Set Up Firm 'Used by North Korea to Sell Weapons," *Guardian*, April 4, 2016.

79. James Pearson, "China-Made Truck Used by North Korea in New Artillery System," Reuters, March 8, 2016, www.reuters.com/article/northkorea-nuclear-truck-idUSL4N16G4Q6.

80. Melissa Hanham, "North Korea's Procurement Network Strikes Again: Examining How Chinese Missile Hardware Wound Up in Pyongyang," *NTI (Nuclear Threat Initiative)*, July 31, 2012, www.nti.org/analysis/articles/north-koreas-procurement-network-strikes-again-examining-how-chinese-missile-hardware-ended-pyongyang/.

81. Andrei Lankov, "Is Byungjin Policy Failing? Kim Jong Un's Unannounced Reform and Its Chances of Success," *Korean Journal of Defense Analysis* 29, no. 1 (March 2017): 25–45.

82. Choe Sang-Hun, "South Korea Says North Korea Has Capacity to Put Nuclear Warhead on a Missile," *NYT*, April 6, 2016.

83. Committee for Human Rights in North Korea, "North Korea Leadership Watch," March 8, 2016, https://nkleadershipwatch.wordpress.com/2016/03/08/kim-jong-un-meets-with-nuclear-weapons-personnel/.

84. This program, which may have been responsible for some North Korean missile test failures, was reportedly launched in 2013 in an effort to head off further development of an ICBM capability. David E. Sanger and William J. Broad, "Trump Inherits a Secret Cyberwar Against North Korean Missiles," *NYT*, March 4, 2017.

85. For example, James R. Clapper Jr., US director of national intelligence under Obama, said: "I don't think, really, [Kim Jong-un] has much of an endgame other than to somehow elicit recognition from the world and specifically, most importantly, the United States, of North Korea as a rival on an international scene, as a nuclear power, and that that entitles him to negotiation and to accommodation, and presumably for aid." Thom Shanker, David E. Sanger, and Eric Schmitt, "Pentagon Finds Nuclear Strides by North Korea," *NYT*, April 11, 2013.

86. The hackers also threatened to attack movie theaters that showed the film. Sony executives decided in December 2014 not to release the film immediately, though they later did so. The student, twenty-two-year old Otto Warmbier, was imprisoned based on his apparently having stolen a political poster from his hotel room. During his captivity he sustained life-threatening injuries and fell into a coma. The North Koreans finally released him in June 2017, and shortly after returning home he died without regaining consciousness.

87. Mike Mullen and Sam Nunn, "How to Deal with North Korea," *Washington Post*, September 15, 2016.

88. Joel S. Wit, at Johns Hopkins University's School of Advanced International Studies, also advocates a new deal with North Korea that would stop and eventually eliminate its nuclear arsenal ("How the Next President Can Stop North Korea," *NYT*, September 13, 2016). He endorses negotiating a permanent peace treaty with North Korea as well as suspension of annual US-South Korea military exercises. But like Mullen and Nunn, Wit calls for enhanced sanctions against the North and supports the Obama administration's decision to deploy the THAAD regional missile defense system—a decision that China has vigorously opposed in the belief the system is actually directed at neutralizing its missiles. David Straub, a former State Department official, also favors enhanced sanctions and a US military buildup unless North Korea agrees to move toward full denuclearization. He approves of a peace treaty with the DPRK as an incentive, but disapproves of formal high-level talks or humanitarian

assistance. Straub, "North Korea Policy: Recommendations for the Trump Administration," Korea Economic Institute of America, December 7, 2016, www.kei_aps_straub_final.pdf.

89. Some North Korea watchers seem to think the North's nuclear and missile tests are designed for offensive rather than deterrent purposes. I strongly disagree. See Max Fisher, "Maybe North Korea's Nuclear Goals Are More Serious Than Once Thought," *NYT*, July 13, 2016.

90. Robert A. Wampler, "Engaging North Korea: Evidence from the Bush I Administration," National Security Archive, November 8, 2017, https://nsarchive.gwu.edu/postings/briefing-books.

91. The war game was sponsored by *The Atlantic* magazine. See Scott Stossel, "North Korea: The War Game," *Atlantic* (July–August, 2005), www.theatlantic.com/magazine/archive/2005/07/north-korea-the-war-game/304029/. Gallucci said, in response to the point that the North Koreans had cheated on the 1994 Agreed Framework, that "the Soviets cheated on virtually every deal we ever made with them, but we were still better off with the deal than without it."

92. Both China and Russia have made clear in the UN Security Council that they will not support what they call the "four nos": any US proposal that might lead to regime change in North Korea, regime collapse, accelerated reunification of the two Koreas, or a US military deployment north of the 38th parallel.

93. For a concise evaluation, see Clemens, *North Korea and the World*, 198–206.

94. Robert Carlin and John W. Lewis, *Negotiating with North Korea: 1992 – 2007* (Stanford, CA: Center for International Security and Cooperation, 2008). Texts of all the agreements just mentioned may be found in that publication. On the Six Party Talks (2003–2009), see Jayshree Bajoria and Beina Xu, "The Six Party Talks on North Korea's Nuclear Program," Council on Foreign Relations, September 30, 2013, www.cfr.org/proliferation/six-party-talks-north-koreas-nuclear-program/p13593.

95. See Tae-ho Kang, "North Korea Inches Toward Negotiations on Its Nuclear Ambitions," *Global Asia* 9, no. 1 (Spring 2014): 58–67.

96. Chung-in Moon and Ildo Hwang, "Identity, Supreme Dignity, and North Korea's External Behavior: A Cultural/Ideational Perspective," *Korea Observer* 45, no. 1 (Spring 2014): 1–37.

97. Bill Richardson, "Five Steps for Engaging with North Korea," *Time*, July 22, 2015, http://time.com/3968478/bill-richardson-5-steps-for-engaging-with-north-korea/. Also valuable is Walter C. Clemens Jr., "From Prisoner Release to Normal Links with North Korea?," *Diplomat*, October 8, 2014, http://thediplomat.com/2014/10/from-prisoner-release-to-normal-links-with-north-korea/.

98. A major element in the direct talks was a visit to North Korea headed by William J. Perry, special adviser to President Clinton and a former defense secretary. Perry and a high-level team conducted an eight-month review of US policy toward the DPRK that led to a report in October 1999 that is far more clear-eyed about North Korea than anything that has been produced since. The report was based essentially on the notion of common security: "mutual threat reduction," a "cooperative ending of DPRK nuclear weapons- and long-range missile activities," and US preparedness "to establish more normal diplomatic relations with the DPRK and join in the ROK's [South Korea] policy of engagement and peaceful coexistence [then being pursued by President Kim Dae-jung]." The text of the Perry report may be found in Carlin and Lewis, *Negotiating with North Korea*, 30–42.

99. According to a memo from Bill Clinton's meeting with Kim Jong-il in 2009, Kim said Bush's "axis of evil" speech in 2002 was the reason for North Korea's focus on nuclear weapons. Kim also said that "if the Democrats had won in 2000 the situation in bilateral relations would not have reached such a point." Elizabeth Shim, "Leaked Memo Shows North Korea's Kim Jong Il Sought Friendlier U.S. Relations," UPI, October 31, 2016, www.upi.com/Top_News/World-News/2016/10/31/Leaked-memo-shows-North-Koreas-Kim-Jong-Il-sought-friendlier-US-relations/9371477964869/.

100. Based on an off-the-record account by a Clinton administration source involved in North Korean affairs.

101. Phrases of these kinds may be found in numerous official DPRK statements. For example, see the DPRK foreign ministry statement of October 25, 2002, cited by Samuel S. Kim, *The Two Koreas and the Great Powers* (New York: Cambridge University Press, 2006), 258–259; the DPRK statement reported by the Korean Central News Agency, *Monthly [Weekly] Report on North Korea,* January 27, 2006, 92; and the statement of the foreign ministry spokesman in Korean Central News Agency and *Chosun Sinbo,* June 27, 2008. (My thanks to Sam Kim and Yurim Yi for these citations.)

102. For this discussion I have especially benefited from Walter C. Clemens Jr., "How to Deal with Kim Jong Un," *Global Asia* 10, no. 4 (Winter 2015): 68–78; Clemens, *Getting to Yes in Korea* (Boulder, CO: Paradigm, 2010); and Moon, *The Sunshine Policy.*

103. Joan Hoff, *A Faustian Foreign Policy from Woodrow Wilson to George W. Bush: Dreams of Perfectibility* (Cambridge, UK: Cambridge University Press, 2007), 163.

104. Nathan, "Who Is Kim Jong-un?," *New York Review of Books,* August 18, 2016, www.nybooks.com/articles/2016/08/18/who-is-kim-jong-un/.

105. See my "Averting War in Northeast Asia: A Proposal," *Asia-Pacific Journal* 9, no. 2 (January 10, 2011), http://japanfocus.org/-Mel-Gurtov/3467.

106. Early in 2017, as deployment of THAAD neared, there was talk in China about a boycott of South Korean goods and even more serious diplomatic and military measures to express China's displeasure.

107. "US Provides First Humanitarian Aid to North Korea in Five Years," *Hankyoreh* (Seoul), January 25, 2017, http://english.hani.co.kr/arti/english_edition/e_national/780225.html.

108. United Nations, Department of Political Affairs, "Security Council Briefing on the Situation in the Democratic People's Republic of Korea,"www.un.org/undpa/speeches-statements/10122015/DPRK.

109. When Secretary of State Rex Tillerson, in October 2017, held out hope for direct talks with North Korea, noting ongoing use of two or three channels of communication, Trump tweeted: "I told Rex Tillerson . . . that he is wasting his time trying to negotiate with Little Rocket Man."

110. As Vice President Mike Pence said on a visit to South Korea following yet another North Korean ballistic missile test in April 2017: "All of those negotiations and discussions [in 1994 and 2005] failed, miserably. The time has come for us to take a fresh approach. And the approach President Trump has taken is not engagement with North Korea but renewed and more vigorous engagement with North Korea's principal economic partner [China]." Josh Rogin, "Pence: The United States Is Not Seeking Negotiations with North Korea," *Washington Post,* April 19, 2017.

111. The North Korean theme that the United States must end its "hostile policy and nuclear threat" was again in evidence during the height of US-DPRK tensions in the summer of 2017. But that view was misreported in the US press to suggest that North Korea had no interest in talks on its nuclear and missile programs. Asia Unhedged, "Did Media Miss Story in North Korea's War of Words?," *Asia Times,* August 11, 2017, www.atimes.com/article/media-miss-real-story-north-koreas-war-words/.

112. David E. Sanger and William J. Broad, "North Korean Tests Add Urgency for U.S. to Fix Defense Flaws," *NYT,* May 29, 2017.

113. In September 2017 Trump addressed the UN General Assembly and vowed to "totally destroy" North Korea, calling Kim Jong-un "rocket man." Kim made an unprecedented personal response, saying Trump was "deranged" and a "dotard," and threatening "the highest level of hard-line countermeasure in history." The full text of Kim's message is in *NYT,* September 22, 2017.

114. Daniel Ellsberg, *The Doomsday Machine: Confessions of a Nuclear War Planner* (New York: Bloomsbury, 2017), 12–14.

SIX

Trapped by History

China-Japan, Israel-Palestine

CHINA AND JAPAN: THE ROCKY ROAD TO RECONCILIATION

A Framework for Transforming Sino-Japanese Conflict[1]

Relations between China and Japan encompass a long-running, dangerous, and seemingly intractable conflict. They are not immune to positive change, but they are constantly vulnerable to backtracking and intensification of rivalry. Both kinds of changes have occurred regularly since normalization of relations in the early 1970s. The issues in dispute are well known: historical grievances—Japan's invasion and occupation of China before and during World War II, the Nanking Massacre, and Japan's refusal to accept full responsibility for Nanjing and other atrocities committed by the Imperial Army; a territorial dispute in the East China Sea; Japan's gradual rearmament in spite of constitutional limitations; and China's uncertain ambitions as it becomes a powerful force in regional and world affairs. My aim is not to retread well-covered ground but to explore opportunities for cooperation that may ease tension and eventually lead to reconciliation.

Intractable conflicts by their nature acquire a life of their own; the longer they go on, the more vested in conflict the parties become. In the case of China and Japan, moreover, history envenoms the relationship to an extraordinary degree, infecting both high-level dialogue and public opinion. Official rhetoric about the importance of Sino-Japanese peace and cooperation notwithstanding, in the public arena we rarely find groups or individuals speaking out on behalf of reconciliation, even when (as in the case of business leaders) they benefit from peaceful rela-

129

tions. In fact, influential people in both countries, especially academics and journalists, have been attacked for advocating reconciliation.

Because China-Japan conflict operates at so many levels—structural, societal, psychological, and of course political—any effort to move toward reconciliation needs to look at both *policies* and *processes*. Moreover, we should be audacious in thinking of reconciliation as involving something more than "simple coexistence." As David Crocker has written with respect to warring parties, but applicable to other kinds of conflict, reconciliation is a healing process:

> In the most minimal account . . . reconciliation is nothing more than "simple coexistence" in the sense that former enemies comply with the law instead of killing each other. Although this *modus vivendi* is certainly better than violent conflict, transitional societies . . . should aim for more. . . . Among other things, this implies a willingness to hear each other out, to enter into give-and-take about matters of public policy, to build on areas of common concern, and to forge principled compromises with which all can live. The process, so conceived, may help to prevent a society from lapsing back into violence as a way to resolve conflict.[2]

Yet if reconciliation is the goal, China and Japan have a long road to travel.

The appropriate starting point on that road is not further debate over grievances but practical steps that serve common interests. In chapter 2 I discussed Japan's apology problem, which is certainly a major obstacle to reconciliation. But that does not make improvement in China-Japan relations impossible. Dealing with the proximate causes of conflict is often more productive than attempting to resolve past grievances. As has happened often in the case of China and Japan, whenever Japanese politicians reopen the wounds of war, they invite a Chinese response, thus feeding competitive nationalisms and pushing the history issue to center stage, precisely where it should not be. As one prominent Chinese scholar noted after a particularly insensitive statement by a Japanese official, historical issues have "become a main or perhaps even the only obstacle to Sino-Japanese engagement and cooperation at the moment, like a fish bone stuck in the throat. Only if this problem is appropriately resolved will China further discuss potential cooperation programs with Japan and specify its policy on Japan's role in international and regional security."[3] Nevertheless, as with relations between Israel and the Palestinians, history is better off being shelved until such time as a sense of true partnership emerges—that is, when concerted cooperation occurs over a lengthy period. Only then, when mutual trust is implicit because of habitual dialogue and policies that serve common interests, is reconciliation possible and apologizing politically feasible.

Needless to say, shelving history is extremely difficult. It keeps coming back to haunt the best efforts of officials on both sides. China-Japan dialogue is thus consistently inconsistent; every positive step may quickly be undermined by a negative one. For example, when Prime Minister Koizumi expressed "deep remorse" to President Hu Jintao in April 2005 for Japan's aggression in China, Hu accepted the words as an apology. But once Koizumi announced that he would visit the Yasukuni Shrine for Japan's war dead, all the goodwill dissipated.[4] Anguish over history infects other Sino-Japanese problems that might otherwise be effectively dealt with, such as the Chinese fishing trawler incident in 2010 that occurred in the East China Sea (discussed below).

The "history issue" goes beyond legitimate grievances, however. There is reason to suspect that grievances are deliberately exploited for political gain, as leverage against the other and as spurs to popular nationalism. Amy King writes about how Chinese officials have long used the phrase "harming the Chinese people's feelings" to express hurt over other countries' (Japan's most of all) lack of respect for China's status, perhaps with the aim of creating guilt feelings.[5] The historian Yinan He shows how "national mythmaking" about history in China and Japan can be instrumental, "to justify national security policy or address domestic political concerns such as regime legitimacy, social mobilization needs, and factional and organizational interests."[6] In short, history can be a very useful political weapon.

To attempt to get around historical grievances and their attendant politicization, we need to dig into the toolbox of engagement. Three approaches seem particularly pertinent in the case of China and Japan: *dialogue*, especially a focus on the legitimacy of the parties, the diversity of formats for discussion, and the process of "getting to yes"; *positive incentives* for bringing parties to the table or otherwise making contact; and *confidence building*, relying on preventive diplomacy and transparency. What these approaches offer is the possibility of focusing on establishing greater trust, widening common ground, and managing differences between disputants. Rivalry is not treated as unalterable, nor is one side to a dispute assumed (for purposes of a settlement) to bear greater responsibility than the other. The domestic political element is of central importance; the roles of powerful bureaucracies, parties, and political leaders, as well as of public opinion and civil society, must weigh in any usable approach to conflict management.[7] Leadership and society in China and Japan must come to recognize their mutual dependence, as a source of common prosperity and as a restraint on nationalistic outbursts.

Problems of Sino-Japanese Conflict Management

Managing differences between China and Japan presents a number of special problems. One is that neither Beijing nor Tokyo seeks an honest

broker who might mediate the conflict. Another is the lack of self-criti-
cism in each society, hence also the seeming inability of each to establish
a new domestic consensus regarding the other party. Third, none of the
multilateral forums to which Japan and China belong, such as the Asia-
Pacific Economic Cooperation (APEC) forum and the ASEAN Regional
Forum, has the capacity or the authority to act preventively or as a concil-
iator in the dispute. Nor does Northeast Asia, unlike Southeast Asia, have
a security dialogue mechanism—an NEASDM such as I proposed in
chapter 4—that the two countries might use to discuss their disputes.

The fourth problem is the growing asymmetry of Japanese and Chinese power. While much is made these days of the fact that the two
countries, for the first time in their modern history, are simultaneously
strong, their strengths lie in different areas. Japan retains strong security
ties with the United States and is stretching Article 9 of its constitution to
include combat involvement overseas. Beijing is busy not only expanding
its military capacity and reach but also cultivating its own multilateral
groups and becoming the lead economic power in the Asia-Pacific region.
As time goes on, the power gap will widen as China becomes militarily
stronger as well as more economically dominant.

Finally, the United States is a formidable obstacle in the path of China-
Japan reconciliation. In the eyes of many Chinese specialists, US partiality
to Japan is a major reason that the two countries' relations are typically
tense.[8] Their argument is that Japan's deployments in the Middle East, its
enhanced military firepower, its interest in constitutional revision, its
strategic partnership with Australia, and its revival of national spirit have
all come at the behest of the United States and thus have the appearance
of balance-of-power politics directed at China. Yet as one Chinese specialist on Japan has admitted, Beijing must choose between the lesser of
two evils:

> The Chinese academic community is somewhat conflicted about the
> future of the U.S.-Japanese alliance. On one hand, although it does not
> expect the alliance to become stronger, an invigorated U.S.-Japanese
> alliance may join hands against China. On the other hand, a looser U.S.-
> Japanese alliance may lead to its ultimate collapse, leaving a Tokyo
> unbound by Washington. It remains uncertain whether an indepen-
> dent Japan would employ a friendly China policy. The direction and
> future of the alliance, however, is ultimately up to Washington and
> Tokyo.[9]

Accenting the Positive

Up until now, the official bilateral level has been the locus of most
discussions of problem areas in China and Japan's relationship. A positive side to this circumstance is that Japanese and Chinese leaders have
embraced East Asian regionalism, at least in terms of deepening econom-

ic integration and joint consultations.[10] They and the other key actors in Northeast Asia have also accepted the idea of creating a regional dialogue mechanism for dispute resolution.[11] Moreover, the high and growing degree of economic interdependence between Japan and China—in trade, Japan's direct investment in China, and (until 2008) Japan's official development assistance (ODA)—remains the crucial asset for preventing open conflict. As of 2016, Japan ranked third among China's export customers and fourth in imports from China. Statistics vary depending on the reporting authority, but their total trade was roughly around $300 billion for 2015, with Japan running about a $50 billion trade deficit (as it typically does). China's share of Japan's total trade is about 21 percent, placing China first ahead of the United States.[12] Japanese foreign direct investment (FDI) in China (including Hong Kong) peaked at about $15 billion in 2012 before shifting to Southeast Asia. But FDI is still around $10 billion annually.[13] Despite the end of Japan's ODA loans to China, technical cooperation and grant aid continue. Total Japanese ODA to China as of 2016 was $29 billion (¥3.3 trillion), of which $1.38 billion (¥157.2 billion) was in grants and $1.59 billion (¥181.7 billion) in technical cooperation.[14]

Viewed from the perspective of conflict management, another positive sign is that the same issues that divide the two countries and peoples may be converted into areas of cooperation. There are ways in which *China and Japan need one another*, such as to protect common air and sea environments, to promote China's "peaceful rise" in ways conducive to both domestic and international stability, to prevent military confrontations, to ensure the safety of nuclear energy plants, and to sustain regional political and economic stability. Such mutual dependence helps reduce potentially aggressive forms of nationalism. Thus, rather than interpret China-Japan relations exclusively in terms of competition for influence, we might think about the significant *opportunity costs* that occur as the result of their friction.[15]

To illustrate the positive possibilities as well as the difficulties in following through on them, we might contrast events in 2006–2007 with 2014. In October 2006, on the occasion of Prime Minister Abe Shinzo's official visit to the PRC, the two sides proclaimed that they would "strive to build a mutually beneficial relationship based on common strategic interests." "Contact and dialogue" were promised, including "frequent" talks between the top leaders. Explicit reference was made to four areas of cooperation: the East China Sea negotiations over the disputed islands (the Senkakus or Diaoyudao), "Japan-China security dialogue," ASEAN+3 (China-Japan-South Korea), and the Six Party Talks on North Korea. Japan and China also promised to "strengthen mutually beneficial cooperation particularly in the areas of energy, environmental protection, finance, information and communication technology, and protection of intellectual property."[16] When Hu Jintao returned Abe's visit in April

2007, he won great applause with a speech, "For Friendship and Cooperation," before the Japanese Diet. As he had in the past, Hu stressed "seeking agreement while minimizing differences" (*qiutong cunyi*). Mention was again made of energy and environmental cooperation.[17]

In December 2007 Prime Minister Fukuda Takeo visited China, following a visit to the United States, and (like Abe) stressed mutual interest.[18] The two governments reportedly reached a basic understanding on global warming, with Japan agreeing to provide China with technological assistance to help cut greenhouse gas emissions.[19] On the military side, the Chinese missile destroyer *Shenzhen* visited Tokyo Bay in November 2007, with a Japanese return visit scheduled for sometime later.[20] These high-level exchanges show that when dialogue focuses on functional areas, progress on improving relations is possible.

Shift to 2014 and a meeting in Beijing between Abe, now in his second tour as prime minister, and China's president Xi Jinping, following two tense years of standoff over the Senkaku/Diaoyudao dispute. Quiet diplomacy between foreign ministries preceded their encounter. The result was a four-point "consensus" that reflected a mixture of resolve and wariness: (1) both countries will continue efforts at "mutually beneficial strategic relations," with due regard for prior agreements; (2) both will seek to "overcome political obstacles" to their relations, relying on the spirit of "due regard for history, and looking to the future"; (3) both recognize that the East China Sea dispute resides in "different viewpoints" and agree to consultations to establish a mechanism for avoiding worsening the situation; and (4) both sides will use various channels of dialogue to promote mutual confidence.[21]

After the meeting Abe was upbeat, characterizing the talks as a "big step forward" in the countries' diplomacy. He pointed out that Japan and China "need each other" and are "inseparably bound together." And he said a "maritime communication channel"—a hotline, in short—had been decided on to help prevent a clash in the East China Sea. The Chinese press and Chinese officials, however, were much less effusive about the new agreement or confident that Japan would fulfill it. As has happened in the aftermath of past tensions, Chinese sources blamed Japan for them, reminded Japan of its wartime aggression, and said moving in a peaceful direction depended on Japan rectifying its behavior. For example, Foreign Minister Wang Yi said that while China "respects" Japan's desire for improved relations, China "hopes that Japan will seriously regard, fully respect, and faithfully implement" the four-point agreement.[22] Likewise, when two of the countries' top foreign policy specialists—one from China's state council, the other representing Japan's national security council—met in Beijing, a Chinese report again put the burden on Japan to fulfill the terms of the four-point agreement. "It is well recognized that the four-point agreement all depends on the implementation," said the news report.[23]

Nevertheless, in a sign that high-level Sino-Japanese diplomacy has indeed resumed, a senior Japanese advisory group, the 21st Century Committee for China-Japan Friendship, visited Beijing on December 4 and met with two top officials, including Premier Li Keqiang. Yet there again, the Chinese hedged, saying that the history issue was still an obstacle the Japanese would have to overcome if improvement of relations were to happen. Thus, it was (and remains) too early to celebrate a new era in relations between China and Japan. Yet the very facts that their leaders finally resumed talking, that Japan acknowledged the existence of a territorial dispute, and that a confidence-building mechanism would be set up to avoid a clash at sea were signs of progress, particularly as they came at a time when Japan was experiencing economic woes that surely complicated Abe's discussions with China.

Reconciling: Potential Avenues and Resources

In keeping with the cooperation matrix I offered in chapter 1, I consider some modest steps on Tracks I, II, and III to promote improvement in China-Japan relations. Some steps may not stand much chance of being implemented any time soon, but each one may generate the kind of goodwill and trust that will lead to other positive steps. Thus, I have sidestepped issues of historical grievance in favor of those in which mutual interests coincide—a win-win approach.[24]

Regularization of High-Level Diplomacy (Track I)

Chinese and Japanese leaders should pledge to make direct dialogue a regular occurrence. A counterpart of such diplomacy might be creation of a prevention-focused bilateral group to, for example, provide advance notification of troop or ship movements, similar to what the Organization for Security and Co-operation in Europe (OSCE) has accomplished. Conflict prevention in the East China Sea must be at the top of the list when it comes to mutual security, since (as discussed in the next section) the territorial dispute is a major flash point.

Mutual Appreciation (Tracks I and II)

Chinese government, media, and other institutions (including schools) can contribute to a positive atmosphere by expressing appreciation for Japan's contributions to China's economic rise. Some Chinese commentators agree that the country has been lax in this regard.[25] As mentioned, Japan was very generous with yen loans and continues to provide aid in grants and technical assistance. When Beijing has expressed appreciation, it has often been diluted by bitter reminders of the past and suggestions that Japanese business has also benefited from the aid and investments. [26] The Japanese side therefore also has an obligation: to acknowledge the benefits *it* has received.

Affirmations of Good Intentions (Track I)

Although words can never replace deeds, professions of friendly intentions and mutual respect, apologies for past conduct, and a positive common vision of future relations do serve good purposes. The Sino-Indian joint declaration of November 2006 is a model forward-looking statement. It specifies areas of actual and potential cooperation, as well as the agencies that will undertake it; it assigns roles for specialists; and it stresses mutual involvement in regional and global activities. These functional areas are framed with rhetoric suggesting positive intentions toward the other party: India and China "are not rivals or competitors" but rather have a "strategic and cooperative partnership," says the joint declaration. [27] Recent events in relations between China and India show that nice words cannot overcome rivalry. Still, the 2006 declaration offers a positive vision that China and Japan might incorporate in an updating of their 1998 agreement, with a new spirit of cooperation and attentiveness to specific areas of cooperation.

Creating a Northeast Asia Security Dialogue Mechanism (Track I)

For China and Japan, the NEASDM would provide an opportunity to work together on any number of common security issues, such as their long-running territorial dispute, security guarantees for the Korean peninsula, and a Northeast Asia nuclear-weapon-free zone. The common forum would also provide an institutional basis for greater transparency in military affairs, such as arms acquisitions and deployments. The Japan-China Fisheries Agreement that went into force in June 2002, and ongoing bilateral "security consultations" since 1994, provide positive reference points and building blocks for a regional dialogue mechanism. [28]

Putting Balance into US Policy [29]

As two knowledgeable experts argued some time ago, the United States has a large stake in a moderation of China-Japan relations. If US policy continues to promote "normal nation" status for Japan in ways that seem to China to amount to containment, a new cold war in Asia might result, with the two countries engaged in an arms race, forcing other countries (notably in ASEAN) to take sides. Rather than backing expansion of Japan's international security role and sounding alarm bells about China's military modernization, the United States "should declare its unambiguous opposition to worsening Sino-Japanese relations and exert its considerable influence with both Tokyo and Beijing to establish a cooling-off period."[30] Instead, Japan has shed some restrictions on its military deployments, China's military capabilities in nearby waters have greatly improved and become more audacious, and US support of Japan has remained rock solid.

Washington could adopt a more balanced position between China and Japan—something influential Chinese analysts say China wants[31] — while maintaining its security alliance with Japan. Tokyo could be given reassurances that the United States is not moving to a "pro-China" policy, a shift that Japanese leaders have feared in the past but that Chinese analysts themselves do not demand.[32] What China wants, and what is surely in Japan's interest as well, is *cooperativeness in US-China relations, which is vital to East Asia's future*. Japan may well need to hedge against a rising China, but it should not be perceived as seeking to contain it.[33]

Track II Gatherings

Apart from high-level diplomacy, Chinese and Japanese media, business, academic, and scientific circles have much that they could explore with each other. A gathering of such specialists, drawn from private and public institutions, might promote mutual understanding, reduce stereotyping, and change popular opinion in both countries. For example, a scientific meeting might be arranged to come up with initiatives on global warming and energy cooperation or a joint plan for dealing with transboundary pollution.[34] A joint East Asia television history project is a second example, following on publication in 2006 of a joint Chinese-Japanese-Korean history text. Track II gatherings might also encourage particular groups to lobby their governments for improvements in China-Japan relations, as Japanese business groups have already done on the Yasukuni issue. The two governments might convene an eminent persons group to advise on solutions to specific issues in dispute.[35]

Track III Civil Society and People-to-People Exchanges

Improving mutual perceptions and counteracting distorted imagery require remedies at the grassroots level as well as among political leaders. For policy makers, nationalism is a two-edged sword; if they appear to be going against it, they face domestic opposition to "softness" when dealing with the enemy. Thus, Hu Jintao is sometimes said to have been a target of the April 2005 demonstrations against a permanent Japanese seat on the UN Security Council for not being as tough with Japan as his predecessor, Jiang Zemin, had been, and the China hands in Japan's foreign ministry have often been criticized in the Japanese press for being too "pro-China."

At the popular level, the problem is more complex. In China's case, anti-Japanese nationalism clearly has grassroots dimensions; the fact that the 2005 protests were driven by the Internet showed that new reality very plainly. But official approval of anti-Japanese feelings (as long as they do not get out of control) is just as clearly involved, not only in popular demonstrations but also in the "patriotic education campaigns" carried on numerous television stations. Social media now also play a role, such as in September 2010 when a Chinese fishing trawler collided with a Japanese patrol boat in the East China Sea, leading to the arrest of the Chinese captain and his crew and seizure of the trawler.[36] Japan released all the prisoners except the captain, but China, besides vigorously protesting, arrested four Japanese employees of a construction company in China on espionage charges and banned export of rare earth minerals to Japan. Demonstrations occurred in both countries, encouraged by nationalistic blogging. A promising agreement for joint exploration of gas fields in the East China Sea never materialized.

Just as certain domestic groups in China probably valued a strong stance on the trawler incident more than cooperative development, Japan had (and has) its counterparts when it comes to playing to or promoting anti-Chinese feelings and not appearing to cave in to Chinese demands. In fact, the incident was something of a watershed in moving China-Japan relations into a new phase of soft-power competition, with the disputed islands the centerpiece.[37] Japanese courts consistently reject suits that challenge officially sanctioned history textbooks and ask for compensation for Chinese (and all other) war victims, revisionist historiography still has an audience (and is rarely criticized by public officials), and the archconservative *Sankei News* and popular comic books often depict China in the most evil terms.[38]

Civil society, though nascent in China and still rather weak in Japan, needs to be encouraged to explore, systematically and practically, how Chinese and Japanese can learn to be more accepting of one another. At least one study of Japanese NGOs in China—which are far more numerous there than in any other country—suggests that they can be very effective people-to-people diplomats, particularly in the environmental field.[39] *Yomiuri*'s reevaluation of Japan's war responsibility exemplifies what the mass media can do to dispose of historical myths.[40] *Yomiuri* and its liberal newspaper counterpart, *Asahi Shimbun*, might cosponsor a media summit with their Chinese counterparts on ways to avoid stereotyping and report objectively on events in the other country.[41] The editors of these two newspapers have called for building a secular war memorial to replace the Yasukuni Shrine, but to no effect.[42] In academia, scholarly gatherings should be held regularly to reevaluate historical sources of grievance.

If some of these ideas are implemented, they may lead to other positive developments.[43] For example, China might support a Japanese seat on the UN Security Council. Suspicions about the force modernizations of their militaries might abate as new confidence-building mechanisms are devised. China and Japan might establish a standing crisis management body. Private groups might be prevented by their governments from interfering in territorial disputes. In the end, China and Japan must reach the point of recognizing that security for one is really security for the other, as happened between the United States and the Soviet Union during the Cold War and when two progressive South Korean governments decided to engage the North. Again, the role of the United States is crucial, particularly if it were to adopt a more balanced position in relations with China and Japan.

Managing the China-Japan Territorial Dispute

China and Japan have attempted to sidestep the sovereignty issue in the East China Sea islands by presenting proposals for joint development of undersea resources, Japan in September 2005 and China in June 2004 and March 2006. But basic issues of territorial control and jurisdiction stand in the way of a resolution.[44] Self-righteous nationalism animates both sides, and when put together with China's new assertiveness and Japan's aspirations for "normalcy," the prospects rise for a serious confrontation. Security ties to Japan put the United States in the middle of this situation.

What can be done to keep this dispute from boiling over? Like the South China Sea dispute, this one can at least be frozen if China and Japan agree to shelve the sovereignty issue, not make use of the islands, and cease active military patrolling around them. One positive development occurred in 2014, when China, Japan, the United States, and a number of other countries agreed to a naval and air communications protocol.

Settlement of the dispute requires additional political confidence-building acts and mutual concessions,[45] such as the following:

- Japan acknowledges the existence of a dispute over sovereignty, but agrees with China on the principle of joint ownership and concedes the need for joint administration on petitions for access to the islands, for example by tourists.
- Entry of military or nonmilitary vessels into disputed waters is forbidden, and the two sides agree to establish a special communication channel to avoid miscalculations and escalation of incidents at sea.
- China and Japan avoid other provocative acts and words, such as proclamation of an air defense zone over the islands and visits by Japanese leaders to the war shrine at Yasukuni.
- Japan continues its "3 no's" policy: not to build, not to land, and not to investigate.
- High-level diplomacy is accepted to develop confidence-building measures.

Even then, however, the shadow of mutual disrespect still hangs over Sino-Japanese relations. As China's foreign minister Chen Yi said at a news conference in 2017: "We naturally want to improve relations with Japan and work for the common prosperity of our two peoples. But Japan must cure its 'heart disease' and rationally view and accept the fact of China's continuous development."[46]

The United States also has an important role to play. It might communicate to the Japanese government that it does not have US carte blanche when it comes to defense of the Senkakus. Such a communication is necessary, inasmuch as President Obama for the first time said in 2014 that the United States does indeed have an obligation to come to Japan's defense in case of an outbreak of fighting around those islands. Washington should also continue to facilitate China's and Japan's participation in trilateral and other multilateral formats for security talks.[47]

Prospects in the Trump Era

The election of Donald Trump and political uncertainty in South Korea created new security issues for the Abe administration. Abe's strong relationship with Obama gave him confidence in the US commitment to the alliance and to a new era in Pacific trade—the Trans-Pacific Partnership (TPP). Abe expended a great deal of political capital on the agreement and relied on Obama to get the TPP passed by Congress. From a strategic angle, both leaders agreed with TPP's other aim: to constrain the Chinese from becoming dominant in Asia trade. That aim melded with a bill pushed through the Japanese Diet in September 2015 allowing the Self-Defense Forces to go into combat abroad, though with important qualifications. Washington had long advocated such a step, even though the bill aroused Abe's political opposition and raised questions about its constitutionality.

With Obama gone, the US commitments on trade and security were suddenly in question, which is undoubtedly why Abe was the first foreign leader to talk with Trump after the election. During his campaign, Trump had suggested that Japan (and South Korea) might bear more of the burden of defense and might even want to consider acquiring nuclear weapons. The Trump team later seemed to walk back such talk, reaffirming the importance of the alliance. But Trump also vowed to withdraw support of the TPP, and he followed through. Thus, Trump's reliability and predictability were in question with Japan.

Reliability is essential to Japan at a time when China is ratcheting up its naval and air presence in nearby areas. Abe, who may well be able to rule into the 2020s, is determined to revise the constitution and make Japan fully independent in national defense. During 2016 tension in the East China Sea increased as both Chinese and Japanese air patrolling became more vigorous, each side apparently testing the other's capabilities near the disputed islands. If the Trump administration's relationship with China deteriorates, will Washington still have Japan's back—and will Tokyo have America's back—in a crisis with China? Will Trump come to Japan's aid if North Korean missiles become more threatening? Will Japan and the United States be able to agree on a new bilateral trade pact now that Trump has ended US support of the TPP? As of mid-2017, there were more questions than answers.

ISRAEL AND PALESTINE: A FIGHT OVER SACRED GROUND

Anything but Peace

Probably no conflict is more freighted with symbolism than that between the Palestinians and Israelis. For both sides the land is sacred and not to be shared: the Zionist dream for many Israelis, Biblical Judea and Samaria, Eretz Israel; the homeland, the resting place for Palestinian independence. Nationalism feeds off these dreams; national security means fulfillment of them. Each side's identity rests on recognition of its *people's* God-given right to the land, and each side's security rests on the insecurity of the other side.

Nowhere else in the world is politics so central to peacemaking and so devastating to the prospect of engagement. In the course of fifty years of Israeli occupation of the West Bank, three points stand out. First, a two-state solution is further away than ever before, and a binational solution is only slightly more realizable. Second, Israeli-Palestinian engagement has no strong advocates in Israeli politics. Third, the United States has failed to be an honest broker of peace. One may say that the fundamental explanation for these negatives is strategic: the threat each side poses to the other, as demonstrated by frequent violence and Arab-Israeli wars. But underneath the threats lies the politics of fear and loathing: each side's conditioning of generations to distrust the other, to arm against it, and to reject as unreliable proposals for accommodation. "Political leaders are the obstacles to peace," former President Jimmy Carter has said of the Israel-Palestine conflict.

Numerous points might be chosen along the Israeli-Palestinian conflict timeline to illustrate how both parties have rejected peace in preference for war. These missed opportunities start with the Palestinians' rejection in 1948 of a partition plan that would have created two states, instead going to war with support from the Arab countries against the newly established State of Israel. The failure of the Camp David summit in September 1978 is another; recognition of Palestinian autonomy might have evolved into statehood had the Palestinians been present and had Israeli and Palestinian leaders not operated on bad-faith models.[48] A third missed opportunity, discussed below, is the failure to implement the agreements reached at Oslo, Norway, in 1993.

I have chosen a more recent occasion to reflect on missed opportunities: the fighting in Gaza, a strip of land with roughly 1.5 million people, controlled by Hamas. In mid-2014 conflict between Hamas and Israeli forces broke out after the kidnapping and killing of three Israeli boys by people associated with Hamas. Israeli settlers retaliated, killing and burning a Palestinian. These two outrages resulted in absurdly disproportional responses by both sides as both the Israeli and the Hamas leaderships came to believe that peacemaking would yield few gains, whereas fighting might achieve gains that had been unachievable before. Rather than meet with Hamas on a truce, Israel announced it would wind down its assault in Gaza on its own terms, which allowed for more indiscriminate bombing. When a UN school-turned-shelter was hit, Secretary-General Ban Ki-moon called the attack "a moral outrage and a criminal act." But the larger outrage surely is the free-fire orders to Israeli soldiers against civilians.[49]

Many reports from Israel at the time pointed to an increasing conviction among its leaders that now was the time to eliminate Hamas once and for all. The tunnels had to be entirely wiped out and the rockets silenced, the Hamas leadership had to be discredited, and Gaza had to have a permanent Israeli military presence. For Hamas, continued fighting justified its existence and established its legitimacy as a negotiating partner. It was also the only way Hamas leaders saw, apparently, to end Israel's blockade of Gaza, to open border crossings with Egypt, and thus to free Gazans from the economic squeeze that had dramatically reduced their quality of life. In short, revenge once again triumphed over clear thinking and dialogue.

This war was particularly anguishing because it was avoidable, as Nathan Thrall of the International Crisis Group argued.[50] Thrall pointed the finger at Israel, with US support, for obstructing the reconciliation agreement reached in April 2014 by the Palestine Liberation Organization (PLO), based in the West Bank, and Hamas, which might have laid the groundwork for a new peace accord with Israel. Hamas was in a weakened condition then, and the "national consensus" that it agreed to put the Palestinian Authority (PA; Fatah) in the driver's seat in Gaza as well as in the West Bank. A few generous acts by Israel and the United States at that time, such as enabling Gaza's civil servants to be paid, might well have produced entirely different reactions to the kidnappings and murders earlier in the month.

The background to that failure to seize the moment is worth recalling. In 2006 the George W. Bush administration urged the PA to hold national legislative council elections, only to witness a Hamas victory. It was a watershed event. Neither Bush nor the Israelis could stomach the unexpected outcome. Israeli artillery and air strikes in Gaza, met by Hamas rockets, ended a brief postelection truce. Thus began a new round of the war in Gaza as the Bush administration rejected advice to talk with Hamas and the PA.[51] Not only did the United States bear substantial responsibility for the war;[52] it paid a heavy political price, since opposing the election results totally undermined professed US commitments to democratization.[53] Washington and Tel Aviv misread Fatah's defeat, refusing to accept that Hamas had won because of "its perceived honesty, service to the community, and nationalist credentials."[54] Hamas became the new power in Gaza. In 2007 Israel imposed an economic blockade there, and in 2008 it set restrictions for security reasons on substantial portions of Gaza's agricultural and fishing areas.

Israel's use of disproportionate and indiscriminate force in Gaza earned it international condemnation. The UN Human Rights Council issued a report early in 2009 that condemned Israel's violations of international law, including "willfully causing grave suffering to protected persons." The Israeli government refused to cooperate with the investigation headed by the renowned jurist Richard Goldstone, arguing that his report was one-sided. But in fact the report raised the issue of war crimes for both Israeli and Hamas actions.[55] As for the economic blockade imposed in Gaza, a UN report issued in August 2010—"Between the Fence and a Hard Place"[56]—said it had "devastating" consequences for people's livelihoods, citing (for example) the homes, farms, water wells, and schools destroyed since 2005. But the blockade also enhanced Hamas's standing there as an alternative to Israel's continuing assault on living standards and personal security. A few prominent Israelis, such as David Grossman, argued that war was not the answer, and that Israel should negotiate with Hamas.[57] His deep conviction is that Israel's leadership had failed its people by rejecting a peace that has long been within reach. But nobody in Tel Aviv was listening.

And what of the US role at that time? The Israeli air attacks were met with "understanding" by the president, the secretary of state, and other high US officials. Yes, they expressed "concern" about the "heartbreaking" toll on the Palestinians these attacks caused, more than eighteen hundred dead and eight thousand wounded. (Israel lost sixty-three soldiers and three civilians.) But US leaders did not directly criticize Israel's conduct. On the contrary, President Obama told Prime Minister Benjamin Netanyahu in a telephone call July 24 that he "underscored the United States' strong condemnation of Hamas' rocket and tunnel attacks against Israel and reaffirmed Israel's right to defend itself," according to the White House statement. Evidently the Palestinians have no such right. And whereas Obama demanded the unconditional release of an Israeli soldier wrongly believed to have been captured by Hamas, calling it a "barbaric" act, no Israeli action was so characterized. Public and congressional opinion in the United States seemed to support the official view that Hamas was to blame for the fighting, so Obama was just where a US president wants to be, on politically safe terrain.

Secretary of State John Kerry said the US goal in Gaza was "an unconditional humanitarian cease-fire." But the Israelis were never really interested even in that minimal step. As newspapers reported, Netanyahu upbraided the US ambassador to Israel, saying the Obama administration should never "second guess me again" on dealing with Hamas. You have to hand it to Netanyahu; he knows how to manipulate the Israel-US relationship to his advantage. He knows how rarely Washington follows up its "concern" about Israeli military and political actions with any withdrawal or reduction of support. Thus, he lets the US leadership fret (or pretend to fret) for awhile and engage in endless shuttle diplomacy, while he goes about his business. This time around, Netanyahu got a bonus: for their own reasons of state, the Egyptians—meaning the military junta that had seized power in July 2013 and has been busy suppressing human rights ever since, with barely a murmur from Washington—were perfectly content to watch the demise of Hamas, and they were rewarded with resumption of US military aid. If nothing else, Washington knows how to keep its friends in the Middle East happy.

The bottom line is that although Netanyahu says he supports a two-state solution, and although a poll in December 2016 found that 61 percent of Israelis favor a Palestinian state with East Jerusalem as its capital,[58] the reality is that Netanyahu is beholden to hard-line politicians and ultra-Orthodox settlers who regard Greater Israel as beyond negotiation.[59] Accordingly, over the years every effort to bring the two sides together around the idea of two people, two states has been thwarted by the attachment of conditions that make such a step impossible. Thus, when Netanyahu at the end of 2013 insisted that any agreement with the Palestinians must include specific reference to Israel as a *Jewish* state, the Palestinians naturally reacted angrily. At issue was not just a questioning of the need for such a statement, but the existential challenge it raised about whose homeland the state of Israel occupies. In present circumstances, therefore, the options in Israel narrow to two: more settlements that overwhelm the Palestinian population or another intifada.

The Biased Broker

For decades the United States, under both Democratic and Republican administrations, has tried to broker a final settlement of the conflict between Israel and Palestine. Not only has Washington failed in that role; it has left Palestinians and the Arab world persuaded that an honest broker's role is not credible, a failure not just of US policy but also of its public diplomacy on democracy and human rights.[60] Many Palestinians and other Arab observers accept that the United States will always support Israel's security and right to exist, but they fail to see why the United

States cannot also be evenhanded when it comes to Palestinian rights. No amount of US shuttle diplomacy and, since George W. Bush's statement in 2002, promised support of a Palestinian state, has convinced Arab governments and people of US reliability. The reasons are easy to identify: support of Israel is a given in US politics across the spectrum; terrorism, especially since 9/11, has turned the focus of US policy away from understanding Palestinian and Arab histories and cultures; Saudi Arabia's dependence on US oil companies to market their oil precludes a break with Washington over the Israel-Palestine issue; and US policy in the Middle East, at least in Arab eyes, is fixed on interventions and military power.[61]

Consequently, as Rashid Khalidi argues, the political vocabulary on the Palestine-Israel issue distorts reality. Words such as "security," "terrorism," and the "peace process" are not neutral, for various US administrations have consistently sided with Israel's interpretation of them. And because the United States has been the pivotal outside actor in the Middle East drama, its interpretation has been decisive in determining the issues most critical to Palestinians: borders, Jerusalem, settlements, use of force, and restitution to refugees. To be sure, there have been plenty of US-sponsored peace "road maps," summits, and conferences. But actual policy has deviated from all these efforts.

Not that Israel always gets what it wants, as Khalidi's study acknowledges. American arms sales to the Saudis and other Arab states, especially during the Cold War, have always raised Israeli objections. But Israel's qualms have usually been eased by large arms sales—in 2007, for example, a ten-year arms aid agreement worth $30 billion, justified as "an investment in peace" by the undersecretary of state, Nicholas Burns, but actually a payoff so that Washington could keep both the Saudis and the Israelis happy.[62] Since Khalidi's study, perhaps the biggest exception to US satisfaction of Israeli interests was Obama's pursuit of a nuclear agreement with Iran, despite Netanyahu's vigorous objections and very undiplomatic criticism of the agreement while he was on a visit to the United States and afterward.

But the balance in US policy is unquestionably on the side of Israel. American leaders have never *conditioned* aid to Israel, the world's top recipient of total US aid, on Israel's acknowledging its nuclear weapons program and opening it to international inspection, abandoning its settlements in occupied lands, or addressing its human rights violations. The US vetoes of UN Security Council resolutions that sought to sanction Israel or were critical of it have been crucial to sustaining Israel's occupation of the West Bank. And US aid to Israel has been virtually automatic, delinked from Israeli conduct.

The scope of US aid is extraordinary. American arms sales and other arms aid to Israel, from the 1967 June War to 2016, amounted to over $38 billion.[63] From 1949 through 2013, total direct US economic and military aid (grants) was about $130.2 billion (adjusted for inflation). In the most recent years Israel has been by far the top recipient of US military assistance. But US military aid figures do not tell the whole story; omitted are many "perks" not available to other US aid recipients, such as loan guarantees (which enable Israel to borrow at lower rates), shipments of excess military equipment, US weapons stockpiled in Israel and accessible to Israeli forces, and support of Israel's defense industry (by allowing Israel to use about 26 percent of US military aid to purchase weapons produced at home).[64] The Occupation has boosted Israel's defense industry; without it, writes Jeff Halper, "Israel would have neither the drive nor the conditions by which to develop, deploy, test and export world-class weaponry and models of control."[65]

American support of Israel also includes political action committee donations to pro-Israel US officeholders and candidates, votes in the UN, and tax-deductible contributions to Israel via US charities. The pro-Israel lobby is perhaps the best organized and financed of any in the United States, and the Jewish community there is large, generally focused on Israeli interests, and frequently reminded of the intimate relationship between Israel's founding and US support. Punishing Israel is politically taboo. Occasional US attempts to use aid to induce Israeli concessions on land-for-peace proposals, in keeping with the Oslo agreements, have not worked. As Roger Cohen writes: "Seldom has Moshe Dayan's old dictum—'Our American friends offer us money, arms and advice. We take the money, take the arms, and decline the advice'—been more vividly illustrated."[66] This situation will get worse under the Trump administration.

Disunity in Two Camps

The Palestinian cause cannot avail itself of US largesse. The Palestinians' suffering under the Israeli occupation goes unrelieved and largely unremarked upon in the United States and is rarely a matter of true outrage even among the Arab states. The PA is constantly put in the position of supplicant, desperately seeking economic assistance from abroad and heavily dependent on Israel for jobs, water, and other vital items. The PA has some support in Europe, such as in aid and sanctions against Israel for human rights abuses, but in the United States the pro-Palestinian constituency is largely confined to left-leaning academics and a few members of Congress. Palestinian efforts to gain political standing at the UN have failed to get far, even when (as by the Goldstone report) Israeli military actions are widely condemned.

The Palestinian cause is further weakened by its own disunity. The PA leadership, under longtime president Mahmoud Abbas, must deal with charges of corruption; failure to provide sufficient support to schools and social services; high unemployment; and lack of favor with Egypt, Saudi

Arabia, and other mainline Arab states. Its harshest critics say the PA has lost legitimacy, has become an arm of the Israeli occupation army, and therefore must be replaced.[67] This inner turmoil makes the PA a weak candidate for pursuing engagement, a reality of which the Israeli leadership has taken full advantage. Without strong public backing, and under pressure from Hamas, the PA lacks the standing that is necessary to confront Israeli counterparts.

The Israelis are also deeply divided, but by demography and identity. As the president of Israel, Reuven Rivlin, said in a speech in 2015, there is a "new Israeli order" characterized by a major change in Israeli identity.[68] Secular Zionists no longer are the clear majority. Referring to first-grade education, he said Israel now has four "tribes," each with its own culture, values, and political orientation. The very different schooling children receive, and the limited exposure they have to what the other tribes read and think, translate into entirely different outlooks on Israel's future and call into question whether Israel can remain committed to being a liberal and democratic state. "Israeli politics to a great extent is built as an inter-tribal zero sum game," Rivlin wrote, with Arabs "not really part of the game" and the Haredim (the ultra-Orthodox) also outside the Zionist mainstream. Yet both those groups form fully half the population already and are the fastest growing.

Israel's pioneer leaders envisioned it as a secular state, and that view prevailed into the 1990s. But in the new century, religious Zionism and, consequently, hostility toward Arabs and denial of their basic rights, have become increasingly powerful. Rivlin was courageously calling for the creation—or re-creation—of Israeli civil society based on security, partnership, and mutual respect. But he didn't sound too optimistic. Based on their relative strengths, an Israel truly interested in engaging Palestine would make the first tangible moves toward a final settlement. But the opposite is true: Israel under right-wing rule is marching toward deeper disengagement, in defiance of Rivlin's message and, more important, in defiance of the logic of mutual security.

A New Role for the United States

The United States, despite its lengthy diplomatic involvement in the dispute between Israel and Palestine and its major aid programs to both sides (though obviously lopsided in Israel's favor), has not been especially helpful or even well-informed in bringing the two sides together. The United States has failed to use the leverage it possesses, either with Israel to press for a two-state solution or with Palestine to insist on recognition of Israel's right to exist within secure boundaries.

For the United States (or any other country) to be an honest broker, it must speak on behalf of a just peace, which is to say the human interest. That interest lies in *cooperative security*: joint recognition by Israel and

Palestine of their common right to the land; dramatic improvement in Palestinians' quality of life, starting with a major increase in international development aid to the PA; shared jurisdiction in Jerusalem, with assured access to all religions; exchanges of diplomatic relations and security assurances; demilitarization of relations and a shift of funding from weapons to programs and projects that promote Palestinian-Israeli cooperation and mutual understanding of their common future; and US support of these principles without constant deference to the position of either the Israeli government or its American backers.

In 2011 a virtual who's who of the US foreign policy establishment endorsed these and other goals in a five-point proposal that would be the basis for an Israel-Palestine settlement that the United States could support. The essence of each point is first, creation of a viable Palestinian state based on the 1967 borders, subject only to minor land swaps; second, resolution of the Palestinian refugee problem on the basis of two states, two peoples, with assistance for their resettlement; third, support for a nonmilitarized, sovereign, and secure Palestine and a secure Israel, with a US-led multinational presence to oversee mutual security; fourth, division of Jerusalem into two sovereign neighborhoods, each controlling holy places that are accessible to both; and fifth, reconciliation of Fatah and Hamas.[69]

Perhaps a sixth condition should be added: that Israel declare itself a nuclear weapons state, subject to international inspection, if it is to continue receiving US military aid. For many years, as Henry Kissinger once said, "the Israelis have persistently deceived us" about their nuclear weapons program, which is generally believed to encompass about eighty weapons. In fact, Washington has been aware of the Israeli bomb from its origins. American policy has essentially been "don't ask, don't tell": Israel won't talk about its nuclear weapons program, and the United States won't press Israel to reveal it or sign the Nuclear Nonproliferation Treaty.[70] That posture creates a double standard of US policy toward other nuclear-weapon aspirants, such as North Korea and Iran, and it gives Arab states such as Saudi Arabia latitude to one day develop their own nuclear weapons. Thus, working toward a Middle East nuclear-weapon-free zone should be among the US goals.

Settling, and Engaging

Ultimately, it is up to the disputing parties to determine the choice of war or peace. The rightward lurch of the Israeli political body in recent years obscures and even silences voices for peace, coexistence, and engagement. Netanyahu has become an extreme nationalist, catering to the religious right and comfortable with decisions that are humiliating to Palestinians. Tzipi Livni, a former foreign minister, is one voice of reason who has not been silent. She says that "making peace is painful" and involves "real security risks"; "whoever makes it will be criticized as a traitor." But doing nothing will only give the "temporary illusion" of a manageable situation.[71] Though Livni shares the view of Israeli entitlement to all of Eretz Israel, she believes in compromise, which can be achieved only if both sides abandon their historical claims and work for the future.[72]

Getting to "yes" has long been an especially vexing question in the Middle East. But there was a time, in 1993 in Oslo, Norway, when Israeli and Palestinian representatives made a historic breakthrough to cooperative relations.[73] The process counted as much as the final product: mutual acceptance of partnership and equality in the search for peace; recognition of the other's humanity, suffering, and grievances; and mutual dependence on each other's security and therefore political stability, sound institutions, and prosperity. Nevertheless, in the end the Oslo agreement, though responsive to Israel's quest for security and the Palestinians' aspirations for statehood, could not overcome political and historical obstacles back home. "There was little talk of reconciliation, even less of the other side's [political] predicaments."[74]

A fascinating dialogue among eight prominent Israeli and Palestinian citizens in the pages of *Harper's Magazine* illustrates the high barriers to a negotiated settlement, starting with the observation that "we live so close to each other, yet we know so little about each other."[75] One striking point is that Israelis and Palestinians cannot get past the divide between the important and the attainable. For Israelis, "the important" is clear recognition by the PA and Hamas of Israel's right to exist within secure borders, whereas for Palestinians "the important" is ending the occupation, stopping settlements on their land, and building a state. "Simply put," said a Palestinian industrialist and former office holder, "for almost half a century we Palestinians have been living in a big prison. . . . One and a half million people locked in an area of 365 square kilometers." Economic, social, and other Israeli concessions divorced from steps to end the Occupation will never be accepted by the Palestinians. Unless it ends, either another round of armed struggle will occur or radical Islamists will become dominant among the Palestinian population, which will mean an even more violent future and an end to talk of a two-state solution.

But what is "the attainable?" It might best be defined as solving small matters first, but with the clear understanding that the endgame is an end to the occupation and illegal settlements in the West Bank. This outcome can only happen in a post-Netanyahu government, since Netanyahu, faced with pressure from the extreme Right, is highly unlikely to call for a halt to settlements.[76] President Obama discovered this in 2016 when he announced a ten-year military aid program amounting to $38 billion, the unspoken hope being that Israel would finally rein in the settlements. It didn't, Obama retaliated at the UN, and Netanyahu felt betrayed.[77] John

Kerry followed up with a major final speech defending the US vote, arguing that a two-state solution is the only road to peace—"if the choice is one state, Israel can be either Jewish or democratic, it can't be both"— and that the Obama administration had been Israel's greatest friend. Kerry pointed to the large and "systematic" increase in the number of settlements since Obama took office: 100,000. He condemned violence by all sides, but saved his strongest words for Netanyahu's government, calling it "the most right-wing in Israel history with an agenda driven by the most extreme elements," meaning the settlers and the politicians who cultivate their support.[78] The reaction of Netanyahu and Donald Trump was equally angry. But as Rashi Khalidi wrote, Kerry's speech was "too little and too late."[79]

Less ambitious steps might still be possible. An Israeli leader of parliament once proposed that rather than attempt a final settlement of security issues, negotiators might first agree on confidence-building measures on a whole range of economic and social issues. One of these of great consequence would be relaxing restrictions on Palestinians' movement—the roadblocks, checkpoints, travel permits—and seriously addressing what Jimmy Carter called Palestinian apartheid: the intolerable living and working conditions in Gaza.[80] That would mean taking down the wall in the West Bank, which the International Court of Justice ruled illegal in 2004.[81] Israel should be prepared to address the terrible quality of life in Gaza and the ultimate need (in a two-state solution) for a land bridge between Gaza and the West Bank.[82] The Israeli government should also drop the insistence on making Israel an ethnoreligious ("Jewish") state, which not only limits peacemaking opportunities with the Palestinians but also alienates many Israelis and forces them to consider emigrating.

A second achievable goal is for Israel to abide by international law and end illegal settlements on Palestinian land. About 570,000 Israelis now live in the West Bank and East Jerusalem. Article 49 of the Fourth Geneva Convention forbids the transfer of populations out of occupied territory—in other words, forcing Palestinian civilians to leave the West Bank so that Israelis can settle there. We now know that the Israeli authorities were aware as far back as 1968 of the illegality of the settlements, demolition of Palestinian homes, and deportation of terror suspects.[83] The land should be returned to its rightful residents, preferably as part of a two-state formula. In return, the PA would give up the "right of return" by all Palestinians driven out of Israel after 1948. But they would have a state to return to, with appropriate compensation from Israel.

A third achievable goal is US, Israeli, and international support of independent Palestine's quest for legitimacy and dignity. In 2015, for example, the PA, having been thwarted in the UN Security Council when a vote to end Israel's occupation of the West Bank went against it, decided to sign several international conventions, most importantly the Rome Statute, which established the International Criminal Court in

2002. As an expression of national dignity and exasperation with the peace process, the PA's signing was understandable. The Netanyahu government and the Israeli Right used the occasion to argue that the Palestinians had abandoned the peace process and could not be trusted. Washington warned the PA not to do so as well. (Neither Israel nor the United States has ratified the Rome Statute, making their protests all the more disingenuous.) The PA has every right to seek the attributes of statehood, and it is the Israelis who have abandoned the peace process. Support of the PA's quest would be a positive trust-building step, as well as support for important principles of international law.

But as former president Jimmy Carter has written, the United States does not have to wait on Israel or any other country to grant independent Palestine diplomatic recognition.[84] More than 130 countries have already taken that step. Doing so would enable Palestine to become a UN member, would give citizenship to the 4.5 million people who do not have it in Israel, would elevate the international status of Palestine, would compel adherence to UN Security Council Resolution 242 (November 1967) on restoring pre-1967 war borders[85] (and thus also compel reversal of illegal Israeli settlements), and would jump-start a major international aid program to improve the quality of life of Palestinians.

The human interest agenda proposed here would distance the United States from Israeli priorities but would actually benefit Israel's security while also promoting broader US interests in a Middle East peace. The new approach would also lend hope to the Palestinian people that they, like their Israeli neighbors, can live a decent life with personal security. Carried out step by step to build mutual confidence, this agenda would aim to gradually demilitarize both sides, turn the dialogue from terrorism to democracy, and change the minds of Israelis who believe that only continued and expanded occupation can ensure their security.

Achieving a final peace settlement in the Middle East is a Track I responsibility. The Geneva Accord,[86] unveiled at the end of 2003 after three years of talks between one-time Israeli and Palestinian officials, demonstrates that a just peace can be constructed if only the various parties have the will to do so and the political support within their own communities to forge ahead. Like the Oslo agreement, that support did not materialize. But whether or not a negotiated settlement works depends on trust building, and that requires consistent engagement among civil societies: educators, lawyers, businesspeople, students, and political activists. As Kerry said in his last speech: "In the end, I believe the negotiations did not fail because the gaps were too wide, but because the level of trust was too low. Both sides were concerned that any concessions would not be reciprocated and would come at too great a political cost. And the deep public skepticism only made it more difficult for them to be able to take risks."[87]

Yet neither Kerry nor the Obama administration paid much attention, or provided meaningful funding, to civil society efforts.[88] Considering the signal importance of reconciliation between Palestine and Israel at the ground level, that omission is beyond unfortunate. Track III has plenty of examples of solidly grounded projects. One is the Geneva Initiative, a follow-on to the Geneva Accord. Founded by leading Israeli and Palestinian figures, it brings together a wide array of people from both sides, sometimes with support from US entities such as the Agency for International Development.[89] Herbert Kelman's Interactive Problem Solving Workshops, a Track II project, have for many years brought Israelis and Palestinians together with the goal to "discover the underlying needs and fears of workshop participants as representatives of the macro conflict, as well what they can tell us about the collective needs and fears in both societies and their manipulation and politicization through politics."[90] Kelman, a distinguished sociologist, has made the personal proposal that a political two-state solution should be accompanied by agreement on "one country": the notion that the entirety of Israel-Palestine land should be accepted and treated as a common community, with implications for people's movements, the environment, and water management, among other areas of concern.[91]

Joint Israeli-Palestinian projects, such as development of Gaza's gas fields and establishment of industrial and high-tech zones, could be an important component of promoting mutual understanding. As Thomas Friedman writes, the key to a nonviolent future is "relationships of trust that create healthy interdependencies." Water is a particularly crucial subject for cooperation. Friedman cites EcoPeace Middle East, a group that is addressing water quality and international cooperation to keep a common waterway, the Jordan River, clean.[92] There are many other joint projects, but we rarely hear of them.

Palestinian and Israeli leaders might exchange apologies. Palestinians would want an Israeli apology for their suffering since 1948, while Israelis might want an apology for attacks on settlements and cities that caused their suffering. Apologies would be a step in the spirit of Oslo: recognition of a common humanity. The Arab Israeli community could play a role here, for it contains peacemakers like Ayman Odeh, a member of the Knesset (the Israeli parliament), fluent in Hebrew, accepting of each people's roots in the Holy Land, and dedicated to Arab-Jewish coexistence.[93]

The sad news is that the Trump administration is likely to roll back the few diplomatic and Track III gains that have been made in favor of a decisively pro-Israel stance. Trump signaled as much before taking office, tweeting in response to John Kerry's speech at the end of 2016 that Israel should wait until January 20, 2017, when it would get a better deal. That will mean even more military aid to Israel and an uncritical response to new Israeli settlements in the West Bank. Israel in fact announced new construction of more than five thousand homes there within a few days of Trump's inauguration, and Israel's parliament retroactively legalized some land grabs by settlers. Under Trump we can expect US rejection of UN Security Council resolutions critical of Israel, such as on Israeli settlements in occupied territory, and accommodating Israel's views on regional Middle East issues such as Iran's nuclear program and terrorism. His administration could also very well mean watching as Israel annexes the West Bank altogether, putting an end to talk of a two-state solution by absorbing the Arab population into Israel proper. Indeed, when Netanyahu visited Washington in February 2017, Trump said at a joint news conference that either a two-state or one-state outcome would be fine with him.[94]

In short, Israel-Palestine engagement is even less achievable now than before. And that means a resumption of violence is more likely than before.

NOTES

1. This section draws on my chapter, "Reconciling China and Japan: A Menu of Alternatives," in *Sino-Japanese Relations: The Need for Conflict Prevention and Management*, ed. Niklas Swanstrom and Ryosei Kokubun (Newcastle upon Tyne, UK: Cambridge Scholars Publishing, 2008), 96–111.

2. David Crocker, "Reckoning with Past Wrongs: A Normative Framework," *Ethics and International Affairs* 13 (1999): 43–64.

3. Yang Bojiang, "Redefining Sino-Japanese Relations after Koizumi," *Washington Quarterly* 29, no. 4 (Autumn 2006): 131.

4. See Tok Sow Keat, "Neither Friends Nor Foes: China's Dilemmas in Managing Its Japan Policy," *China: An International Journal* 3, no. 2 (September 2005): 297–298.

5. King, "Hurting the Feelings of the Chinese People," Woodrow Wilson Center, February 15, 2017, www.wilsoncenter.org/blog-post/hurting-the-feelings-the-chinese-people.

6. He, "Remembering and Forgetting the War: Elite Mythmaking, Mass Reaction, and Sino-Japanese Relations, 1950–2006," *History and Memory* 19, no. 2 (2007): 44–45.

7. See Reinhard Drifte, "Engagement Japanese Style," in *Chinese-Japanese Relations in the Twenty-first Century: Complementarity and Conflict* (New York: Routledge, 2002), 53. See also Murata Koji, "Domestic Sources of Japanese Policy towards China," in *Japan's Relations with China: Facing a Rising Power*, ed. Lam Peng Er (London: Routledge, 2006), 39.

8. See also Wang Jisi, "China's Search for Stability with America," *Foreign Affairs* 84, no. 5 (September–October, 2005): 44.

9. Yang Bojiang, "Redefining Sino-Japanese Relations," 133.

10. Sueo Sudo, "It Takes Two to Tango: The Conflict as Japan Sees It," in *China and Japan at Odds: Deciphering the Perpetual Conflict for the Future*, ed. James C. Hsiung (New York: Palgrave, 2007), 43–57.

11. This was one element of the Joint Statement of Principles of the Six Party Talks in September 2005, and it was repeated in subsequent meetings. The text may be found in Northeast Asia Peace and Security Network (NAPSNet) Special Report, September 20, 2005, at http://nautilus.org.

12. See Japan External Trade Organization, "JETRO Survey: Analysis of Japan-China Trade in 2015," www.jetro.go.jp/en/news/releases/2016/c52b1f3efe0aa231.html; Global EDGE, "China: Trade Statistics," https://globaledge.msu.edu/countries/china/

tradestats; and Japan Ministry of Finance, "Trade Statistics of Japan," www.customs. go.jp/toukei/srch/indexe.htm.

13. Keiko Ujikane, "Japan Shifts Investment from China to Southeast Asia," *Bloomberg*, May 30, 2016, www.bloomberg.com/news/articles/2016-05-30/southeast-asia-is-winning-more-japanese-investment-than-china.

14. Ministry of Foreign Affairs, Japan, "Overview of Official Development Assistance (ODA) to China," February 1, 2016, www.mofa.go.jp/policy/oda/region/e_asia/china/.

15. I am indebted for this point to Prof. Peter Van Ness of the Australian National University.

16. "Japan-China Joint Press Statement," October 8, 2006, www.mofa.go.jp/region/asia-paci/china/joint0610.html.

17. Chinese text in *Renmin gang* (People.com), April 13, 2007, http://politics.people.com.cn/GB/1024/5608346.html.

18. Fukuda cited three areas: promoting mutual benefit (such as energy), mutual understanding (such as security), and international society (such as terrorism and North Korea). See Kazuyo Kato, "China-Japan Rapprochement in Perspective," *China Brief* 8, no. 1 (January 4, 2008), https://jamestown.org/program/china-japan-rapprochement-in-perspective/.

19. "Japan, China Reach Deal on Anti-Global Warming Project," *Yomiuri Shimbun*, November 30, 2007, in NAPSNet (Nautilus Institute), November 30, 2007, https://nautilus.org/napsnet/napsnet-daily-report/napsnet-daily-report-30-november-2007/#item17.

20. "Japan: Chinese Warship Visits," *NYT*, November 28, 2007, A16.

21. "China and Japan Arrive at Four-point Consensus in Principle on Handling and Improving Sino-Japanese Relations," *Renmin wang* (The People's Net), November 7, 2014, http://world.people.com.cn/n/2014/1107/c1002-25993302.html.

22. "Wang Yi: Hopes That Japan Seriously Treats, Fully Respects, and Faithfully Implements," *Renmin wang*, November 8, 2014, http://world.people.com.cn/n/2014/1108/c1002-25996194.html.

23. "The Four-Point Consensus Is a Test of Japan's Sincerity," *Renmin gang*, November 8, 2014, http://japan.people.com.cn/n/2014/1108/c35469-25994839.html.

24. This focus on interests draws inspiration from Roger Fisher, Elizabeth Kopelman, and Andrea Kupfer Schneider, *Beyond Machiavelli: Tools for Coping with Conflict* (Cambridge, MA: Harvard University Press, 1994).

25. See Shi Yinhong, "Sino-Japanese Rapprochement as a 'Diplomatic Revolution,'" www.uscc.gov/hearings/2003hearings/written_testimonies/031030bios/singjapprochement.htm. Shi urges that "the Chinese government, represented by our top leader, should frequently use appropriately strong language to express gratitude to Japan for its large scale economic assistance to China since the beginning of our 'Reform and Opening' in the late 1970s" (p. 4).

26. Ralph Jennings, "Japanese Aid Message Lost on Deaf Chinese Ears," *Japan Times*, January 11, 2005, www.asiamedia.ucla.edu/article.asp?parentid=19388; "Japan's Aid to China Is Not Unilateral Benefaction: FM Spokeswoman," *People's Daily Online* (Beijing), December 2, 2004. Moreover, PRC repayments of Japanese loans have regularly surpassed loan amounts since 2003.

27. Press release from the prime minister's office, "Joint Declaration by the Republic of India and the People's Republic of China," November 21, 2006, http://pib.nic.in/release/release.asp?relid=22168.

28. The fisheries agreement established a joint commission to manage overlapping fishing areas. The security dialogues, of which there have been seven (through 2006), also include exchanges of visits by military personnel. On the latter, see Christopher W. Hughes, *Japan's Security Agenda: Military, Economic, and Environmental Dimensions* (Boulder, CO: Lynne Rienner Publishers, 2004), box 5.3, p. 196.

29. For an extensive treatment of this issue, see my "U.S. Policy and Sino-Japanese Rivalry," in Hsiung, *China and Japan at Odds*, 113–131.

30. Minxin Pei and Michael Swaine, "Simmering Fire in Asia: Averting Sino-Japanese Strategic Conflict," *Policy Brief* [Carnegie Endowment for International Peace], no. 44 (November 2005): 7.

31. As Wu Xinbo writes: "If China has normal relations with the United States as well as Japan and trilateral relations are largely stable, Beijing will be less suspicious of a Washington-Tokyo axis . . . " Wu, "The End of the Silver Lining: A Chinese View of the U.S.-Japanese Alliance," *Washington Quarterly* 29, no. 1 (Winter 2005/2006): 128–129.

32. Japanese concerns about Washington's China policy were rife in the Nixon years, at the time of the visit to China, and when the Clinton administration established a "strategic partnership" with China. See Gerald L. Curtis, "U.S. Policy toward Japan from Nixon to Clinton: An Assessment," in *New Perspectives on U.S.-Japan Relations*, ed. Gerald L. Curtis (Tokyo: Japan Center for International Exchange, 2000), 9–19. On China's perspective, Yang Bojiang ("Redefining Sino-Japanese Relations," 135) writes that "the best choice for the United States would be to continue its alliance with Japan and South Korea and keep benign relations with China but also to transition to active promotion of multilateral cooperation throughout the region. Looking forward, the only way to resolve the regional security dilemma in East Asia completely is to promote multilateral security structures."

33. See Kenneth B. Pyle, *Japan Rising: The Resurgence of Japanese Power and Purpose* (New York: PublicAffairs, 2007), 337–38, 348.

34. Kent E. Calder, in "China and Japan's Simmering Rivalry," *Foreign Affairs* 85, no. 2 (March–April 2006): 136, suggests that energy cooperation provides an especially fruitful avenue for promoting Track II cooperation between China and Japan.

35. Mark J. Valencia, "The East China Sea Dispute: Context, Claims, Issues, and Possible Solutions," *Asian Perspective* 31, no. 1 (2007): 127–67.

36. A comprehensive study of the incident is Robert Y. Eng, "State Policy, Cyber-nationalism, and Popular Protest in the Senkaku-Diaoyu Territorial Dispute: Revisiting the 2010 Trawler Collision Incident" (unpublished manuscript, University of Redlands, Department of History, August 26, 2014).

37. Linus Hagström, "The Sino-Japanese Battle for Soft Power: Pitfalls and Promises," *Global Affairs* 1, no. 2 (2015): 129–137.

38. Minxin Pei and Danielle Cohen "A Vicious Sino-Japanese Cycle of Rhetoric," December 21, 2005, http://carnegieendowment.org/2005/12/21/vicious-sino-japanese-cycle-of-rhetoric-pub-17811. On *Sankei Shimbun*'s ability to silence critics of Japan's policies toward China, see David McNeill, "Softly, Softly," *Japan Focus*, July 18, 2007, www.japanfocus.org/products/topdf/2466.

39. Akio Takahara, "Japanese NGOs in China," in Lam, *Japan's Relations with China*, 166–179.

40. James Auer, ed., *From Marco Polo Bridge to Pearl Harbor: Who Was Responsible?* (Tokyo: The Yomiuri Shimbun, 2006).

41. China's official newspaper, the Beijing *People's Daily*, has certainly published its share of anti-Japanese articles, but it has also published positive commentaries, such as one endorsing "rational" and "moderate" nationalism in the two countries. See "Role of Nationalism in Sino-Japanese Relations," *People's Daily Online*, February 16, 2007.

42. Wakamiya Yoshibumi and Watanabe Tsuneo, "Yomiuri and Asahi Editors Call for a National Memorial to Replace Yasukuni," *Japan Focus*, February 28, 2006, www.japanfocus.org/article.asp?id=524.

43. Two other groups that have made proposals concerning China-Japan reconciliation are the International Crisis Group, "North East Asia's Undercurrents of Conflict," Report No. 108, December 15, 2005, www.crisisgroup.org/home/index.cfm?l+1&id=3834); and the Japan Forum on International Relations, Policy Council, "Japan and China in the Changing Asia" (Tokyo, 2006).

44. For specific proposals to resolve the East China Sea dispute, see Valencia, "The East China Sea Dispute."

45. I am indebted for these ideas to the stimulating article by Akikazu Hashimoto, Michael O'Hanlon, and Wu Xinbo, "A Framework for Resolving Japan-China Dispute Over Islands," *Los Angeles Times*, December 1, 2014, www.latimes.com/opinion/op-ed/la-oe-ohanlon-china-japan-senkaku-diaoyu-islands-20141130-story.html. See also International Crisis Group, "Old Scores and New Grudges: Evolving Sino-Japanese Tensions," Asia Report No. 258, Brussels, July 24, 2014.

46. Foreign Ministry of the PRC, Press Conference of Wang Yi, March 8, 2017, www.fmprc.gov.cn/web/zyxw/t1444028.shtml.

47. Chu Shulong of Qinghua University makes a similar suggestion in "A Mechanism to Stabilize U.S.-China-Japan Trilateral Relations in Asia," Brookings Institution, Center for Northeast Asian Policy Studies, Washington, DC, January 2008.

48. See Bernard Avishai, *A New Israel: Democracy in Crisis 1973–1988, Essays* (New York: Ticknor & Fields, 1990), 86–88. The Camp David Accords brought together Egyptian president Anwar el-Sadat and Israeli prime minister Menachem Begin in a meeting at Camp David, Maryland, presided over by US president Jimmy Carter. The summit produced a "Framework for Peace in the Middle East" that included a peace treaty between Egypt and Israel, which went into effect in 1979, and arrangements for eventual Palestinian self-rule in the West Bank and Gaza. However, neither the Palestinians or the Jordanians (both of whom were not represented at Camp David) nor other Arab states or the UN supported the latter agreements.

49. Breaking the Silence, *This Is How We Fought in Gaza: Soldiers' Testimony and Photographs from Operation "Protective Edge"* (n.p., 2014).

50. Nathan Thrall, "How the West Chose War in Gaza," *NYT*, July 17, 2014.

51. Advice, for example, from the former national security adviser, Zbigniew Brzezinski, who said: "I think we have to talk to everyone that's involved in this conflict, directly or indirectly. One doesn't gain anything by ostracism; it's a self-defeating posture." Zbigniew Brzezinski, interview by Jim Lehrer, *NewsHour*, PBS, July 18, 2006, www.pbs.org/newshour/bb/middle_east/july-dec06/mideast_07-18.html.

52. David Rose, "The Gaza Bombshell," *Vanity Fair*, April 2008, www.vanityfair.com/politics/features/2008/04/gaza200804.

53. Emile Nakhleh, *A Necessary Engagement: Reinventing America's Relations with the Muslim World* (Princeton, NJ: Princeton University Press, 2008), 92.

54. Nakhleh, *A Necessary Engagement*, 92.

55. See United Nations General Assembly, Report A/HRC/RES/S-9/1, https://unispal.un.org/DPA/DPR/unispal.nsf/0/404E93E166533F828525754E00559E30; and the Goldstone report at http://www2.ohchr.org/english/bodies/hrcouncil/specialsession/9/docs/A-HRC-S-9-2.doc. Goldstone subsequently expressed regret over one aspect of the report, namely, Israel's supposedly indiscriminate killing of civilians.

56. United Nations Office for the Coordination of Humanitarian Affairs and World Food Programme, "Between the Fence and a Hard Place," August 2010, www.ochaopt.org/documents/ocha_opt_special_focus_2010_08_19_english.pdf.

57. www.nytimes.com/2014/07/28/opinion/david-grossman-end-the-grindstone-of-israeli-palestinian-violence.html.

58. Kol Israel (national radio service) poll in December 2016, cited in www.geneva-accord.org/mainmenu/most-israelis-support-the-establishment-of-an-independent-palestinian-state. Other polls reported at www.geneva-accord.org likewise show strong Israeli support for negotiation of a two-state solution.

59. See David Remnick, "The Party Faithful," *New Yorker*, January 21, 2013, 38–49; and Hussein Agha and Robert Malley, "The Two-State Solution Doesn't Solve Anything," *NYT*, August 11, 2009, A17.

60. See the excellent account by a former senior US CIA analyst, Emile A. Nakhleh, *Necessary Engagement*, 92–97.

61. See Nakhleh, *Necessary Engagement*; Rashid Khalidi, *Brokers of Deceit: How the US Has Undermined Peace in the Middle East* (Boston: Beacon Press, 2013). See also Roger Cohen, "Why Israel Refuses to Choose," *NYT*, October 28, 2016.

62. Steven Erlanger, "Israel to Get $30 Billion in Military Aid from U.S.," *NYT*, August 17, 2007, A5.

63. SIPRI, http://armstrade.sipri.org/armstrade/html/export_toplist.php.

64. Shirl McArthur, "A Conservative Estimate of Total U.S. Direct Aid to Israel," *Washington Report on Middle East Affairs*, October–November, 2013, www.wrmea.org/2013-october-november/congress-watch-a-conservative-estimate-of-total-u.s.-direct-aid-to-israel-more-than-$130-billion.html. The remaining 74 percent of US military aid to Israel must be used to buy US weapons. In 2019 Israel will have to start buying US weapons with US aid.

65. Halper, *War Against the People: Israel, the Palestinians and Global Pacification* (London: Pluto Press, 2015), 36.

66. Cohen, "Why Israel Refuses to Choose."

67. Diana Buttu, "Why the Palestinian Authority Should be Shuttered," *NYT*, May 26, 2017.

68. "President Reuven Rivlin Address to the 15th Annual Herzliya Conference," http://www.president.gov.il/English/ThePresident/Speeches/Pages/news_070615_01. aspx. See also David Remnick, "The One-State Reality," *New Yorker*, November 17, 2014, 53.

69. Henry Siegman, "Can Obama Beat the Israel Lobby?," *Nation*, January 13, 2011, 11–15.

70. David Stout, "Israel's Nuclear Arsenal Vexed Nixon," *NYT*, November 29, 2007, A14.

71. Remnick, "The Party Faithful," 49.

72. Roger Cohen, "Her Jewish State," *New York Times Magazine*, July 8, 2007, 70.

73. I rely here on the account of Uri Savir, *The Process: 1,100 Days That Changed the Middle East* (New York: Random House, 1998).

74. Savir, *The Process*, 311.

75. "Israel and Palestine: Where to Go from Here," *Harper's*, September 2014, 29–43.

76. To some observers, prospects for a two-state solution seemed virtually nil at the end of 2016, because under Netanyahu "the political and cultural drift is toward ever more assertive and intolerant nationalism." Cohen, "Why Israel Refuses to Choose"; Isabel Kershner, "Israelis Wonder How Long Netanyahu Can Back Settlements and Two-State Solution," *NYT*, December 25, 2016.

77. Obama had the United States abstain on an otherwise unanimous UN Security Council resolution at the end of 2016 that was critical of the Israeli settlements and urged a return to negotiation of a two-state solution. Ordinarily, the United States would have vetoed the resolution. It was the first time in thirty-six years that such a resolution had passed.

78. Kerry, "Remarks on Middle East Peace," December 28, 2016, https://2009-2017. state.gov/secretary/remarks/2016/12/266119.htm.

79. Khalidi, "John Kerry and Israel: Too Little and Too Late," *NYT*, December 31, 2016.

80. Carter, *Peace Not Apartheid* (New York: Simon & Schuster, 2006); Gideon Levy, *The Punishment of Gaza* (London: Verso, 2010).

81. The wall, 85 percent of which goes through Palestinian land, currently is about 280 miles long, with another 170 miles yet to be constructed. Israel considers the wall a deterrent to "terrorist" attacks, but Palestinians say the wall not only prevents free movement but also obstructs access to water. A permit is required to pass through, which Palestinians consider humiliating. Where a gap in the wall exists, Palestinians cross illegally, but Israel's own figures indicate that very few attacks on Israelis occur near those locations, suggesting that the wall has very little value. Kamel Hawwash, "Israel's 'Apartheid Wall' Inspires More Violence Than It Deters," *Middle East Eye*, September 12, 2016, www.middleeasteye.net/columns/israels-apartheid-wall-inspires-more-violence-than-it-deters-2003696254.

82. In November 2012, by vote in the UN General Assembly, a Palestinian state received international recognition.

83. An Israeli foreign ministry lawyer delivered this opinion, which was not discovered in government archives until 2015. See Gershom Gorenberg, "Israel Knew All Along That Settlements, Home Demolitions Were Illegal," *Haaretz*, May 19, 2015, www.haaretz.com/misc/article-print-page/.premium-1.657167.

84. Carter, "America Must Recognize Palestine," *NYT*, November 28, 2016.

85. SC Resolution 242, passed unanimously in November 1967, asserted "the inadmissibility of the acquisition of territory by war" and Israeli withdrawal from territory occupied in the Six Day War.

86. The Geneva Accord calls for an end to the Occupation, restoration of the pre-1967 war borders, and creation of a Palestinian state, among other things. The text is in *Tikkun*, January–February 2004, 33–45, and at www.tikkun.org/article.php/JanFeb2004TOC.

87. Kerry, "Remarks on Middle East Peace."

88. Joel Braunold and Sarah Yerkes, "Is a Peace Deal Possible if Israelis and Palestinians Simply Don't Trust Each Other? January 3, 2017, www.brookings.edu/blog/markaz/2017/01/03/is-a-peace-deal-possible-if-israelis-and-palestinians-simply-dont-trust-each-other/.

89. See www.cartercenter.org/news/documents/doc1556.html.

90. From the Herbert C. Kelman Institute, "Conference Report: The Transformation of Intractable Conflicts: Perspectives and Challenges for Interactive Problem Solving," March 27–29, 2014, 7, http://kelmaninstitute.org/wp-content/uploads/2014/05/Harvard-Conference-Report-Intractable-Conflicts_web.pdf.

91. Kelman Institute, "Conference Report," 11.

92. Thomas L. Friedman, "The Last Train," *NYT*, October 26, 2014.

93. David Remnick, "Seeds of Peace: Ayman Odeh's Unlikely Crusade," *New Yorker*, January 25, 2016, 24–30.

94. Netanyahu's tenure may be shorter than expected, however. A corruption scandal had by mid-2017 implicated some of his closest advisers as well as his wife. Netanyahu himself may face corruption charges.

SEVEN

Engagement

Lessons for Policy Makers and Peacemakers

TAKING RISKS

In an interview with President Obama in 2015, Thomas L. Friedman asked if the president could define his doctrine. Obama responded:

> We are powerful enough to be able to test these propositions without putting ourselves at risk. And that's the thing . . . people don't seem to understand. . . . You take a country like Cuba. For us to test the possibility that engagement leads to a better outcome for the Cuban people, there aren't that many risks for us. It's a tiny little country. It's not one that threatens our core security interests, and so [there's no reason not] to test the proposition. And if it turns out that it doesn't lead to better outcomes, we can adjust our policies. The same is true with respect to Iran, a larger country, a dangerous country, one that has engaged in activities that resulted in the death of U.S. citizens, but the truth of the matter is: Iran's defense budget is $30 billion. Our defense budget is closer to $600 billion. Iran understands that they cannot fight us. . . . You asked about an Obama doctrine. The doctrine is: We will engage, but we preserve all our capabilities. [1]

Two points are worth underlining in Obama's statement. The first is that engagement may be thought of as a test of an adversary's intentions. It is revocable; if engagement doesn't draw out the adversary, or if the adversary seeks to take advantage of engagement's "softness," the stronger party can withdraw the offer. The peace community often proclaims, "give peace a chance." Obama said on January 21, 2013: "We will show the courage to try and resolve our differences with other nations peacefully—not because we are naïve about the dangers we face, but because

159

engagement can more durably lift suspicion and fear."[2] Testing the possibility of a peaceful outcome is a crucial element of an engagement strategy. But to be a fair test, engagement must be pursued consistently, even doggedly, with the immediate aim of conflict management rather than conflict resolution.

The second point is that the stronger party can always move to a tough policy. The gun remains in the holster, but is available for use. In the Cuban case, the "gun" was (and remains) the US embargo, which Obama eased by executive action. But it is still in place on many items. With Iran and North Korea, the "gun" was (and remains) real: "all options are on the table" has been the US fallback position for a long time.

For a diplomatic strategy of engagement to be credible, the key is handling the gun so that it isn't a threat that draws attention away from the offer to engage. At the very least, "getting to yes" with an adversary takes the use of force off the table. Force is always available, but as a deterrent; its punitive use should never have equal status with efforts to stimulate talks and reciprocal concessions. The same is true regarding threats to use of force; they often backfire, leading not only to counterthreats but also to solidifying the other side's posture as a victim and strengthening its domestic support against the enemy. We see this counterproductive effect of threats in US-DPRK and US-Iran relations today; it has also been the case in US relations with Cuba, China, and Russia.

Whether or not an effort to engage an adversary will yield fruit, the argument here is that a government is usually better off making the attempt before deciding on sanctions or use of force. I have mentioned numerous approaches for engaging without loss of face or fear that engagement will be taken for weakness. Apologizing, taking symbolic steps, and stopping use of negative stereotypes and demonizing language are among those options. Intercultural research has shown that sensitivity to cultural distinctions in international relationships can be a major contributor to progress in dialogue.[3] Likewise, the choice of format, procedures, and participants in international dialogue may also have much to do with outcomes.[4] As the Iranian, Cuban, and other cases have shown, engagement-minded NGOs operating under Tracks II and III do shape the policy environment. All these forms of engagement play into official steps under Track I, when only a government's decision can take engagement to a higher level. Negative security assurances, exchanges of diplomats, confidence-building measures such as military redeployments, and offers of aid or other material inducements then become critical. The bottom line is that engagement of an adversary, once set in motion, may yield unexpected benefits. Call it a positive domino effect.

Underlying engagement diplomacy is a more fundamental key to success, empathy: seeing the world through the eyes of the other party.

Obama clearly understood the role of historical grievances in Iran's and Cuba's views of the United States, and while he surely did not agree with every element of that view, he (and those who supported him) knew that effectively reaching out to those countries' leaders would require responding directly and humanely to their viewpoints. And we can deduce from the response to Obama—for example, Raúl Castro's commendation of Obama for his "respect and acknowledgment of our people"—that empathy is rewarded. Where empathy is lacking, as in Sino-Japanese relations, or where it gets buried, as in Israeli-Palestinian relations after Oslo, past grievances will be exceptionally difficult to overcome.

The ultimate aim of engagement is to transform a relationship.[5] Transformation does not have to mean friendship, but it does imply acceptance of change to mutual advantage. Israelis and Palestinians, and Americans and North Koreans, may never see eye to eye on many issues, but if they accept each other's international legitimacy, acknowledge each other's grievances, and understand each other's security needs—all of which, again, requires empathy—a genuine transformation is possible. Relying on regime change on the assumption that different leaders will increase the odds of accommodation is a fool's errand. In the possibly long period before a new leader emerges, new sources of grievance can arise, deepening tensions and suspicions. And that new leader may prove even less malleable than the previous one.

A critical part of any effort by adversaries to design a new relationship is accepting that *the two sides need each other*. China and Japan, the United States and China, even Israelis and Palestinians can gain mutual advantages from improving relations—economically first of all, but also culturally, educationally, and certainly strategically. The advantages sometimes extend to third parties and to regional or global issues, where a common position enhances their perspective. The essential argument here is that peaceful, cooperative relations are in everyone's best interest, and that there is a high and increasing price to be paid for indifference to the consequences of ongoing rivalry.

NOTHING SUCCEEDS LIKE SUCCESS: EVALUATING ENGAGEMENT

How should engagement be evaluated? If a country repeatedly rejects incentives to talk or takes actions that suggest it has no interest in being engaged, has engagement therefore failed? On the other hand, if negative responses to engagement clear the way for tough actions, such as sanctions, should engagement be judged a success (because it brought out the other side's true motives) or a failure (because it proved naïve)? Clearly, not every form of diplomatic outreach really constitutes *engagement*. Principles of engagement are neither well defined nor uniformly applied, making an assessment of policies using a single set of standards rather difficult. Context matters; if attempts to engage the adversary are coupled with threats or shows of force, can the policy properly be characterized as engagement? Barack Obama's foreign policy in his second term, in contrast with his first, was said to be based on a "light footprint" but also on "coercive diplomacy."[6] Such a dual track does not suggest a fundamental departure from US foreign policy as it has been practiced for many years. Yet he did have two successful ventures in engagement.

The successes with Iran and Cuba are by their nature different in many respects, starting with the geopolitical facts that Cuba lies just off US shores and thus falls within "America's backyard," while Iran is embedded within the complexity of Middle East politics and the primary US interest in Israel's security. Then there are special features such as Iran's nuclear weapons potential, Cuba's socialism, the Cuban-American diaspora, Iran's direct or indirect involvement in nearby conflicts, and the Israeli factor in US relations with Iran.

Nevertheless, engagement strategies bring the two cases together. Political obstacles within Cuba, Iran, and the United States have been paramount, making it very difficult for a US leader interested in engagement to stick to a consistent approach and equally difficult for a Cuban or Iranian leader to entertain the idea of engagement. Incentives were crucial to bringing the parties together, but finding the right ones proved a challenge. Overcoming historical memory was then and always will be a major barrier, yet the key point is that history was not allowed to stand in the way of agreement. Backsliding is certainly possible in both the Cuban and Iranian cases, especially with Iran because the level of mutual trust is so low, the nuclear issue isn't fully resolved, and relations between the United States and Iran are deeply embedded in unresolved wars next door to Iran. Thus, the margin for error is likewise larger with Iran and would be even if Obama's successor were not predetermined to scrap the nuclear agreement.

Ideally, the nuclear agreement with Iran and the formal ties with Cuba should be followed by further incentives to deeper engagement: with Iran to normalize diplomatic and economic relations, and with Cuba to end the embargo and speed up mutually beneficial economic ties. Unfortunately, all these actions seem like distant possibilities at this writing.

CHALLENGES

One challenging part of an engagement strategy is finding the right menu of incentives and being able to implement them. The incentives themselves require sensitivity to what is most meaningful to one's adversary and not merely consideration of what one is willing to give up. Implementing incentives also requires paying close attention to one's own political scene and determining which ones will pass muster and/or generate the least criticism. Navigating on the domestic front is especially hazardous because engagement efforts are fairly easy to derail or dilute by methods such as exaggerating their demerits and insisting on inserting conditions into agreements that opponents know will be deal breakers.

A second challenge is correctly reading an adversary's actions and intentions. Take Iran's and North Korea's missile tests, for example. Iran carried out ballistic missile tests in 2017 that led the Trump administration to impose sanctions, even though Iran maintained (correctly) that the tests fell outside the nuclear agreement, did not involve missiles with a nuclear weapon capability, and were intended to bolster deterrence of hostile states nearby. North Korea's ballistic missile tests violated various UN Security Council bans, and each series lengthened the missiles' range and destructive capacity. Like the Iranians, the North Koreans claimed that the aim of the tests was to be able to deter a US attack, which US shows of force and Trump's belligerent language made credible. The missile tests complicated diplomacy, but should they have been taken as grounds for abandoning engagement efforts? I think not; as long as the engagement project is promising, the inevitable bumps in the road should not deter moving ahead.

Time is a third challenge. Engagement is not an easy road to travel; it takes great patience and perseverance, qualities that government leaders usually don't have.[7] Officials will insist that they have made an honest effort, only to be thwarted by an adversary that won't be forthcoming or has no interest in engaging. That may sometimes be so, but more often than not the real problem is that engagement has not been consistently pursued or has been undermined by domestic opposition. As I said in chapter 2, engagement is much more than talking or even formally negotiating. It is a lengthy, multilevel process, measured in years, not months; witness the roughly nine years of on-again, off-again talks between the United States and Iran. Talking includes avoiding (and ignoring the other side's) threats and hostile language, seeking common ground, and especially identifying meaningful incentives. Government officials often seem content to try dialogue and give up when talking doesn't quickly yield the concessions they demand. That practice is far from what I mean by engaging an adversary.

A fourth challenge is the competence of the people who make decisions about carrots and sticks. Time and again we encounter credible critiques of higher-level officials who have ignored the foreign-policy professionals, reacted to situations abroad on ideological and personal rather than empirical grounds, and thus reached for the gun before trying diplomacy.[8] People whose work on other countries is grounded in history, language, and cultural studies don't necessarily have all the answers; we might recall the failure of expertise in US relations with the former

Soviet Union, as opposed to ignoring or underappreciating expertise in US decision making on conflicts in the Middle East. Still, the country experts cannot be casually dismissed by leaders who have an ax to grind and are viscerally opposed to the idea of engagement, as was apparent among George W. Bush's inner circle in the decision to attack Iraq after September 11, 2001. In general, the problem here may be that the closer adversaries come to violent conflict, the less expertise is valued or consulted.

FACILITATING ENGAGEMENT

Apologizing, or at least accepting responsibility for, a wrongful act can work wonders. Two lessons emerge from my study of using apologies to advance international relationships. They both come from the US-Iran case. The first is that engagement before apologizing stands a much better chance of being effective than apologizing without engaging. The nuclear deal between Tehran and the United States and other parties clearly facilitated the quick release of the US sailors. That deal cemented positive relations between Secretary of State Kerry and Foreign Minister Zarif, promoted trust as both sides fulfilled their commitments under the deal, and at least temporarily isolated hard-liners opposed to the deal in the United States and Iran. As one consequence, Iran's seizure of ten US sailors whose patrol boats entered Iranian territorial waters did not, literally, muddy the waters. The nuclear agreement held.

A second lesson about apologizing is that domestic politics rules when leaders consider apologizing. Iran's release of the US sailors was carried out after a minimal apology from their commander, not from the US government itself. That was possible because both countries' leaderships did their due political diligence, ensuring that critics in both countries had no opportunity to garner support for punitive action. The Pentagon admitted that the two patrol boats had violated Iran's territory and that mechanical failure was not the reason.

Facilitating engagement requires searching for avenues of cooperation, and one fruitful issue is global warming and other immediate threats to the environment. That common ground has been so difficult to achieve speaks to the mixture of denial, uncertainty, and especially national economic interests that together undermine agreements with real teeth. The Paris accord, with its pledge to keep global temperature rise to 1.5 degrees Celsius, is probably unattainable, as evidenced by the continuing rise in carbon particles in the air (the highest in recorded history) and average world temperatures (the hottest on record). Thus we see the West Antarctic ice sheet disintegrating; coral reefs being damaged beyond repair; floods and hurricanes becoming more frequent than ever;

unprecedented species loss; and rising oceans that threaten island nations and, soon, major cities worldwide.

If the major powers were to make environmental protection, starting with climate change, a top-priority national security issue, it could provide the foundation for engagement between adversaries. Relations between the United States and China could be the starting point, taking off from pledges made by Barack Obama and Xi Jinping on climate change and building with increased investments in soft energy sources; reduced petroleum consumption; and cooperative research to protect threatened species, forests, and water supplies. All of the cases explored in this book offer opportunities for cooperation on important common environmental problems, such as water in Israeli-Palestinian relations, fisheries in Chinese-Japanese relations, and biodiversity on the Korean peninsula. Where governmental agreements are not feasible, NGOs may fill the gap; where countrywide coverage is not possible, city and county action may be possible.

Every country's public diplomacy would also benefit from effective engagement. On its own, public diplomacy directed at any adversary may lack credibility, particularly if actions on the ground belie professions of support for social justice, human rights, and other universal values. Engagement efforts may provide that credibility by demonstrating commitment to reducing tensions and willingness to embark on a more respectful and stable relationship. As engagement deepens, opportunities for public diplomacy may open up, even in countries where it would otherwise be treated as "enemy propaganda." For example, Track III people-to-people programs that provide meaningful services in a targeted country, if combined with inducements to engage at other levels, may alleviate official suspicions there while at the same time serving as useful elements of public diplomacy.

Other lessons that emerge from the case studies provide lessons for conducting diplomacy in the human interest. Leave grievances at home. Tackle the easiest (win-win) issues first. Practice mutual respect. Avoid stereotyping and demonizing an adversary; instead, acknowledge the adversary's legitimacy. The Oslo experience teaches that even the most intractable conflicts are capable of transformation, that even the most hardened enemies can become partners in the search for a just peace and can achieve mutual respect once they perceive one another as human beings with valid histories rather than irremediably evil intentions. After all, *for whom* do we want engagement? Not so much for states, institutions, or other units of international affairs as for real people caught in the middle of conflict—innocent people who want nothing so much as to live in peace where they wish.

Having said that, not all international conflicts are amenable to peaceful solutions or to engagement. Peace is a wonderful idea, peace with justice even better. But we must be clear in our own minds what peace means in particular circumstances and how it may have to be qualified to reach an agreement or simply ruled out as unattainable for now. For example, US relations with North Korea and Russia, and China-Japan and Israel-Palestine relations, are all fraught with the potential for violent new confrontations. None of them has built-in mechanisms for conflict management, and none have honest brokers available to mediate disputes. Moreover, domestic politics in every one of the parties in these rivalries weighs against finding common ground or taking risks for peace. From the outside we can suggest various ways these adversaries might engage one another, but as I have shown, prospects are dim for acceptance of an engagement strategy.

THE FUTURE OF ENGAGEMENT

The margin for error on engagement is slim. It is subject to dilution or outright reversal once the practitioner leaves office. Such is the case in 2017. Notions of partnership and collaboration on many crucial international issues are fast disappearing. International politics resembles anarchy far more than it does engagement. A hard-edged nationalism is on the rise in Europe and elsewhere. Most unfortunate is that the momentum on engagement created under Barack Obama seems to be withering away. The Trump administration has favored all the standard actions typical of US-style crisis management: reprisals, sanctions, warnings, force deployments, and threats. These actions violate a cardinal rule of diplomacy: threats will most likely produce a reaction exactly opposite to the one desired. They will incite nationalist fervor, invite counterthreats, and obstruct dialogue.

History's lessons can easily be misread or ignored, however. Simon Critchley tells of the "moral responsibility of knowledge" that he learned from a television series in the 1970s hosted by Dr. Jacob Bronowski.[9] There is no such thing as scientific certainty said Bronowski, a Polish-born British mathematician whose parents were murdered at Auschwitz. A "tolerance principle" should apply in science as in everyday life to allow for margins of error. We always know less than we think we know. Fundamentalists, fascists, and others who preach with scientific certainty are thus particular dangers, now as then. Those who today think they *know* for a fact who is the devil and who is the angel—who *are certain* about historical cycles and God's will—are the same people who gave us Auschwitz, the gulag, apartheid, and Sarajevo, not to mention Hiroshima, Nagasaki, and Vietnam.

And now "radical Islamic terrorism." With demagoguery in vogue today in the United States and Europe, the lessons of Auschwitz are in danger of being unlearned. Leaders have turned inward and turned on immigrants and refugees as scapegoats for enduring social and economic problems. Doors are closing, civil society is being disrupted, and violence against "the other" is on the rise. All this is being done in the name of national and ethnic pride—"America First," for example—and while globalism has produced more than its share of inequities, it has also become a convenient target for those who reject international cooperation on human rights, alleviation of poverty, environmental protection, and common security. For some observers, international politics today bears frightening resemblances to the 1930s.

But international relations are cyclical. A period of intense competition and conflict can suddenly give way to cooperation and peacemaking. It all depends on core values, leadership, and interpretations of national interest. Richard Nixon's trip to China started a new era in US-China relations. The fall of the Soviet Union created opportunities for changing East-West relations. And Barack Obama reached out to Iran, Cuba, and other countries in search of reduced tensions and new exchanges. So prospects for engagement may appear suddenly. But only farsighted leaders can grasp the opportunity to change history.

Martin Luther King Jr. said, "The arc of the moral universe is long, but it bends toward justice." Advocates of engagement must believe that, and carry on.

NOTES

1. Friedman, "Obama Makes His Case on Iran," *NYT*, July 15, 2015.
2. Inaugural Address, January 21, 2013, https://obamawhitehouse.archives.gov/the-press-office/2013/01/21/inaugural-address-president-barack-obama.
3. See Raymond Cohen, *Negotiating Across Cultures: International Communication in an Interdependent World* (Washington, DC: US Institute of Peace, 1997).
4. See Harold Saunders, *A Public Peace Process: Sustained Dialogue to Transform Racial and Ethnic Conflicts* (London: Palgrave Macmillan, 2001), and Herbert C. Kelman, "The Problem-Solving Workshop in Conflict Resolution," in *Communication in International Politics*, ed. Richard L. Merritt (Urbana: University of Illinois Press, 1972), 168–204.
5. On transforming the relationship between disputing parties, see Louis Kriesberg, *Constructive Conflicts: From Escalation to Resolution*, 2d ed. (Lanham, MD: Rowman & Littlefield, 2003).
6. David E. Sanger, "In Step on 'Light Footprint,' Nominees Reflect a Shift," *NYT*, January 8, 2013.
7. Obama, when asked in December 2013 about the odds that a nuclear agreement with Iran would succeed, put them at no better than 50–50. But he added: "What we do have to test is the possibility we can resolve this issue diplomatically. If at the end of six months it turns out we can't make a deal, we are no worse off." Bradley Klapper and Darlene Superville, "Obama on Iran: Diplomacy Is the Best Approach," *Huffington Post*, December 7, 2013, www.huffingtonpost.com/2013/12/07/obama-iran-diplomacy_n_4404991.html.
8. See, for example, John Nixon's study of Saddam Hussein and Iraq, based on years of work for the CIA: *Debriefing the President: The Interrogation of Saddam Hussein* (New York: Blue Rider Press, 2016).
9. Simon Critchley, "The Dangers of Certainty: A Lesson from Auschwitz," *NYT*, February 2, 2014.

Selected Bibliography

Included here are the principal books, journal articles, research reports, and official documents consulted for this book. Omitted are numerous news articles and some less-used publications that are cited in the endnotes.

BOOKS

Bustamante, Michael J. "Obama's Move on Cuba." In *Cuba Libre? U.S.-Cuban Relations from Revolution to Rapprochement*, edited by Gideon Rose, 304–311. New York: Foreign Affairs, 2016.

Carlin, Robert, and John W. Lewis, eds. *Negotiating with North Korea: 1992–2007*. Stanford, CA: Center for International Security and Cooperation, 2008.

Clemens, Walter C., Jr. *Getting to Yes in Korea*. Boulder, CO: Paradigm, 2010.

———. *North Korea and the World: Human Rights, Arms Control, and Strategies for Negotiation*. Lexington: University Press of Kentucky, 2016.

Cohen, Raymond. *Negotiating Across Cultures: International Communication in an Interdependent World*. Washington, DC: US Institute of Peace, 1997.

Gurtov, Mel. *Global Politics in the Human Interest*. 5th ed. Boulder, CO: Lynne Rienner Publishers, 2013.

———. *Will This Be China's Century? A Skeptic's View*. Boulder, CO: Lynne Rienner Publishers, 2013.

Hoff, Joan. *A Faustian Foreign Policy from Woodrow Wilson to George W. Bush: Dreams of Perfectibility*. Cambridge, UK: Cambridge University Press, 2007.

Kelman, Herbert C. "The Problem-Solving Workshop in Conflict Resolution." In *Communication in International Politics*, edited by Richard L. Merritt, 168–204. Urbana: University of Illinois Press, 1972.

Kim, Samuel S. *The Two Koreas and the Great Powers*. New York: Cambridge University Press, 2006.

Kriesberg, Louis. *Constructive Conflicts: From Escalation to Resolution*. 2d ed. Lanham, MD: Rowman & Littlefield, 2003.

Legvold, Robert. *Return to Cold War*. Cambridge, UK: Polity, 2016.

LeoGrande, William M. "Cuba: Public Diplomacy as a Battle of Ideas." In *Isolate or Engage: Adversarial States, US Foreign Policy, and Public Diplomacy*, edited by Geoffrey Wiseman, 231–258. Stanford, CA: Stanford University Press, 2015.

LeoGrande, William M., and Peter Kornbluh. *Back Channel to Cuba: The Hidden History of Negotiations between Washington and Havana*. Chapel Hill: University of North Carolina Press, 2014.

Limbert, John W. *Negotiating with Iran: Wrestling the Ghosts of History*. Washington, DC: United States Institute of Peace Press, 2009.

Moon, Chung-in. *The Sunshine Policy: In Defense of Engagement as a Path to Peace in Korea*. Seoul: Yonsei University Press, 2012.

Nakhleh, Emile. *A Necessary Engagement: Reinventing America's Relations with the Muslim World*. Princeton, NJ: Princeton University Press, 2008.

Nincic, Miroslav. *The Logic of Positive Engagement*. Ithaca, NY: Cornell University Press, 2011.

Nixon, John. *Debriefing the President: The Interrogation of Saddam Hussein*. New York: Blue Rider Press, 2016.

Osgood, Charles. *An Alternative to War and Surrender*. Urbana: University of Illinois Press, 1962.

Parsi, Trita. *Losing An Enemy: Obama, Iran, and the Triumph of Diplomacy*. New Haven, CT: Yale University Press, 2017.

———. *A Single Roll of the Dice*. New Haven, CT: Yale University Press, 2013.

———. *Treacherous Alliance: The Secret Dealings of Israel, Iran, and the United States*. New Haven, CT: Yale University Press, 2007.

Pei, Minxin. *China's Crony Capitalism: The Dynamics of Regime Decay*. Cambridge, MA: Harvard University Press, 2016.

Rose, Gideon, ed. *Cuba Libre? U.S.-Cuban Relations from Revolution to Rapprochement*. New York: Foreign Affairs, 2016.

Saalman, Lora, ed. *China-Russia Relations and Regional Dynamics: From Pivots to Peripheral Diplomacy*. Stockholm: Stockholm International Peace Research Institute, 2017.

Saunders, Harold. *A Public Peace Process: Sustained Dialogue to Transform Racial and Ethnic Conflicts*. London: Palgrave Macmillan, 2001.

Shambaugh, David, ed. *Tangled Titans: The United States and China*. Lanham, MD: Rowman & Littlefield, 2013.

Swaine, Michael, and Zhang Tuosheng, eds. *Managing Sino-American Crises: Case Studies and Analysis*. Washington, DC: Carnegie Endowment for International Peace, 2006.

Wiseman, Geoffrey, ed. *Isolate or Engage: Adversarial States, US Foreign Policy, and Public Diplomacy*. Stanford, CA: Stanford University Press, 2015.

ARTICLES

Baek, Jieun. "The Opening of the North Korean Mind: Pyongyang Versus the Digital Underground." *Foreign Affairs* 96, no. 1 (January–February 2017): 104–113.

Bajoria, Jayshree, and Beina Xu. "The Six Party Talks on North Korea's Nuclear Program." Council on Foreign Relations, September 30, 2013. http://www.cfr.org/proliferation/six-party-talks-north-koreas-nuclear-program/p13593.

Berger, Andrea. "The New UNSC Sanctions Resolution on North Korea: A Deep Dive Assessment." 38 North, March 2, 2016. http://38north.org/2016/03/aberger030216/.

Bonsal, Philip. "Cuba, Castro and the United States." *Foreign Affairs* (January 1967). http://www.foreignaffairs.com/articles/cuba/1967-01-01/cuba-castro-and-united-states.

Bruck, Connie. "Exiles." *New Yorker*, March 6, 2006, 46–63.

Calder, Kent E. "China and Japan's Simmering Rivalry." *Foreign Affairs* 85, no. 2 (March–April 2006): 29–39.

Chan, Melissa K. "Reporting from China: 400 Reports, on 1.4 Billion People, in One Authoritarian State." *International Journal of Communication*, no. 11 (2017). http://ijoc.org/index.php/ijoc/article/view/5155/1976.

Clemens, Walter C., Jr., "From Prisoner Release to Normal Links with North Korea?" *Diplomat*, October 8, 2014. http://thediplomat.com/2014/10/from-prisoner-release-to-normal-links-with-north-korea/.

———. "How to Deal With Kim Jong Un." *Global Asia* 10, no. 4 (winter 2015): 68–78.

Clifton, Eli, and Ali Gharib. "The Iranophobia Lobby Machine." *Nation*, August 4–11, 2014, 21–24.

Cockburn, Andrew. "The New Red Scare." *Harper's*, December 2016, 25–31.

Cohen, Stephen F., and Katrina vanden Heuvel. "Coalition or Cold War?" *Nation*, December 21–28, 2015. http://www.thenation.com/article/coalition-or-cold-war-with-russia-2/.

Delury, John. "The Disappointments of Disengagement: Assessing Obama's North Korea Policy." *Asian Perspective* 37 (2013): 149–182.

Economy, Elizabeth. "Beijing Is No Champion of Globalization." *Foreign Affairs*, January 22, 2017. http://www.foreignaffairs.com/articles/china/2017-01-22/beijing-no-champion-globalization.

Etzioni, Amitai. "The Asian Infrastructure Investment Bank: A Case Study of Multifaceted Containment." *Asian Perspective* 40, no. 2 (2016): 173–196.

Fukuyama, Francis. "Reflections on Chinese Governance." Center on Democracy, Development, and the Rule of Law. February 2016. http://fsi.stanford.edu/sites/default/files/fukuyama_feb.16_wp_0.pdf.

Fyffe, Steve. "Hecker Assesses North Korean Hydrogen Bomb Claims." *Bulletin of the Atomic Scientists*, January 7, 2016. http://thebulletin.org/hecker-assesses-north-korean-hydrogen-bomb-claims9046#.

Gordon, Joy. "El Bloqueo." *Harper's*, July 2016, 49–55.

Gurtov, Mel. "Are We in a 'Post-American Era'?" *China-US Focus*, November 1, 2017, https://www.chinausfocus.com/foreign-policy/2017/1101/15635.html.

———. "Averting War in Northeast Asia: A Proposal." Asia-Pacific Journal 9, no. 2 (January 10, 2011). http://japanfocus.org/-Mel-Gurtov/3467.

———. "Rules and Rocks: The US-China Standoff Over the South China Sea."http://apjjf.org/2015/13/23/Mel-Gurtov/4330.html.

———. "Trouble at Sea." http://apjjf.org/-Mel-Gurtov/4795/article.html.

———. "Trump and Xi in Beijing: A Snapshot," China-US Focus, November 17 , 2017, https://www.chinausfocus.com/foreign-policy/trump-and-xi-in-beijing-a-snapshot.

———. "Trump Faces China: Some Unsettling Thoughts." *China-US Focus*, December 22, 2016. http://www.chinausfocus.com/foreign-policy/trump-faces-china-some-unsettling-thoughts.

———. "The Uncertain Future of US-China Relations." *Asia-Pacific Journal—Japan Focus* 11, no. 52 (December 27, 2013). http://apjjf.org/2013/11/52/Mel-Gurtov/4052/article.html.

Hanham, Melissa. "North Korea's Procurement Network Strikes Again: Examining How Chinese Missile Hardware Wound Up in Pyongyang." *NTI (Nuclear Threat Initiative)*, July 31, 2012. http://www.nti.org/analysis/articles/north-koreas-procurement-network-strikes-again-examining-how-chinese-missile-hardware-ended-pyongyang/.

He Weiwen, "What's Next After Beef?" *China-US Focus Digest* 14 (June 2017): 34–38.

Hersh, Michael. "North Korea's Kim Jong Il." *Newsweek*, October 21, 2006. http://www.newsweek.com/north-koreas-kim-jong-il-111871.

Hersh, Seymour. "The Coming Wars." *New Yorker*, January 24–31, 2005, 40–47.

———, "The Iran Plans." *New Yorker*, April 17, 2006, 30–37.

———. "The Next Act." *New Yorker*, November 27, 2006, 94–107.

Jannuzi, Frank. "Roadblocks Removed: Can the US Travel the Diplomatic Path with the DPRK?" November 9, 2014. http://38north.org/2014/11/fjannuzi110914/.

Jervis, Robert. "Getting to Yes with Iran: The Challenge of Coercive Diplomacy." *Foreign Affairs* 92, no. 1 (January–February, 2013): 105–115.

Johnson, Keith, and Dan De Luce. "U.S. Gears Up to Challenge Beijing's 'Great Wall of Sand.'" *Foreign Policy*, September 22, 2015. http://foreignpolicy.com/2015/09/22/u-s-gears-up-to-challenge-beijings-great-wall-of-sand-obama-xi-south-china-sea/.

Kang, Tae-ho. "North Korea Inches Toward Negotiations on Its Nuclear Ambitions." *Global Asia* 9, no. 1 (Spring 2014); 58–67.

Kell, John. "Trump Tower Funded by Rich Chinese Who Wanted Visas." *Forbes*, March 7, 2016. http://fortune.com/2016/03/07/trump-tower-chinese-visas/.

Kotkin, Stephen. "Russia's Perpetual Geopolitics." *Foreign Affairs* 93, no. 3 (May–June 2016): 2–9.

Kornbluh, Peter. "A New Deal with Cuba." *Nation*, January 12–19, 2015, 4–8.

———. "Obama in Cuba." *Nation*, April 25–May 2, 2016, 14–18.

———. "US-Cuban Diplomacy, *Nation* Style." *Nation*, April 29, 2013, 20–23.

Kornbluh, Peter, and William M. LeoGrande. "Cuba Confidential: Inside the Crazy Back-Channel Negotiations That Revolutionized Our Relationship with Cuba." *Mother Jones*, September–October 2015. http://www.motherjones.com/politics/2015/07/secret-negotiations-gross-hernandez-kerry-pope-obama-castro-cuba.

Kramer, Mark. "The Myth of a No-NATO-Enlargement Pledge to Russia." *Washington Quarterly* 32, no. 2 (April 2009): 39–61.

Kupchan, Charles A. "Enemies into Friends: How the United States Can Court Its Adversaries." *Foreign Affairs* 89, no. 2 (March–April 2010): 120–134.

Lankov, Andrei. "Is Byungjin Policy Failing? Kim Jong Un's Unannounced Reform and Its Chances of Success." *Korean Journal of Defense Analysis* 29, no. 1 (March 2017): 25–45.

Lieberthal, Kenneth, and Wang Jisi. "Addressing U.S.-China Strategic Distrust." Brookings Institution, John L. Thornton China Center Report no. 4 (March 2012).

Lukyanov, Fyodor. "Putin's Foreign Policy: The Quest to Restore Russia's Rightful Place." *Foreign Affairs* 95, no. 3 (May–June 2016): 30–37.

Lynch, Colum. "To Assuage Russia, Obama Administration Backed Off Syria Chemical Weapons Plan." *Foreign Policy*, May 19, 2017. http://foreignpolicy.com/2017/05/19/to-assuage-russia-obama-administration-backed-off-syria-chemical-weapons-plan/.

———. "U.N. Panel: North Korea Used Chinese Bank to Evade Nuclear Sanctions." *Foreign Policy*, March 7, 2016. http://foreignpolicy.com/2016/03/07/u-n-panel-north-korea-used-chinese-bank-to-evade-nuclear-sanctions/?wp_login_redirect=0.

Maloney, Suzanne. "How to Contain a Nuclear Iran." Brookings Institution. March 12, 2012. http://www.brookings.edu/opinions/2012/0305_nuclear_iran_maloney.aspx?p=1.

Moon, Chung-in, and Ildo Hwang. "Identity, Supreme Dignity, and North Korea's External Behavior: A Cultural/Ideational Perspective." *Korea Observer* 45, no. 1 (Spring 2014): 1–37.

Nathan, Andrew. "Who Is Kim Jong-un?" *New York Review of Books*, August 18, 2016. http://www.nybooks.com/articles/2016/08/18/who-is-kim-jong-un/.

Osnos, Evan, David Remnick, and Joshua Yaffa. "Active Measures." *New Yorker*, March 6, 2017, 40–55.

Parsi, Trita. "Iran Deal More than a Nuclear Issue." *Middle East Eye*, December 7, 2014. http://www.middleeasteye.net/columns/iran-deal-more-nuclear-issue-1767492686.

———. "Pen-Palling with the Ayatollah." *Foreign Policy*, November 7, 2014. http://foreignpolicy.com/2014/11/07/pen-palling-with-the-ayatollah/.

Pei, Minxin, and Danielle Cohen. "A Vicious Sino-Japanese Cycle of Rhetoric." December 21, 2005. http://carnegieendowment.org/2005/12/21/vicious-sino-japanese-cycle-of-rhetoric-pub-17811.

Peksen, Dursun, and A. Cooper Drury. "Economic Sanctions and Political Repression: Assessing the Impact of Coercive Diplomacy on Political Freedoms." *Human Rights Review* 10 (2009): 393–411.

Perkowski, Jack. "Trump on China." *Forbes*, April 5, 2011. http://www.forbes.com/sites/jackperkowski/2011/04/05/trump-on-china/#153401d040ca.

Pomerleau, Mark. "DoD Plans to Invest $600M in Unmanned Underwater Vehicles." *Defense Systems*, February 4, 2016. https://defensesystems.com/articles/2016/02/04/dod-navy-uuv-investments.aspx.

Richardson, Bill. "Five Steps for Engaging with North Korea," *Time*, July 22, 2015. http://time.com/3968478/bill-richardson-5-steps-for-engaging-with-north-korea/.

Rotberg, Robert I. "Mugabe Über Alles: The Tyranny of Unity in Zimbabwe." *Foreign Affairs* 89, no. 4 (July–August, 2010): 10–18.

Sadjadpour, Karim. "How America Could Stumble Into War with Iran." *Atlantic*, February 9, 2017. http://www.theatlantic.com/international/archive/2017/02/iran-trump-nuclear-deal/515979/?utm_source=nl-atlantic-weekly-021017.

Sahlins, Marshall. "China U." *Nation*, October 30, 2013, https://www.thenation.com/article/china-u/.

Samaranayake, Nilanthi, Michael Connell, and Satu Limaye, "The Future of U.S.-India Naval Relations." Center for Naval Analyses. February 2017. https://www.cna.org/cna_files/pdf/DRM-2016-U-013938-Final2.pdf.

Shugart, Thomas. "China's Artificial Islands Are Bigger (and a Bigger Deal) Than You Think." https://warontherocks.com/2016/09/chinas-artificial-islands-are-bigger-and-a-bigger-deal-than-you-think/.

Smithson, Amy E. "Assad's Phony Farewell to Arms." *Foreign Affairs*, October 26, 2016. http://www.foreignaffairs.com/articles/syria/2016-10-26/assads-phony-farewell-arms.

Smeltz, Dina, Stepan Goncharov, and Lily Woitowicz. "US and Russia: Insecurity and Mistrust Shape Mutual Perceptions." November 4, 2016. http://www.thechicagocouncil.org/publication/us-and-russia-insecurity-and-mistrust-shape-mutual-perceptions.

Soeya, Yoshihide. "A View from the Inside on Japan's Perpetual Trust Gap." *Global Asia* 8, no. 3 (Fall 2013): 38–41.

Stossel, Scott. "North Korea: The War Game." *Atlantic* (July–August 2005). http://www.theatlantic.com/magazine/archive/2005/07/north-korea-the-war-game/304029/.

Straub, David. "North Korea Policy: Recommendations for the Trump Administration." Korea Economic Institute of America. December 7, 2016. http://www.kei_aps_straub_final.pdf.

Takeyh, Ray. "Time for Détente with Iran." *Foreign Affairs* (March–April 2007). http://www.foreignaffairs.com/articles/iran/2007-03-01/time-d-tente-iran.

Taub, Ben. "The Assad Files." *New Yorker*, April 18, 2016, 36–49.

Treisman, Daniel. "Why Putin Took Crimea." *Foreign Affairs* 95, no. 3 (May–June 2016): 47–54.

Valencia, Mark J. "The East China Sea Dispute: Context, Claims, Issues, and Possible Solutions." *Asian Perspective* 31, no. 1 (2007): 127–67.

———. "Toe to Toe: The China-US Struggle Over the South China Sea Grows." *Global Asia* 11, no. 4 (Winter 2016): 86–92.

Wang Jisi, "America in Asia: How Much Does China Care?" *Global Asia* 2, no. 2 (Summer 2007): 24–28.

———. "Inside China." *Global Asia* 5, no. 2 (Summer 2010): 8–9.

Wang Yizhou. "China's Path: Growing and Learning." *Global Asia* 5, no. 1 (Spring 2010): 12–16.

Wheeler, Nicholas J. "Trust-Building in International Relations." *Peace Prints*. http://www.wiscomp.org/pp-v4-n2/nick%20wheeler.pdf.

Williams, Ian. "North Korean Missile Launches: 1984–Present." Center for Strategic and International Studies, Washington, DC. April 20, 2017. https://missilethreat.csis.org/north-korea-missile-launches-1984-present/.

Wright, Robin. "The Adversary." *New Yorker*, May 26, 2014. http://www.newyorker.com/magazine/2014/05/26/the-adversary-2.

———. "Tehran's Promise." *New Yorker*, July 27, 2015. http://www.newyorker.com/magazine/2015/07/27/tehrans-promise.

Wu Xinbo. "The End of the Silver Lining: A Chinese View of the U.S.-Japanese Alliance." *Washington Quarterly* 29, no. 1 (Winter 2005/2006): 119–30.

Yang, Keeho. "The South Korea-Japan Agreement on Comfort Women: Mending the Past, Building a Future." *EAF Policy Debates*, July 11, 2017. http://www.keaf.org/book/EAF_Policy_Debate_The_South_Korea-Japan_Agreement_on_Comfort_Women:_Mending_the_Past_Building_a_Future?ckattempt=1.

Yao Yunzhu. "The 'New Normal' in China-U.S. Military Relations." *China-US Focus Digest* 12 (December 2016): 25–28.

Yeo, Andrew I. "Evaluating the Scope of People-to-People Engagement in North Korea, 1995–2012." *Asian Perspective* 41, no. 2 (2017): 309–339.

Zhang Feng. "Provoking Beijing in the South China Sea Will Only Backfire on Washington." *Foreign Policy*, May 21, 2015. http://foreignpolicy.com/2015/05/21/united-states-provoke-beijing-south-china-sea-air-defense-identification-zone/.

Zhang Tuosheng. *"Ruhe goujian Zhong-Mei xin xing daguo guanxi* [How to construct a new China–US great power relationship]." Nautilus Institute Special Report. July 23, 2013. http://www.nautilus.org.

———. "The Shifting US-China Balance of Power in the Western Pacific: Getting the Transition Right." *Global Asia* 11, no. 1 (Spring 2016): 18–22.

DOCUMENTS AND REPORTS

"Ambassador Jang Il Hun on Human Rights in North Korea." October 20, 2014. http://www.cfr.org/north-korea/ambassador-jang-il-hun-human-rights-north-korea/p33642.

Arms Control Association. "Nuclear Weapons: Who Has What at a Glance." July 2017. https://www.armscontrol.org/factsheets/Nuclearweaponswhohaswhat.

Bermudez, Joseph S., Jr., Andy Dinville, and Mike Eley. *North Korea Camp No. 25—Update 2*. The Committee for Human Rights in North Korea. November 29, 2016. http://www.hrnk.org/uploads/pdfs/ASA_HRNK_Camp25_Update2.pdf.

Committee for Human Rights in North Korea. "North Korea Leadership Watch." March 8, 2016. https://nkleadershipwatch.wordpress.com/2016/03/08/kim-jong-un-meets-with-nuclear-weapons-personnel/.

Engler, Richard. Interview with Javad Zarif. http://www.nbcnews.com/video/javad-zarif-foreign-minister-of-iran-full-interview-with-richard-engel-880666691718.

Garwin, Richard, et al. Letter to the President, August 8, 2015. http://www.nytimes.com/interactive/2015/08/08/world/document-iranletteraug2015.html.

ICEF Monitor. "A Record Number of Chinese Students Abroad in 2015." April 6, 2016. http://monitor.icef.com/2016/04/a-record-number-of-chinese-students-abroad-in-2015-but-growth-is-slowing/.

Iran Project. "Strategic Options for Iran: Balancing Pressure with Diplomacy." April 2013. http://www.scribd.com/doc/136389836/Strategic-Options-for-Iran-Balancing-Pressure-with-Diplomacy.

Katzman, Kenneth, and Paul K. Kerr. "Iran Nuclear Agreement." Congressional Research Service, Washington, DC. December 5, 2016. https://fas.org/sgp/crs/nuke/R43333.pdf.

Kerry, John. "U.S. Vision for Asia-Pacific Engagement." August 13, 2014. http://www.state.gov/secretary/remarks/2014/08/230597.htm.

Lawrence, Susan V., and Mark E. Manyin. "China's February 2017 Suspension of North Korean Coal Imports." Congressional Research Service, Washington, DC. April 25, 2017. https://fas.org/sgp/crs/row/IN10659.pdf.

Letter from Retired Generals. "The Iran Deal Benefits U.S. National Security." http://apps.washingtonpost.com/g/documents/world/read-an-open-letter-from-retired-generals-and-admirals-on-the-iran-nuclear-deal/1689/.

Ludes, James N., and Mark R. Jacobson. "Shatter the House of Mirrors: A Conference Report on Russian Influence Operations." Newport, RI: Salve Regina University, Pell Center for International Relations and Public Policy. October 2017. http://pellcenter.org/wp-content/uploads/2017/09/Shatter-the-House-of-Mirrors-FINAL-WEB.pdf.

Meick, Ethan. "China-Russia Military-to-Military Relations: Moving Toward a Higher Level of Cooperation." U.S.-China Economic and Security Review Commission Report. Washington, DC. March 20, 2017.

Morrison, Wayne M. "China-U.S. Trade Issues." Congressional Research Service, Washington, DC. February 9, 2017. https://fas.org/sgp/crs/row/RL33536.pdf.

National Intelligence Estimate, Iran: Nuclear Intentions and Capabilities. Washington, DC: National Intelligence Council. November 2007. https://graphics8.nytimes.com/packages/pdf/international/20071203_release.pdf.

Office of the Secretary of Defense. *Annual Report to Congress: Military and Security Developments Involving the People's Republic of China 2017.* Washington, DC: Office of the Secretary of Defense, 2017.

Organization for International Investment. *Foreign Direct Investment in the United States.* Washington, DC: OII, 2016.

People's Republic of China, Ministry of Foreign Affairs. "Foreign Ministry Spokesperson Hong Lei's Regular Press Conference on March 4, 2016."http://www.fmprc.gov.cn/mfa_eng/xwfw_665399/s2510_665401/2511_665403/t1345253.shtml.

Permanent Court of Arbitration on the West Philippine Sea. Press Release, July 12, 2016. http://www.scribd.com/document/318075282/Permanent-Court-of-Arbitration-PCA-on-the-West-Philippine-Sea-Arbitration#download.

Presidential Policy Directive on Cuba. http://www.nytimes.com/interactive/2016/10/14/world/americas/document-Presidential-Policy-Directive-on-Cuba.html.

Rumer, Eugene, Richard Sokolsky, and Andrew S. Weiss. "Guiding Principles for a Sustainable U.S. Policy Toward Russia, Ukraine, and Eurasia: Key Judgments from a Joint Task Force." Carnegie Endowment. February 9, 2017. http://carnegieendowment.org/2017/02/09/guiding-principles-for-sustainable-u.s.-policy-toward-russia-ukraine-and-eurasia-key-judgments-from-joint-task-force-pub-67893.

United Nations, Department of Political Affairs. "Security Council Briefing on the Situation in the Democratic People's Republic of Korea."http://www.un.org/undpa/speeches-statements/10122015/DPRK.

United Nations, Human Rights, Office of the High Commissioner. *Report of the Commission of Inquiry on Human Rights in the Democratic People's Republic of Korea.* February 7, 2014. http://www.ohchr.org/EN/HRBodies/HRC/CoIDPRK/Pages/ReportoftheCommissionofInquiryDPRK.aspx.

United Nations Security Council. "Report of the Panel of Experts Established Pursuant to Resolution 1874 (2009), Summary."http://undocs.org/S/2017/150.

———. SC Resolution 2371. August 4, 2017. http://www.un.org/en/ga/search/view_doc.asp?symbol=S/RES/2371(2017).

———. "Security Council Resolutions."http://www.un.org/en/sc/documents/resolutions/2016.shtml.

———. SC Resolution 2321/2016. http://www.un.org/en/ga/search/view_doc.asp?symbol=S/RES/2321(2016).

Wampler, Robert A. "Engaging North Korea: Evidence from the Bush I Administration," National Security Archive, November 8, 2017, https://nsarchive.gwu.edu/postings/briefing-books.

Wertz, Daniel. *Track II Diplomacy with Iran and North Korea.* June 2017. National Committee on North Korea. http://www.ncnk.org/sites/default/files/NCNK_Track_II_Conference_Report_0.pdf.

Index

THAAD (Terminal High Altitude Air
Defense), 80, 83, 118, 119
Thrall, Nathan, 142
threats, 16, 160
Thucydides Trap, 63–64, 64
Trans-Pacific Partnership (TPP), 140
Trump, Donald, 65; bad-faith model of,
79; Israeli-Palestinian conflict and,
152–153; nationalism and, 166; Sino-
Japanese conflict and, 140–141; on
Taiwan, 80; US-China relations and,
63–64, 66–67, 70, 79–81, 84, 89n58;
US-China trade and, 79–80; US-
Cuba relations and, 54; US-Iran
relations and, 49–51; US-North
Korea relations and, 118–119; Xi
and, 63–64, 70, 89n58. *See also* US-
Russia relations
Trump, Donald, Russia and, 18, 81, 96,
99; crisis management of, 166;
criticism and, 98; real estate
financing and, 98–99; on Russian
interference in election (2016), 96,
97, 98, 98–99; Syria chemical
weapons attack and, 98
trust building, 31n25; Sino-Japanese
conflict and, 130; US-China relations
and, 86; for US-North Korea
relations, 116
Turkey, 10
Tutu, Desmond, 15

Ukraine intervention, 92, 93–94
UN. *See* United Nations
UNCLOS. *See* United Nations
Convention on the Law of the Sea
UN Commission of Inquiry on Human
Rights in North Korea, 102
United Nations (UN), 8
United Nations Convention on the
Law of the Sea (UNCLOS), 73;
China and, 74, 75, 76, 78; US and, 74
United States (US): apologies by, 28,
29; arms sales of, 67, 80, 83, 145;
Cheney and, 36; Clinton
administration and, 115–116,
126n98; engagement and foreign
policy of, 7; foreign policy language
of, 7; income inequality in, 71; Iran

hostage crisis and, 36, 41–42, 48;
Israel aid from, 145–146; Israeli-
Palestinian conflict and, 141, 142,
143–144, 144–146, 147–148, 152–153;
military of, 67, 75, 76, 77, 84; Nixon
and, 22, 167; Philippines and, 76–77;
Sino-Japanese conflict and, 132,
136–137, 139, 140; UNCLOS and, 74;
Vietnam and, 8, 76, 80; war on terror
and, 8, 28, 82. *See also* Bush
administration; Kerry, John;
Obama, Barack; Russian
interference in presidential election
(2016); Trump, Donald; US-China
relations; US-China trade; US-Cuba
relations; US-Iran relations; US-
North Korea relations; US-Russia
relations
Universal Declaration of Human
Rights (1948), 1, 6n1
US. *See* United States
US-China relations, 23, 73, 109; C-2
and, 64, 81; climate change and, 165;
code of conduct for, 85; Cold War
thinking and, 65; common security
and, 85–86; communication issues
and, 67; cooperation in, 81–86;
cybersecurity and, 63, 66, 83; direct
clash and, 63–64; halfway
engagement and, 2; international
relations levels and, 63, 66, 84; Kerry
on, 75; military imbalance in, 67–68,
72; mistrust in, 61; new type of great
power relations and, 61, 64, 65, 68;
Nixon and, 22, 167; nuclear
weapons and, 66–67; peaceful
development in, 65; regional
security in Northeast Asia and, 83,
113; responsible stakeholder and,
64, 68; SDM and, 84; security and,
85–86; self-conceptions and, 65;
Thucydides Trap, 63–64, 64;
transactions in, 63; Trump and,
63–64, 66–67, 70, 79–81, 84, 89n58;
trust building and, 86; Zhang
Tuosheng on, 66. *See also* China,
weaknesses of; South China Sea
dispute

About the Author

Mel Gurtov is professor emeritus of political science at Portland State University, Oregon, and senior editor of *Asian Perspective*, which he served as editor in chief from 1994 to 2017. Dr. Gurtov's graduate education was at Columbia University's School of International Affairs and University of California Los Angeles. He has published twenty-five books on international affairs, US foreign policy, and East Asia, among them *Will This Be China's Century? A Skeptic's View* (2013); *Global Politics in the Human Interest* (5th ed., 2007); *Superpower on Crusade: The Bush Doctrine in US Foreign Policy* (2006); and *Confronting the Bush Doctrine: Critical Perspectives from Asia-Pacific*, coedited with Peter Van Ness (2005). A former senior Fulbright scholar, RAND Corporation analyst, and an author of the *Pentagon Papers*, he now lives in Deadwood, Oregon, where he blogs on international politics under the title "In the Human Interest" (https://melgurtov.com). He can be reached at mgurtov@aol.com.

WORLD SOCIAL CHANGE

Series Editor: Mark Selden